Aging in Post-Mao China

Westview Replica Editions

The concept of Westview Replica Editions is a response to the continuing crisis in academic and informational publishing. Library budgets for books have been severely curtailed. Ever larger portions of general library budgets are being diverted from the purchase of books and used for data banks, computers, micromedia, and other methods of information retrieval. Interlibrary loan structures further reduce the edition sizes required to satisfy the needs of the scholarly community. Economic pressures on the university presses and the few private scholarly publishing companies have severely limited the capacity of the industry to properly serve the academic and research communities. As a result, many manuscripts dealing with important subjects, often representing the highest level of scholarship, are no longer economically viable publishing projects--or, if accepted for publication, are typically subject to lead times ranging from one to three years.

Westview Replica Editions are our practical solution to the problem. We accept a manuscript in camera-ready form, typed according to our specifications, and move it immediately into the production process. As always, the selection criteria include the importance of the subject, the work's contribution to scholarship, and its insight, originality of thought, and excellence of exposition. The responsibility for editing and proofreading lies with the author or sponsoring institution. We prepare chapter headings and display pages, file for copyright, and obtain Library of Congress Cataloging in Publication Data. A detailed manual contains simple instructions for preparing the final typescript, and our editorial staff is always available to answer questions.

The end result is a book printed on acid-free paper and bound in sturdy library-quality soft covers. We manufacture these books ourselves using equipment that does not require a lengthy make-ready process and that allows us to publish first editions of 300 to 600 copies and to reprint even smaller quantities as needed. Thus, we can produce Replica Editions quickly and can keep even very specialized books in print as long as there is a demand for them.

About the Book and Author

Aging in Post-Mao China:
The Politics of Veneration
Ada Elizabeth Sher

The notion that the Chinese respect the elderly is a well-known cultural stereotype, yet little is known about the extent to which this tradition has survived the sweeping political, social, and economic changes of the past thirty-five years. This case study of Shenyang, the industrial capital of Liaoning Province, explores what it means to be old in the People's Republic of China, especially in terms of religious and ethical traditions, education, health, and current political, economic, and employment trends. Dr. Sher bases her assessments on interviews conducted with elderly members of the community; on observations made of old people at work, at home, and around the city; and on detailed discussions about family relations and the aged with workers from a major iron and steel company. What she reports is largely a success story--for this is one area of which the Chinese are justifiably proud. Nevertheless, the book raises important questions about whether the special status of the elderly can be maintained in the wake of major demographic changes and China's instensive drive toward modernization.

Dr. Sher, vice president of Rural Education and Development, has conducted intensive field work in the People's Republic of China, first as a member of a specialized health study tour during the summer of 1982 and then as a visiting faculty member at the Northeast Institute of Technology in Shenyang.

Aging in Post-Mao China
The Politics of Veneration

Ada Elizabeth Sher

Foreword by Victor W. Sidel and Ruth Sidel

Westview Press / Boulder and London

Cover: *The Chinese character Shòu, symbolizing longevity, is often used as a decoration to wish someone over 50 long life. The author is grateful to Shiue Ling-yunn and Victoria Chee for the design.*

A Westview Replica Edition

Copyright © 1984 by Westview Press, Inc.

Published in 1984 in the United States of America by
   Westview Press, Inc.
   5500 Central Avenue
   Boulder, Colorado 80301
   Frederick A. Praeger, Publisher

Library of Congress Catalog Card Number: 84-51527
ISBN 0-86531-869-7

Printed and bound in the United States of America
10 9 8 7 6 5 4 3 2 1

To all those
who have shared their lives with me,
in appreciation

Contents

Foreword

The elderly, as is well known, have played a central role in Chinese life for thousands of years. In pre-Revolutionary China, in contrast to many other societies, older people had considerable prestige and power in the community and particularly within the family unit. Workers and peasants who had little power in the larger society exercised their authority at home and while authority was for the most part in the hands of men, particularly outside the home, women who had lived most of their lives as powerless pawns finally gained some measure of authority within the home as they grew older, when they took on the role of "mother-in-law." It was the elderly who made the fundamental decisions about family life and the demonstration on the part of the young to the elderly of reverence, respect and often fear was an accepted and central ritual of daily life. As the linchpin of the family, the elderly were, of course, mirroring the structure of the larger society: the patriarchal, often cruel, authoritarianism of traditional China was replicated and supported by a patriarchal, often cruel, authoritarian family structure.

Since the dominant position of the elderly in pre-Revolutionary China was inextricably connected with the maintenance of a hierarchical society in which not only power but also income, goods and services were largely reserved for the elite, the question of what has happened to the elderly in post-Revolutionary China becomes a key factor in understanding the structure and fabric of the society today. While frequent shifts in policy have characterized the 35 years since the founding of the People's Republic, one principle has remained fairly constant: the attempt by the leadership in many areas of Chinese life to turn the society on its head, to reverse the former power structure, to reject the old priorities and formulate new ones. In health care, according to the four principles enunciated by Mao Zedong in 1950, services were to be provided first not to the elite who formerly received the bulk of high quality medical care but rather to the "workers, peasants and soldiers." Women were to take their rightful place in society and to "hold up half the sky." Landlords were overthrown and their land and power turned over to the peasants. In this context, what has happened to the elderly, those who held such a grip on power in traditional China?

From studies published during the 1970s and from the observation of many visitors, it has become clear that while older people in China no longer retain their unquestioned, autocratic role within the family and within Chinese society, they nevertheless do have a respected, often honored status in the New China. While they have lost some of their power to determine directly the lives of others, they retain roles that utilize the traditional respect with which they are still viewed in contemporary Chinese society. They work in neighborhood committees, they work in the area of health care, they help to raise children and during the Cultural Revolution they taught children about the "bitter past." But what about the most recent period, since the death of Mao in 1976? How are the elderly treated during this era of rapid modernization? Are they considered extraneous to China's leap into the 21st century? How do the elderly feel about their own lives? What of those older people who have no children to care for them and must live in "homes for the respected aged"? How do older Chinese people themselves feel about old age?

Ada Sher, who has recently received her Masters in Public Health Policy and Administration and her Doctorate in Education at the University of North Carolina, has had a unique opportunity to observe and analyze the role of the elderly in China today. After making a visit to China with us in the summer of 1982 as part of a group studying health care, Mrs. Sher returned to China during the summer of 1983. She spent her time during this second visit largely in Shenyang and was able to observe older people at work, in their homes and during their day-to-day activities in the city. She conducted interviews with the elderly about their work, their families, about health care, about aging--in short, about their lives. She was also able to interview younger adults about their attitudes on the aged and aging. In her words, she was able to go "backstage" and get to know "one group of old people . . . in one corner of China."

What she has written is an extraordinarily thoughtful, caring description and analysis of the role of the elderly in China today. Mrs. Sher brings to this work an unusual intelligence, sensitivity and a delicate awareness of both cross-cultural differences and the feelings of others, no matter what culture they are from. Ada Sher has added significantly to our understanding of

the role of the elderly in China and has done so with
understanding, tact and with humor. We are all richer
for her fine piece of work.

Victor W. Sidel and Ruth Sidel
New York City
May 1984

Acknowledgments

First of all, I want to thank President Bi Kezhen, Vice-President Su Shiquan and Mr. Lao Zhongkui, Director of the International Center for the Exchange of Learning and Research, for inviting me to the Northeast Institute of Technology (NEIT) in Shenyang and making every attempt to both facilitate my work and help me feel at home. I appreciate the generosity of the Liaoning and Shenyang Foreign Affairs Departments for allowing me this opportunity to do on-site social research--a venture they considered a "first." For their superb assistance and many kindnesses, I owe a great deal to Liaoning provincial psychologist Wang Shumao and Mr. Lao's staff: Sun Lianying, Li Jun and Liu Guixang. Dr. Marvin Williamsen, of Appalachian State University, introduced me to the NEIT officials when they visited North Carolina and helped arrange my participation in the Faculty Exchange Program. I appreciate his efforts on my behalf. Together with my students from the Anshan Iron and Steel Company, these people provided the passageway to a new world.

For their marvelous introduction to, and continuing guidance on, health and social welfare in China, I thank Drs. Vic and Ruth Sidel. In fact, more than thank them, I wish to acknowledge the respect and admiration I have for them both personally and professionally.

Working with the following professors at the University of North Carolina at Chapel Hill was a uniquely satisfying and enriching experience: Moye Freymann, Julio George, George Noblit, James Paul and Harry Phillips. Their help and advice were never restrictive, but rather encouraging, helpful and supportive. The superb typing and conscientiousness of Dr. Karin Gleiter made the preparation of this book pleasurable and rewarding.

I am deeply grateful to all of the above, but the richest help and support were given by my best friend and teacher, my husband Jonathan. I hope that my children, Matt and Evvy, will find in life the kindness, friendship and collegiality offered to me throughout this research effort.

Introduction

The story of aging in the People's Republic of China, a country having a People's Government, <u>People's Daily</u>, the People's Liberation Army, People's money, the National People's Congress and even the People's Great Wall, is best told from a people's point of view. Indeed, one of the fundamental ideological distinctions of China today is the belief that the direction of history is determined by *people*, not by material conditions.

Telling the people's story is a task ill-served by an over-reliance upon traditional quantitative methods of social science research. Statistical evidence is necessary, but not sufficient, to reveal the complexities of the elderly's role and status in contemporary China. In fact, when examining a concept as multidimensional and personal as "well-being," the inherent reductionist bias of statistical data can prove to be as much of a hindrance as a help to one's understanding.

The challenge of qualitative research is captured by Mao's famous dictum to "seek truth from facts."[1] The fieldwork I undertook was intended to help make sense of all the facts uncovered through my secondary source research. Above all, my purpose was to explore the richness of the reality of being old in China today --an exploration that hinged upon the search for the context and meaning lying below and beyond the documentable facts. Qualitative research is, by definition, as much of an art as it is a science. It is highly dependent upon the sensitivity and insight of the observer and the willingness of the observed to reveal themselves in words and actions.

The time I spent in China[2] was an adventure that (like such classic adventure stories as <u>Moby Dick</u>) ought to be told in the first person. I continue to be drawn magnetically to China by fascination, love, and respect. I feel daunted by the seriousness of the Chinese people--a personality characteristic I share-- and by the sense of playfulness--which, thank God, is

1

also inside me to tame and balance the seriousness.

In my mind, the symbol of Shenyang, the site of the case study herein, during the summer of 1983 was the camera. People posed all over. Children knew how to act in front of a camera as if by instinct; young couples tried to immortalize their feelings for one another on film; photographers were assigned to cover events, large and small. Film stands--created to serve the local people, not tourists (of which there were very, very few in Shenyang)--were almost as numerous as popsicle carts. The one being photographed says "thank you," even to the foreigner, as if to say thank you for including me in this new undeclared campaign of "Let a hundred cameras click!"[3]

In China, everyone has a pose. Photography in Shenyang is formal. "It's the Chinese way!" Yet, no more beautiful scene can be found in China today than that of a group who have just *finished* having their portrait taken. They smile and laugh and the feeling that pours out as they let go of their self-consciousness represents the two sides of China: the formal, formidable emerging world power and the sensitive, delicate, intimate people. Perhaps the formal side makes the informal one even more striking. Too much of the writing we've received in the West describes only the formal pose and not the gracious humanity it masks.

Bicycle bells, horns, and "too many people--people everywhere!" are typical reports of tourists. The unique mix of independence, interdependence, and uneven development--an abacus and computer on the same desk, Pierre Cardin fashion mixed with sombre blue or grey uniforms and home visits by physicians in a time when numbers alone dictate against the value of the person and his or her individual needs--cue the visitor to the sometimes jarring reality of a transitional society.

Colin Turnbull suggests that as far as dedication to human relationships and cultivation of a highly tuned social consciousness is concerned, first primitive, and then transitional societies are, in fact, the more developed.[4] The present situation of the elderly in Shenyang is examined here to test this theory. The first question is how to classify China when it seems all three phases of development are concurrently found. She is primitive in her use of human labor, transitional in her planning, and modern in her goals.

For the purposes of this book, Oriental and Occidental (two descriptors having equal mystique in my mind) will be used to distinguish these worlds in a less value-laden way than "developed" and "developing" or "less developed." I shall describe what I came to know and how a cross-section of Shenyangese interpreted their situation. Our viewpoints often came as close as the concepts of "wish" and "hope," or "chance" and "opportunity." I wanted to understand the gap that our

opposite hemispheric upbringings had created in our
being able to fully understand one another and found
nothing more rewarding than reaching a congruence of
meaning. In fact, my happiest moments came when I was
able to truly understand what was meant by stated words.
I find each new concept changes our lives a little bit.
Our grasp of an exterior reality seems to have a domino
effect on our world view. Like *ikebana*, the art of
flower arranging, the inclusion or alteration of one
small object affects the total atmosphere.

What affects the lives of the elderly in China?
Why are the context and reality of their situation ap-
parently so different from those found in Occidental
societies? What are the constructs that have determined a reality of aging seemingly far more reverent
and productive than our own? Is there something for us
to gain, or has our culture become so set on its course
that such lessons are forever lost to us? These were
questions which led me to undertake this study--ques-
tions that became even more pressing as I delved into
the relevant literature and discovered a body of scholarly work and journalistic accounts as diverse and contradictory as the nation they purported to describe.
Unlike many who have written about modern China, I
carried little ideological baggage with me on my journey. It was my purpose neither to reinforce myths
about the Chinese nor to debunk them.

My goal was much more modest. Insofar as possible
--given the very real constraints of time, language,
and culture--I wanted to go "backstage" and get to know
a group of old people from various walks of life in one
corner of China. I did not want to spend the bulk of
my time in Beijing talking with government officials
and assorted experts about how life was supposed to be
for the elderly according to the most recent party line.
Instead I wanted to observe, experience, and discuss
how life actually was and the extent to which "a sense
of well-being" actually occurred in the lives of a
cross-section of Shenyang's aged individuals.

What I discovered and what I describe in the chapters that follow will give little comfort to those who
would prefer to think of the Chinese as an indistin-
guishable mass or as mere pawns in the interplay of
social, economic, and political forces at both national
and international levels. This is not to downplay the
impact of such realities, for the stories I heard from
the elderly I interviewed were nothing if not a testament to the power of these forces to alter (for better
or worse) the lives of everyone in their path--direct
participants and bystanders alike. Yet, by definition,
the aged are the survivors. As survivors they are a
reminder of the resilience and capacity of *individuals*
not only to cope with whatever life may present them,
but also to assert their own humanity and at least

occasionally triumph in so doing.

Similarly, my study will be of little use or so-
lace to those interested in using any new information
about China to reinforce their opinions (positive or
negative) about the Chinese Revolution or the current
national leadership. Nevertheless, no matter what
one's political persuasion might be, there are two sa-
lient facts that have indisputably resulted from the
Chinese revolution: (1) there are more people sur-
viving to old age in China today than ever before and
the proportion of elderly in Chinese society has significantly increased each decade since 1949; and (2) the
material conditions of the elderly, although exceeding-
ly modest by Occidental standards, are notably better
for a greater percentage of the elderly now than was
true in pre-revolutionary China.

What I found in China was not the promised land,
but rather a land of enormous promise. My hope is that
this report will provide the balance so often missing
from the work of Occidental writers prone to either
seeing everything through rose-colored glasses or
simply seeing red. Although few have come before, I
hope many others will be attracted to observing and re-
cording various dimensions of life among the aged in
China. Accordingly, my work should be seen as a relatively early contribution to what I expect to be a
growing Occidental literature on the Chinese elderly.
It is not the last word on the subject. It is only the
latest. If it advances our knowledge and understanding
of China today, and serves as a reminder of the complex
and intensely human stories lying just behind the statistics and policy pronouncements, it will have served
my purposes well.

To make the journey from the bounds of what we
know to an understanding of daily life in an upper corner of China, I would like to begin with a brief macro-
analysis of aging using data from the United States to
represent the Occidental experience and move into a
broad overview of aging in China. The chapter entitled
"The Context of Being Old in China" considers the status of the aged from the perspectives of ethics, education, economics, politics and health. Once this cultural context is established, the focus will shift to
Shenyang--a city in the Northeast and the home of the
old people whose lives provide the core of this case
study. The macroanalytic view of facts and figures
serves to make clear my biases and understanding of the
society and provides a framework from which to analyze
the data from Shenyang. The route of the research effort is thus from a general Occidental reality to a
very specific group of old people in Shenyang, for it
is within her people that the heart of China can be
found.

NOTES

1. To "seek truth from facts" is considered "the quintessence of Mao Zedong Thought" by Deng Xiaoping, head of both the Communist Party Military Commission and the State Military Commission and China's top leader since the death of Mao.

2. I was presented with an extraordinary opportunity to conduct primary source research in China as part of a Faculty Exchange Program between a scientific and technical national key school Dongbei Gongxueyuan (The Northeast Institute of Technology) in Shenyang, Liaoning Province, and Appalachian State University in Boone, North Carolina.
From my formal and informal studies of China, of aging, and of policy development, and from my interest in and appreciation for the value of cross-national studies, I wanted to conduct fieldwork in the PRC. My introduction and consequent research methodology modeling came from a trip I took with the American Medical Students' Association Delegation in June 1982. We were fortunate to have been led by Drs. Victor and Ruth Sidel, both of whom continue to play a prominent role in elucidating Chinese medicine, health and social policy to the West. They set a wonderful example of how to conduct research in China--striving to give back to your hosts at least as much as you receive and to recognize the importance of understanding the context of the "facts" you discern. During the tour I was able to discuss aging with presidents of Chinese medical schools, chairmen of public health facilities, physicians, and citizens, both to learn firsthand and to judge the validity and reliability of what had been reported in the Western press and academic journals.

3. In May and June of 1957, Mao began what became known as the "hundred flowers" campaign: "Let a hundred flowers bloom and a hundred schools of thought contend." The aim of this mass movement, according to Jonathan Spence, The Gate of Heavenly Peace: The Chinese and Their Revolution, 1895-1980, p. 332, was "to restore confidence to those who felt their skills were not valued by the state, whether in the realm of the creative arts and humanities (the flowers) or in the areas of scientific research and practice (the schools of thought)." An "antirightist" campaign the following summer silenced the critics who emerged in the "hundred flowers" movement. However, according to a speech delivered at the Fifth Session of the Fifth National People's Congress on November 26, 1982, and reported by Peng Zhen, "Report on the Draft of the Revised Constitution of the People's Republic of China," Fifth Session of the Fifth National People's Congress, p. 89:

"There is no doubt that 'letting a hundred flowers
bloom and a hundred schools of thought contend' remains
one of the basic principles guiding our scientific and
cultural work and that it must be firmly implemented to
make socialist science and culture flourish."

4. Colin Turnbull, The Human Cycle (New York:
Simon and Schuster, 1983).

I
A Perspective
on Increasing Longevity

MACROANALYTIC FRAMEWORK

All societies proclaim the value, if not the sanctity, of human life. However, the extent to which they actually behave in accordance with this fundamental ethical precept varies dramatically around the world. The commonly held principle of life being precious has not precluded either individuals or nations from treating human life as if it were cheap. The actual quality of life, however defined, for elderly people is very different from country to country, from group to group within the same country, and over time. Contradictions between the rhetoric of respect and the reality of rejection are all too common in the world today.

A brief comparison of China and the United States may prove valuable as a preparatory step in setting our sights on China because, at the level of popular stereotypes, they represent opposite ends of the spectrum --at least as far as the status of their older citizens is concerned. Put simply, the image of the United States is one of providing materially for the basic needs of old people, but simultaneously isolating them socially, politically, economically, and even physically. Closer to the truth, the financial situation of the elderly in the United States remains reminiscent of the famous lyric from "God Bless the Child That's Got His Own," in which "them that's got, shall get, and them that's not, shall lose." Of those over 65, 14.6 percent have incomes that place them under the official poverty line, and about 15 percent have incomes just above it.[1] Still, unlike many aspects of American life, the bottom line is not money, but rather the place and function of the elderly in society. The planned obsolescence we call retirement may be a harsh struggle to survive for some and a period of leisure for others, but for almost everyone over 65 or 70 it is a time of mandated marginality in social, economic, and political terms (with the notable exception of participation in

7

voting). We often think of our elderly as "living in
the past" and yet, for most older Americans, the past
is the only place available to replenish their self-
esteem and rejuvenate their will to live. By systemat-
ically forcing the elderly out of the mainstream, we
have made manifest our belief that they are inconsequential to the present and irrelevant to the future.
The fact that they seek refuge in the past is hardly
surprising--it is, after all, the only safe harbor
we've allowed them to maintain.

China, on the other hand, is seen as providing
comparatively meager material resources, but according
the elderly a position of respect and thoroughly inte-
grating them into the mainstream of society. Put in
cultural terms, the Chinese view old age as a fulfillment rather than a deprivation. Retirement represents
a transition from one socially and economically useful
role to another, equally valuable one. The elderly
continue to hold responsible positions in the family
and community. They continue to help the family economically through their pensions, outside work, or
assumption of household chores that enable the younger
women to work outside the home. In the community, the
elderly are found in great numbers organizing workshops
and special programs, investigating complaints and ar-
bitrating civil disputes, controlling traffic, advising
at their former workplaces, and generally participating
in the life around them. Remaining active is seen as a
civic duty.

In the United States, retirement is widely regarded as a withdrawal not only from a particular occupational role, but also from active participation in
civic or public life. For Americans, retirement is a
time to pursue personal interests and to reap the
fruits of one's past labors as fully as resources and
health permit. Their leadership in community affairs
is rarely solicited--or welcomed.

In the United States, a deficiency model guides
policymaking--a model based upon our cultural perception of what elderly people *lack*.[2] Chinese policy-
making, by contrast, is based upon a maximization model
which stems from the cultural perception of what the
elderly *have* and can contribute to the betterment of
society. The elderly in China are regarded as responsible members of families, kinship networks, and sometimes of production units. They are family and community oriented and self, family, pension, or production
team supported.

Fox Butterfield, in his recent book, China, Alive
in the Bitter Sea, says he feels the greatest contrast
to the West comes with old age.[3] To many Americans it
means the lonely end of life, loss of vitality, income,
friends, and security. In traditional China, though
people's physical powers waned as they aged, they were

thought to still be growing toward wisdom. Butterfield
calls old age in China the summit of existence. The
appelation *Lao* (old) is a compliment. In his book,
Butterfield quotes Confucius:

> At 15, I set my heart on learning.
> At 30, I was firmly established.
> At 40, I had no more doubts.
> At 50, I knew the will of heaven.
> At 60, I was ready to listen to it.
> At 70, I could follow my heart's desire without
> transgressing what was right.

Confucianism was the official ideology of China for approximately 2,200 years--up until Marxism-Leninism and
the Thought of Mao officially took precedence. Even
today, although on a more implicit basis, Confucianism
continues to underlie the country's ethical and normative systems and remains a powerful cultural force.

The available evidence--demographic, analytic, and
anecdotal--makes a convincing case that being elderly
in China and being elderly in the United States are
very different experiences indeed.[4] In absolute terms,
old people in America, as do other age groups, enjoy a
higher standard of material well-being than their counterparts in China. Even given our poverty statistics,
we have far more possessions and higher income levels
than the Chinese. And yet, a consideration of aging
makes it clear that material well-being is not the beginning and end of an overall sense of well-being.
American elderly may be more *valuable* in financial
terms, but Chinese elderly are more *valued* in social
and political ones.

The societal expectations of, policies for, and
behavior toward the elderly are functions of the ethical values and moral codes of the society itself in
that the degree of status conferred upon older people,
the relative quality of care they receive when necessary, the extent to which they are integrated into the
mainstream of both private and public life, the relative proportion of available resources they command,
and the sense of self-esteem they feel are all factors
that both define and determine well-being. The key to
understanding these phenomena lies in unlocking the
operational values and moral choices shaping them.

RELEVANCE OF THE CHINESE EXPERIENCE

The health and productivity of the aged are valuable assets to a country if the energies, talents, and
experiences of this growing population are viewed as
"resources" and creatively utilized. In an increasingly competitive and efficiency-oriented world-wide

economic situation, keeping older people productive
first, through health promotion and disease prevention,
and second, through providing opportunities for meaningful activity, can be a major contribution to both
the nation's economy and the individual's quality of
life.

A *vital* population is an essential component of
development, and health, as we all know, is more than
the absence of disease. Health, as defined in the
West, is "the ability to perform upon requirement or
desire (with a maximum of efficiency and satisfaction
compatible with one's usual capacity) and takes into
account biological, psychological and social aspects of
functioning."[5] The relationship of the health of a
population to the overall process of development has
been well documented by such international agencies as
the World Health Organization, the Economic Development
Institute of the World Bank, and the International
Labor Organization in Geneva. The United Nations con-
vened a World Assembly on Aging in 1982 in Vienna designed "to launch an international action program aimed
at guaranteeing economic and social security to older
persons, as well as opportunities to contribute to national development."[6] One hundred and twenty-four
countries, including China and the United States, participated. Side by side, the developmental and humanitarian aspects of aging were considered in a gathering
representing the continuum from the most traditional
societies to the most modern.

Health is both an input to, and a goal of, development. Expenditures on health (both personally and
societally) become investments in productive capacity.
In other words, while elevating personal health and
social conditions, investments in maintaining the
health and well-being of the members of a society at
the same time enhance national development.

The situation of the elderly in all countries will
shortly be challenged by changing demographies. To use
more familiar figures as a referent for the unfamiliar,
consider the situation in the United States. When the
United States achieved independence in 1776, the average life expectancy at birth was 35. By 1900, it had
increased to 47, and then, due to continuing advances
in education, the control of infectious and the management of degenerative diseases, improved nutrition,
water purification, sanitation, personal health care
and occupational safety, it has continued to rise to an
average life expectancy for infants born in 1982 of
74.5.[7] It is projected that an American child born in
the year 2000 will live to an average age of 86.2, if
female, and 74.3, if male, and it is further believed
by some that in the 21st century, the average life span
will reach a maximum of 95 with death coming as a result of natural biological breakdown rather than from

disease.[8] Others put the inherent life span for the
species at approximately 120.[9] Today, in fact, a married couple in which both partners have survived to age
65 can expect one of the spouses to live to 90 or
above.[10] Those now 65 or older represent 11.3 percent
of the population of the United States,[11] and Census
Bureau projections estimate that in less than half a
century, by 2030, 21.1 percent of the expected national
population of 304.3 million will be over 65.[12]

So too, with the founding of the People's Republic
of China in 1949, the average life expectancy at birth
was 35. By 1958 it had risen to 57 and by 1984 reached
70--a remarkable climb given the history, status of development, and national income per capita.[13] Eight
percent of the population was over 60 in 1980. (Old
age comes sooner in China, statistically speaking.)
Projections show an increase to 11 percent in 2000,
20 percent in 2025,[14] and a whopping 25 percent in
2035.[15] In that year, if country population propor-
tions remain approximately the same and China continues
to hold approximately one-quarter of the world's population, one out of every 16 world citizens will be an
elderly Chinese!

By the year 2000, nearly 60 percent of the world's
elderly will live in developing nations.[16] Global projections indicate that, between the years 1980 and 2000,
the number of adults over 60 will double and those over
80 will increase by 119 percent.[17] Declining death
rates (except for cancer), lower birth rates (increasing the proportion of older people), and higher life
expectancy at birth (due to better health conditions)
all characterize this demographic transition.

As an observer, it was impossible for me to avoid
making comparisons (even if subconsciously) between
what I had seen in the West and what I saw in China.
As a qualitative researcher, however, my attempt was to
view and experience as much as I could from the perspective of the Chinese elderly with whom I interacted.
The result, inevitably, is an Occidental report of a
Chinese reality. Yet, it is not--and was not meant to
be--a formal comparative study between China and the
U.S. or between Shenyang and a comparable American
city, though that would be an interesting comparison at
a later date. It is a study about being old in China,
generally, and in Shenyang, in particular.

Focusing on a specific locality in a culture foreign to one's own is hardly a new idea. It is, in
fact, characteristic of such qualitative research clas-
sics as Margaret Mead's Coming of Age in Samoa and
Colin Turnbull's The Forest People. Issues of generalizability and interpretation are discussed in detail in
Appendix A on methodology. The point of this chapter
and the one that follows is to allow readers to move
more comfortably from the familiar to the unfamiliar

and from the macro-level to the micro-level.

This process of moving from one level to another also describes what I have tried to do in presenting the Chinese experience. My supposition is that one must build a holistic framework beginning with the formal and informal codes that structure the experience of being old in China and extending to the observable, empirical realities of today before an accurate analysis can be made. Thus, I will next seek to explore the meanings and manifestations of well-being among the elderly in a Chinese urban area through an examination of various societal contexts and a case study in an attempt to understand and explain the relevancy of the values, policies, practices, and traditions to the status of the aged in China. To understand the fruit, one must understand the plant--and to understand the plant, one must understand the roots and soil in which the plant grows.

NOTES

1. "U.S. Poverty by the Numbers," Newsweek, 8/15/83.

2. For further reading on policy making and the elderly in the United States, see:
R.H. Binstock and E. Shanas (Eds.), Handbook of Aging and the Social Sciences (New York: Van Nostrand Reinhold Co., 1976).
C.L. Estes, "Austerity and Aging in the U.S.: 1980 and Beyond," Int. J. of Health Services, 1982, 12:4.
L. Lowy, Social Policies and Programs on Aging (Lexington, MA: Lexington, 1980).
H. Thomae and G.L. Maddox (Eds.), New Perspectives on Old Age: A Message to Decision Makers (New York: Springer Publishing Co., 1982).
U.S. Department of Health, Education and Welfare, Older Americans Act of 1965, As Amended. Administration on Aging, Office of Human Development Services, Washington, D.C., July 1979. U.S. DHEW Pub. No. (OHDS) 79-20170.

3. Fox Butterfield, China, Alive in the Bitter Sea (New York: Times Books, 1982), p. 217.

4. For further reading on the elderly in the United States, see:
R.N. Butler, Why Survive? Being Old in America (New York: Harper & Row, 1975).
D.H. Fischer, Growing Old in America (New York: Oxford University Press, 1970).

Eva Salber, Don't Bring Me Flowers When I'm Dead--Voices of the Rural Elderly (Durham, NC: Duke University Press, 1983).
Jeanie Schmidt Kayser-Jones, Old, Alone and Neglected: A Comparison of Being Old in Scotland and the U.S. (Berkeley, CA: University of California Press, 1981).

5. Health as defined at the Salzburg Seminar on Health, Productivity and Aging, June 1983.

6. For summary of proceedings, see "Report of the World Assembly on Aging," United Nations Publication No. E.82.1.16.

7. "Marriage Statistics are Up," The Chapel Hill Newspaper 61:166:2, 10/5/83. Figures are taken from the National Center for Health Statistics.

8. Projections by Eileen Crimmins, University of Southern California gerontologist, as reported in Philip J. Hilts, "Life expectancy rises 3 years, to 74 for men, 86 for women," The Washington Post, May 31, 1983.

9. Lowell D. Holmes, Other Cultures, Elder Years: An Introduction to Cultural Gerontology (Minneapolis: Burgess Publishing Company, 1983), p. 54.

10. Jim Birren, University of Southern California gerontologist. Figures from actuarial tables quoted by Dr. Birren at Salzburg Seminar Session 223, June 1983.

11. "Experts now think America's aged increasing at fast rate," The Chapel Hill Newspaper 61:162:3A, 9/30/83.

12. Ibid.

13. "Life expectancy doubles to 70 since Liberation," China Daily 3:809:3, 2/29/84.

14. Speech by Mr. Yu Guanghan, Chairman of the Chinese Delegation, to the World Assembly on Aging, Vienna, July 1982, p. 6. Mr. Yu is currently chairman of the Chinese National Committee on Aging.

15. Coale's figure predicated on reaching zero population growth by the year 2000. Coale, A.J. "Population trends, population policy, and population studies in China." Population and Development 7 (1): 85-97, March '81, as quoted in Chen, P. and Kols, A. "Population and Birth Planning in the People's Republic of China." Jan.-Feb. 1982. Population Reports. Series J:

25:603. Baltimore: Population Information Program, The Johns Hopkins University, Hampton House, 624 North Broadway, 21205, p. J609.

16. George L. Maddox, "Aging People and Aging Populations: A Framework for Decision-Making," New Perspectives on Old Age: A Message to Decision-Makers, ed. Hans Thomae and George Maddox (New York: Springer, 1982), p. 21.

17. Statistics from U.N. Office of Public Information; World Health Magazine, April 1979; "Aging: The Developed and Developing World," by Walter M. Beattie, Jr., All University Gerontology Center, Syracuse University, New York, as quoted in Baines, J. Aging and World Order, Global Education Associates, East Orange, N.J., Feb. 1980.

II
The Context of Being Old
in China Today

Culture I take to be that local knowledge,
the common sense expectations, the systems
of meanings and values, the norms governing
experience, the taken-for-granted world of
cognitive orientations and group interests
that orient a people to the situations around
them and to their own selves, that orient a
group to their collective life role, the problems in that life role, and to their representation and solution. Culture is embodied in
language--the other major symbolic system, and
in kinship systems, religious systems and
legal systems as well. And indeed, in the very
experience of illness itself. Culture can be
thought of in this last domain as an organized,
and organizing, set of structured principles
that constitute and are expressed by the per-
ceptual, cognitive, affective, behavioral, and
communicative dispositions--dispositions that
at once are anchored in local arrangements of
social relationships and that create particular
local patterns of meaningful experience and
signify value-laden action.[1]

The definition above by medical anthropologist and
psychiatrist Arthur Kleinman takes into account the
psycho-bio-social aspects that work together to form a
culture and a community. In studying the health and
well-being of old people, it is first necessary to get
a sense of the world in which they operate.

No one sector of a society acts in isolation. The
various aspects of the present day Chinese reality--ed-
ucational, ethical/religious, political, economic,
legal, social, medical and environmental--are like
spokes of a wheel. Each has a distinct bearing on the
well-being of China's older citizens, but it is their
interdependence and cumulative impact that are striking
to Occidental observers.

Also like a wheel, the turns (revolutions) can
actually be rapid, yet appear motionless. Don Woods,
an American computer specialist spending his fourth
year living in Shenyang, often observed: "Everyday is
the same, yet everyday is different!" In China, the
sense of timelessness and the sense of rapid change
somehow go hand in hand.

What I report here are 1983 figures and opinions
which I have tried to place in an historical perspective. While fundamental cultural characteristics and
truth transcend time, facts quickly change in Chinese
society today. Information on contemporary life is often outdated before a book can be published in the West.
Thus, although the specific details of each sector discussed herein may also soon be in need of update, the
basic patterns of Chinese society and their implications for the elderly are likely to remain true for the
foreseeable future.

In order to establish the context of being old in
China today, five dimensions of Chinese society as they
relate to the elderly will be examined in this chapter
--ethics and religion, politics and law, education,
economy and employment, and health. By describing
post-Mao China through these five sectors, the societal
forces and factors shaping daily life among the elderly
in Shenyang should become more readily understandable.
Whether one regards the current political system as a
people's democracy, as a totalitarian state, or as an
amalgamation of the two, the government and its policies are an ever-present--indeed inescapable--influence
on the attitudes and behavior of ordinary citizens
throughout the People's Republic of China. The over-
riding importance of the government in the society, and
in even the mundane affairs of individual old people,
makes a firm grasp of these five dimensions imperative
in discerning the objective status and well-being of
the elderly both in Shenyang and across China.

RELIGIOUS/ETHICAL CONTEXT

One evening towards the end of my stay in Shenyang,
five of my students were visiting me when the subject
of religion arose. The most earnest of them repeated
the standard Marxist belief that religion is more akin
to feudal superstition (relying on a supernatural power,
rather than on the ability of people, to transform the
world) than it is characteristic of a modern, developed
nation. To another of my students, religion was something like clairvoyance and the world of spirits which,
though he felt existed on the one hand, seemed prepos-
terous to him on the other. The one most sensitive to
the poetic and literary traditions of China was expect-
ably philosophical but uncommitted. The fourth left,

uninterested, and the fifth, an *aficionado* of the West,
saw religion as part of the Western lifestyle along
with computers, guns, and disco dancing in every home.

As Richard Bush suggests in <u>Religion in China</u>,
sociologists and anthropologists see religion as a cultural institution, while psychologists see it as an
expression of inner human need. He goes on to state
that philosophers define religion as a system of
thought or doctrine, while historians examine it as
part of the intellectual development of an era.[1]

All of the above perspectives are allowed in China.
The policy of the government, though atheistic itself,
is to protect religious beliefs. However, there is
felt to be a concomitant duty to protect China from the
foreign influences and religious missionaries incul-
cated in the pre-revolutionary era. Article 36 of the
new Constitution adopted in December 1982 explicitly
reflects this concern:

> Citizens of the People's Republic of China
> enjoy freedom of religious belief.
> No state organ, public organization or
> individual may compel citizens to believe in,
> or not to believe in, any religion; nor may
> they discriminate against citizens who believe
> in, or do not believe in, any religion.
> The state protects normal religious activ-
> ities. No one may make use of religion to en-
> gage in activities that disrupt public order,
> impair the health of citizens or interfere with
> the educational system of the state.
> Religious bodies and religious affairs are
> not subject to any foreign domination.

What the government does insist upon are the
"three selfs" as far as religion is concerned: self-
administration, self-support, and self-propagation.
Contrary to what one might expect in an avowedly atheistic state, representatives of religions even are
found participating in the administration of the government. For example, a Buddhist nun (Long Lian) is a
member of the Chinese People's Political Consultative
Conference.[2]

Although Western expertise is now allowed to in-
form China's technical, industrial and economic sectors, great pains are taken to ensure that the socio-
cultural side of life remains Chinese. Religion is
certainly included in this category. Socialist morality and ideological reconstruction are believed to be
far more important to Chinese civilization, social
change and development than either the theological concerns of religion or the materialistic preoccupations
of Soviet Marxism. As Article 24 of the 1982 Constitution declares:

The state strengthens the building of
socialist spiritual civilization through spread-
ing education in high ideals and morality, general education and education in discipline and
the legal system, and through promoting the
formulation and observance of rules of conduct
and common pledges by different sections of the
people in urban and rural areas.

The state advocates the civic virtues of
love of the motherland, of the people, of labour,
of science and of socialism; it educates the
people in patriotism, collectivism, internation-
alism and communism and in dialectical and historical materialism; it combats capitalist,
feudal and other decadent ideas.

Today's Chinese elderly were raised and socialized
in the pre-revolutionary culture. Accordingly, they
were subject to forms of religious training and aspects
of ethical indoctrination at variance with those now
received by their grandchildren and great-grandchildren.
Still, for all the changes, some fundamental ethical
precepts have endured into the modern era. For the elderly, one of these core principles of ethical behavior
revolves around the ideal and the reality of "filial
piety." According to Bush, filial piety is:

. . . the primary element or main stream in
Chinese religion, both in the ancient past and
in the present. An amazing variety of currents
move in and out of the main stream of filial
piety with their varying emphases in thought
and activity. Dominant among these are Confucianism, Taoism, Buddhism, and folk religion.
But the main stream of filial piety flows
through them all.[3]

How has filial piety evolved through periods of tradition, revolution, industrialization, and now modernization?

Confucianism, not a religion, but a highly ratio-
nalistic ethical system, was made the official ideology
of the State around 220 B.C.* and lasted to the end of
the Qing Dynasty in 1911. It was enforced by imperial
rule, sustained by an agricultural economy and based
upon the family and kinship structures. Though it is
difficult to say whether the people embraced the
thought or the thought embraced the people, it became

---

*Confucius himself lived from approximately 551 to 479
B.C. and his conversations and sayings--considered the
single strongest cultural influence on Chinese society
were recorded by his disciples in the Analects.

the longest continuous cultural tradition in the history of the world.

The basic tenets of Confucianism are that the universe is orderly rather than chaotic and that there is supposed to be harmony within and among "the five cardinal relationships": emperor and his ministers, fathers and sons, older and younger brothers, husbands and wives, and between friends.[4] Within the family there were supposed to be equal protection and welfare for all members. The family shared both honors and disgrace; thus, a particular orientation to the family as a unit more important than the self evolved.

The authority of age in Confucianism is well documented. As Judith Treas points out:

> Rooted in a complex system of Confucian family ethics, the supremacy of seniority called for the absolute power of parents over offspring, as evidenced by the socially approved practice of infanticide and by parents' arrangement of children's marriages. Although this hierarchical system of age relationships had its basis in the family, it generalized to all dealings of young and old, master and apprentice. C.K. Yang (1974) aptly described the pervasiveness of these values when he wrote: In traditional society an individual from childhood to the end of his life was completely immersed in an atmosphere which compelled the observation of filial piety. The lesson of filial piety was carried in nursery stories, in daily exhortations and reprimands, in tales and novels, in textbooks from the first primer to the most profound philosophical discourse, in the numerous "temples of filial sons and chaste women" which studded the land, in dramatized living examples of extremely filial children.[5]

Within the family, "respect" for the aged was reinforced by coercion and threat of violence.[6] Filial disrespect under Confucianism, according to John King Fairbank, was a capital crime. "In law, a father was entitled to kill a truly impious son, since the son was his social responsibility and filiality was the most important social bond."[7] As Yang is quoted in another article, "Not until the fourth decade in one's life would one begin to gain serious consideration from senior members in the age hierarchy."[8]

Confucianism postulates a government with very limited functions other than the maintenance of law, order and harmony. The government which governs the least is considered the best. People are believed to be able to control and manage a good society without appealing to a Supreme Being and should be allowed to

capitalize on their ingenuity and provide for them-
selves--albeit guided by the exemplary behavior of the
rulers.

In social welfare concerns this is still the case.
The government provides the directives, sets the structure and calls upon officials and Party members to set
the examples, but implementation strategies are expected
to be developed by the local people and made appropriate
to local conditions.

Confucianism has had its challenges. In more modern times, the era between 1880 and 1949 saw conflicting
political and social ideologies arise to compete with
Confucianism. For instance, K'ang Yu-wei (the foremost
scholar of the 1880s) wrote The Great Commonwealth, the
first major blow to the Confucian family system. Questioning the sanctity of marriage, he felt love, not
parents, should be the basis for marriage and, in addition, advocated a repledge of marriage vows yearly. He
proposed communes to replace the private property system, public facilities for the raising of "unselfish"
children, and retirement homes for the aged.

As was his style, Mao took from Confucianism that
which was useful to the Revolutionary cause. As
Ganshow describes:

> Mao believed that the skills of the elderly
> would be beneficial to his Revolution, and he
> called for including the elderly in a coalition
> of people of all ages, and he challenged them
> to continue the Revolution and to build a
> socialistic society. In present-day China, the
> basis for respect has changed from the Confu-
> cian-based ideology to one based on respect for
> the makers of the Revolution. Now the aged are
> valued because they have within their memories
> the facts about the Revolution that young Chi-
> nese want to know. They can tell of personal
> experiences involving the suffering, the strug-
> gle, and the hardships of the Revolution and
> the happiness associated with establishing the
> new order. The elderly are therefore valued
> for their memories not of traditional China but
> of the birth and growth struggles of the new
> China.[9]

Marxism, as adapted by the Chinese, reigns supreme
and is the basis for the present democratic socialist
dictatorship. Nonetheless, the cultural conditioning
of Confucianism, so operative over the centuries, left
more than just remnants. Humanism, rationalism, and
learning from historical experience are dominant Confucian ideals still characteristic of Chinese society.
The role of ideology, structural conventions, and the
position of the ruling elite are still important

concerns as they have been since the time of Confucius. Loyalty, social responsibility and conformity, key Confucian values, are still stressed. The "five constant virtues," as defined by Confucius--benevolence, righteousness, propriety, wisdom and fidelity--continue to be firm foundations of modern Chinese culture. Since 1979, in fact, the government has begun to revive the good name of Confucius. Still, Confucian thought is viewed as incidental to the building of a socialist spiritual civilization with Chinese Communist ideals as the nucleus.

In Confucianism, one's political self is the externalization of one's moral training. A sage internally will have no problem being a wise ruler externally. Another maxim holds that the superior man should take care of the interests of the inferior man. One can see this in the Communist Party today. There is a rigorous selection process in choosing members of the Party. Although the Cultural Revolution era was the exception, the process of becoming a Party member is the ideological/political equivalent to the selection process in becoming a professional ballplayer in the United States. It is supposed to represent an elite group of highly developed, well-trained, exceptionally skilled team players.

In September 1982, in order to overcome "unhealthy tendencies" towards laxity within the Party and individuals putting their own interests above the needs of others and those of the nation, the Party's Twelfth Congress instituted a "rectification campaign" and "consolidation drive." To be conducted over the next three years, it was mandated to help the Party shoulder in a better way the important responsibility of leading the socialist modernization effort.[10] A fundamental turn for the better is felt to be needed in the working style of the whole Party, individually and as a whole, in order both to cement ties to the citizenry and to provide the leadership needed in these next crucial decades.

All 40 million Party members will receive an intense reindoctrination and then must qualify under new ideological standards. The basis upon which they will be judged is knowledge of and commitment to the Party line as contained in the Selected Works of Deng Xiaoping. Addressing "impurities of ideology, style, and organization within the Party" and abuse and misuse of authority, *cadres* will be examined for such detrimental impediments to modernization as "bureaucracy, formalism, red tape, irresponsibility and inefficiency."[11] Through this effort, it is hoped that the Party will be "purified and strengthened."

The Disciplinary Inspection Commission of the Chinese Communist Party's Central Committee will work through local commissions in this examination of Party discipline and will adopt measures to make sure the political quality and professional standards of the *cadres* in charge will be exemplary so that (contrary to Cultural Revolution judgments) each case can "stand the test of history." "Economic criminals, degenerate elements corrupted by bourgeois ideas and those who insist on opposing and endangering the Party will be expelled from it."[12] Those expelled or refused registration, however, will still be provided work, looked after, and encouraged to be good citizens.

The first group to be examined are those who rose to power during the Cultural Revolution on the basis of a strong ideology currently contrary to Deng's pragmatic policies and present day political thought. On such matters as the use of competitive exams to select college students, the encouragement of private enterprise, the dissolution of the commune (as Mao envisioned it) in favor of the responsibility system, and the forced retirement of aged guerilla fighters in the Army, it is believed that these "party dissidents" surreptiously block reforms. People will also be judged on the atrocities they committed during the Cultural Revolution. It is hoped by the present leadership that this movement will achieve as much as the first Yanan rectification campaign which laid the basis for winning the revolutionary war and giving birth to the People's Republic.[13] New members are being solicited from the ranks of the technologically proficient. At the same time the "purification" purge is occurring, an anti-corruption campaign is in full swing. Even Party officials have been found guilty (and imprisoned, expelled from the Party, or executed) of such crimes as smuggling, foreign currency speculation, extortion and embezzlement.[14]

As can be seen from the very real example given above, the ethical underpinnings of present day society are much stronger than overtly religious practices which have little, if anything, to do with political character. In the same vein, the continuing supportive influence of Confucianism on Chinese attitudes towards the elderly is remarkable to witness. Much of the positive predisposition the Chinese--as individuals and as a society--exhibit towards old people can be attributed directly to the abiding, albeit ethereal, heritage of Confucianism.

"Respecting the old" and "nurturing the young" are present day socialist ideals that go hand in hand. The source of what Colin Turnbull would call "Spirit" (i.e., the source of Power, Society, Life, the Unknown)[15] is family (including the "motherland"). The elderly parents of a professor with whom I was discussing Turnbull's work, a doctor and a nurse, have as their greatest source of "Spirit" their grandchildren. Their top priority is equipping their son's children with the

best advantages the society has to offer, and they derive great purpose and pleasure from doing so.

Still it's worth remembering that the effects of a
Confucian ethical code have not always been so benign.
Like any society's ethical code, there is a tension,
and a notable gap, between theory and practice. In the
idealized version of Confucianism, both the young and
the old derive major benefits from such practices as
filial piety and a state of harmony is achieved.

In reality, however, Confucianism spawned numerous
disharmonies and abuses--not the least of which was the
tyranny of the elderly resulting from filial piety tak-
en to extremes. Absolute obedience to the wishes and
will of the old was the norm within Chinese families
and the price paid by the young for their elders' protection and support was often severe--whether in the
form of psychological oppression or in that of physical
abuse.

The Communist revolution allowed the stranglehold
of the elderly to be broken and more equitable relationships formed both in families and across society. The
irony is that the intergenerational harmony Confucianism was intended to inculcate could only be achieved as
Confucianism itself was downgraded from the nation's
official ideology to its current status as an ethical
undercurrent. When filial piety was strictly enforced,
"respect" for the aged became a rationale for intergenerational oppression. Today, however, the Confucian
ideal of intergenerational love and harmony has reemer-
ged from the shadows of its overly strict manifestations in earlier times and its current effects are almost entirely benign.

Put simply, the tyranny is gone, but the bonds of
affection and devotion remain. Families appear to be
very close. The society is certainly very controlled,
but family relationships are not based on authoritarianism as in the old society but on harmony and respect.
Remarkably, not a single Chinese, in formal interviews
or informal conversations, spoke of old people as a
burden. Their observable behavior reinforced, rather
than belied, the notion that filial piety in present-
day China has evolved into an active ethic of devotion,
care and support for one's elders. All this leaves one
with the impression that the revolution purged the ex-
cesses of Confucian practice and, by doing so, has come
closer to manifesting the essence of Confucianism's ethical ideals.

The State has certainly maintained her role of providing moral leadership in this area. As a recent issue of China Reconstructs points out:

A good deal of concern has been expressed about
security in old age. Now urban, working people
and industrial workers are entitled to pensions,

and in the countryside, various measures have
been taken to provide a secure life for the
elderly. The problem is probably to overcome
loneliness and provide home nursing during
sickness. It is already estimated that when
the first generation of only children come of
age and marry some 25 years from now, each
young couple will have to care for two elderly
couples. To establish this custom, it is important that young married couples begin now
to take care of parents on both sides. In the
current "Five-Good Family" campaign, stress is
being laid on the responsibility that the husband and wife have for their respective parents
as well as on the neighborly spirit of caring
for the older people who do not live with their
children.[16]

EDUCATION CONTEXT

With the notable exception of the Cultural Revolution (1965-1976), the top of the Chinese pyramid of social status always has been occupied by those who labored with their minds--scholars. Next in the Chinese
social hierarchy have been those who labored with their
bodies--farmers and artisans. Merchants traditionally
have been seen as parasitically taking advantage of the
labor of others and ranked low in social status, even
though they may have been economically well-off.

Nevertheless, there appear to be fundamental contradictions in the attitudes and behavior toward education found in traditional Chinese society. For example,
women could acquire an extensive education, but until
the modern era, they were not allowed to compete for
the governmental and administrative posts for which
they were qualified. Similarly, despite the long tradition of open examinations for all, *de facto* class
segregation evolved instead of genuinely equal access
to education. After all, the children of landed gentry
had far more time, energy and opportunities to study
and prepare for the national examinations than did the
peasant class who were expected to engage in manual labor from sunrise to sunset.

These facts may not represent a contradiction as
much as they are an explanation of the historic function of education in Chinese society. Because the ten-
sions around what constitutes a "right" education and
for whom within China have been persistent ones--and
because, as will be discussed later, the current cohort
of elderly Chinese have been particularly affected by
the twists and turns of post-revolutionary education
policies--this subject is worthy of further pursuit.

From the 14th century onwards, until the end of

the Qing Dynasty, China's officials and experts were selected from among successful national examination candidates. These positions brought power, privilege and honor not only to the individual but also to the entire extended family. Even before the 14th century the principle of anonymity was used in the copying and grading of exams.[1] (This tradition has been reinstituted and can be seen today in the examination system for colleges and universities. Administrative preparations begin three months in advance for the intense three-day national entrance exams. Committees are set up in all districts and "invigilators" conduct the exams "according to regulations.")

Many jobs in China, as well as entrance to the next level of schooling, are increasingly based once again upon performance in examination exercises and in order to ensure a more equitable representation of educationally disadvantaged populations--women, national minorities and peasants from outlying areas--a quota system has been put into effect.

Under the guise of a meritocracy, education was used as a mechanism of socio-economic class reproduction and control. In principle, everyone was eligible to compete in the examinations leading to the best jobs. In fact, the competition was inevitably weighted in favor of offspring of the already educated (or wealthy) Chinese. In economic terms, education--like any other necessary resource or commodity--was valued, at least partially, on the basis of its scarcity.

The Chinese Revolution left major educational changes in its wake. Education has been viewed as a vital tool not only in fostering economic progress, but also in the political socialization of the Chinese people. Creating the "new Communist man" was the explicit goal of the post-revolutionary education system.

During the Cultural Revolution most schools were closed, then later reopened as a combination of manual labor training centers and political indoctrination units. Intellectualism, technical research and development, and other "elitist" trappings were vigorously cast aside. Egalitarianism was the order of the day and the humiliation/suppression/dissolution of the intellectual class was virtually complete.[2]

With Mao's death and the removal of the Gang of Four, the pendulum swung back. The current ideology of pragmatism and modernization has spurred a restoration of high levels of academic competence and professionalism. Accordingly, university education and other forms of advanced training are strongly supported. So-called "key schools" have been reinstituted for the best and brightest youth and the drive for universal literacy and universal primary education has a feeling of urgency.[3]

At the primary and secondary levels, schooling is

not yet universal for Chinese young people. School enrollment rates have risen in line with the directive
for universal primary education issued by the Party
Central Committee and the State Council. According to
the 1982 census data, however, among those aged 12 and
above, 23.1 percent are illiterate; 34.5 percent received primary school education; 6.6 percent completed
middle school; and 0.6 percent are college graduates.

Liaoning Province (with Shenyang as its principal
city) now has a 96.9 percent enrollment rate among
school-aged children and an 88.7 percent primary school
completion rate. Of the 61 counties and urban/suburban
districts in Liaoning Province, 56 have achieved universal primary education and the rest are under pressure to do so by 1985. To further universalize and
equalize educational opportunities, exceptional teachers are being transferred to what are considered
"underdeveloped" areas to aid in teacher training and
school improvement.[5]

There is a high dropout rate in the rural areas as
children are still expected to help their parents
throughout the agricultural cycle. The new "responsibility system" rewards family effort and thus has created incentives for the use of children in economic,
rather than educational, endeavors. To reduce the
dropout rate of children entering the economic sector
at early ages, two suburban counties in Shanghai (a
leading area in terms of innovative policies and practices) have decided that rural enterprises may employ
only those with at least a junior high education.[6]

Much remains to be done to expand effective access
to education and to redress past inequalities. The
literacy campaigns illustrate both sides of the equa-
tion. In 1949, the adult illiteracy rate was a stag-
gering 80 percent.[7] By 1982, this figure has been reduced to 23.5 percent.[8] Great advances have been realized and yet China remains a nation in which tens of
millions of adults still lack even the most rudimentary
formal education or literacy skills.

Correcting the historic maldistribution of educational opportunities and the legacy of elitism masquer-
ading as meritocracy in an unfinished task for China's
leaders. The distributional challenge in education can
be summed up in one statistic--90 percent of China's
illiterates can be found among the 80 percent of the
population living in rural areas. The December 1982
Constitution mandated that primary education be compulsory and universal and the Ministry of Education has
set the end of the 1980s as its target date for full
implementation. Although 93 percent of all school-age
children have entered school, there are continuing
problems with both dropout rates and graduation standards.[9] As in many other sectors, the Chinese have
done remarkably well with remarkably low funding.

Nonetheless, the fact that China ranks third from the bottom among 151 nations in terms of its per capita education expenditures has constrained full development.[10]

Major education issues also exist beyond the primary level of schooling. The news media reflect the concern that despite the remarkable recovery from the Cultural Revolution, most of Chinese higher education is antiquated, underequipped, and unable to produce the number of specialized graduates the country needs.[11] For every 10,000 people in China, there are 11.6 university students. Compare this to: India, 58.4; the Soviet Union, 106; Japan, 210; and the United States, 507.[12] In 1983, 1.67 million Chinese finished secondary school and competed for 360,000 college and university spots.[13] There were 280,000 college and university students and 3,000 post-graduates completing degrees.[14] Though "innovations" are being tried, these "experts" are routinely distributed across the huge Chinese land mass according to a job assignment system (described in the following section) that places the "socialist good" above family structure or individual preference.

It should be noted that a passing or qualifying grade is not enough to insure acceptance into a university. An individual must be considered to have high moral standards in the eye of his "unit" (*danwei*)* as well. As officials from a well-known medical school explained, "How a person relates to his family is very important, for if he has trouble there, how will he relate to his patients, to larger groups and to the society?" Good intergenerational relations thus receive institutional support. Those who don't respect their elders don't get ahead educationally.

Another example, given by the president of a large university, was that young men and women who are sexually promiscuous do not receive good recommendations from their *danwai* and thus are denied opportunities for educational advancement.[15] Susan Shirk, in her excellent book <u>Competitive Comrades: Career Incentives and Student Strategies in China</u>, calls this system a "virtuocracy" and argues that such moral judgments have superceded the technical judgments typical of a meritocracy.[16] In this way, the state upholds its interests and protects itself from mores that run counter to

---

*Everyone in China has a *danwei* to which he/she belongs. It may be a workplace, office, factory, school, commune or residence structure, but it's the smallest organizational group with which an individual identifies and is identified by the society. Everything (social, economic, and political) is at least initially organized through the *danwei*. Even as a foreigner, I had to identify my "unit" before a hotel reservation could be made.

what it considers "the public good."

The elderly benefit because, in the view of the Chinese, it is "correct," "fitting" and "proper" that they be treated as valuable and important. Many times and in many circumstances I was told in response to my questioning, "It's just the Chinese way!" as if nothing else need be said. "Respect for the elderly" falls into this category in the Chinese mind.

In an attempt to meet the demand for education, the government is developing alternative systems of self and distance education through the use of correspondence courses, TV universities, spare-time studies within factories and enterprises, and literacy classes. For example, Liaoning Province has 39 regular institutions of higher learning and 102 spare-time universities. Technical secondary schools and technical workers' training schools are increasing rapidly in number. It is estimated that over 8 million of the 35 million residents of Liaoning Province are studying at various schools at all levels. Liaoning Provincial TV University has enrolled more than 15,000 industrial management, industrial accounting, and commercial accounting students from factories and enterprises.[17] Liaoning is not atypical in this regard. Nearly 200 million people, or one-fifth of China's population, are presently receiving various forms of regular education according to Vice-Minister of Education Zhang Wen-song.[18]

Thirty-three thousand "self-taught" students in Beijing have applied to take national examinations—including a 74-year-old retired teacher.[19] Those who pass the exams will be awarded diplomas and those who score exceptionally well will be recommended for better jobs or enrolled in the universities. This self-development opportunity only exists in a few major cities at the present time but it is expected to expand.[20] Forty local "day colleges," similar to American community colleges with a two- to three-year curriculum, have been set up to train people to fill local needs. While universities, with a yearly per capita training cost of 1,500 to 2,000 yuan, are tuition-free, the day colleges are charging a tuition of about 500 yuan.[21]

To put these developments in a proper perspective, one must remember the profound effects the Cultural Revolution has had on the entire society. No Chinese was left untouched. In the education sector, many universities were shut down or their curricula altered to focus almost exclusively on Marxist-Leninist-Mao Zedong Thought. Study and research were discouraged, if not altogether prohibited, and many faculty members and students were "sent down" to the countryside to engage in manual labor. "Re-education" camps were established for intellectuals following Mao Zedong's 1966 "May 7th-Directive" and within a few years, over 20,000,000 people (virtually all of China's professional and

university trained population) were assigned to these
cadre schools.[22] The eleven years of the Cultural Revolution created a void both in the development of technical, scientific, and academic knowledge and in the
development of leaders. One hears over and over how
much was lost or interrupted during the Cultural Revo-
lution--work, study, education and, most terribly,
lives.

Ironically, this education gap has kept the elderly in a position of prominence. Those individuals now
of retirement age in state enterprises, factories and
schools have, in many instances, been asked to continue
working as there is a pronounced lack of skilled younger people able to replace them. Although 60 is the
recommended retirement age for university professors,
the regulations state that they may continue working
until 70 (and there are exceptions even to this limit).
This situation exists not only out of current respect
for the profession, but also because their perspective,
experience and knowledge are often irreplaceable in advancing the modernization movement.

Older people in the government, State enterprises
or institutions who possess needed skills rarely "retire" at all--at least in the Occidental sense of
forced leisure time. Instead, they move to another
"line," or layer, of the bureaucracy:

> Those on the "first line" are the actual deci-
> sionmakers; those on the "second line" are the
> senior Party leaders in the highest level di-
> recting the basic orientation of the system;
> the "third line" refers to the advisory posi-
> tions; those on the "fourth line" are retired,
> but still maintain influence on the operations
> of the original units; and the "fifth line"
> refers to complete retirement.[23]

There is a real reluctance among the well-educated and
well-placed elderly to retire. Besides having an out-
let for their dedication and source for their feelings
of productivity, working carries with it continued
power, prestige, and perquisites for the aged.

This situation is only temporary--a stopgap measure designed to keep the momentum of development going
while a new generation of technical and political leaders are trained. The first wave of this post-Cultural
Revolution educated class is just moving into position
and the old *cadres* are being encouraged to move back to
another line. The following excerpt from an August
1983 issue of China Daily heralds the arrival of this
younger cohort. Aside from being an excellent summary
statement, this editorial points out a fact worth keeping in mind--namely, that the "younger" better educated
leaders moving into first line positions are themselves

in their 50s and 60s:

A profound reform in leading organs is taking place in China. With the streamlining of government structure started last year, leading bodies of the central, provincial and most of the prefecture and municipality levels are reorganized. Some 400,000 veteran *cadres* have now stepped down from leading posts. Large numbers of middle-aged and younger *cadres* are being promoted and enabled to play more responsible roles.

Thus China now has two leadership echelons in place. The first is made up of veteran revolutionaries who have participated in the long time legendary struggles of the Chinese revolution and experienced the successes and frustrations in the country's socialist construction. A few of them still need to work in the leading core. They are revolutionaries of the elder generation who have rich experience and enjoy high prestige among the people. But most of them moved back to the second or third line, mainly giving advice and guidance on major policy issues.

The second echelon consists of younger colleagues of the first. They are generally in their 60's on the central level. Most of them are above 50. They take up the heavy task of running day-to-day affairs.

This is an important breakthrough in the rejuvenation of China's leading organs, which is long overdue.

History shows that the problem of succeeding the veteran revolutionaries by the young cannot be easily solved. In the Soviet Union, Stalin failed to handle it well. In China, Comrade Mao Zedong raised the problem in the early 1960s, but he did not manage to do a good job of it either. During the "cultural revolution," the whole Party and State organizations were severely crippled and those who were picked out to replace the veterans hardly shared their minds with the multitudes.

Now China has entered a new period, a correct handling of the problem of successors is all the more imperative and essential for the modernization drive. And this complicated and difficult task has fallen to the still living veteran revolutionaries. Guiding principles and policies have been drawn on the basis of past and fresh historical experience. Requirements set for qualified new leaders can be summed up as: revolutionary minded, young, better-educated

and with professional expertise. A plan was
drawn and has been put into practice earnest-
ly.[24]

What does all of this mean for China's elderly?
In a society which is just creating (or re-creating) an
educated technocratic class, there is an inevitable reliance upon those with the most experience and prior
training. In the case of China today, the well-educated are largely a group of aging elderly. They have
been valued for their wisdom, but they will be replaced
by those with more advanced technical knowledge. The
government now actively encourages its ranking older
functionaries to prepare their younger followers and
move aside for them when they are ready.[25] The current
cohort of elderly Chinese has had a particular place,
purpose and position, but will such high status continue to be accorded to successive generations of elderly
professionals, politicians and technicians? Stated
differently, will respect for (and allegiance to) the
elderly be compromised when, because of greater numbers
of educated and energetic youth, the old no longer are
irreplaceable? Will intergenerational competition for
the same jobs become a frequent occurrence? If so,
will it lead to resentment of the old by the young and,
ultimately, to a marginalization of the elderly--first
economically and then socially as well?
    The answers are by no means certain. In Occiden-
tal countries, the most likely response to all the
aforementioned questions would be affirmative. In
China, deference to the elderly may be both so psycho-
logically engrained and so culturally reinforced that
it will prove impervious to the assumed leveling effects of universal education and literacy.
    One key may rest with the political judgment as to
whether the knowledge and wisdom acquired through experience will take precedence over the technical expertise acquired through formal education and training.
All things considered, however, the best guess one can
make is that while realignments may occur as to who
serves in which lines in which factories, agencies and
other units, the effective demand in the modernization
movement for educated people will remain so high that
everyone capable of contributing (young or old) will be
placed in a position through which their contributions
can be realized.

ECONOMIC/EMPLOYMENT CONTEXT

    Closely allied to the education sector, on a per-
sonal level, is the economic sector--especially given
China's mandatory job assignment system. Employment
policies have a profound social effect, as can be seen

through an examination of: first, current gender differences in retirement age; second, the effects of the
work assignment system on family structure; third, the
position of the elderly in relation to the work force;
and, fourth, the economic roles that the elderly assume
within their families.

Through the so-called "iron rice bowl," lifetime
jobs are guaranteed to all government employees and
workers who have been assigned to State-owned enterprises* and institutions. The national retirement program also extends to members of the Chinese Communist
Party, career soldiers and mass organizations from the
county level up. The age of eligibility and the pre-
cise financial arrangements vary according to gender,
occupational status and length of employment.

Regardless of work performance, the "iron rice
bowl" never breaks! The system affects some 83 million
people--19 percent of the work force.[2] There is presently a great deal of controversy over the "iron rice
bowl." On one hand, with State control and distribution of personnel, the system guarantees jobs to those
within the system and protects against unemployment.
On the other hand, it rewards equally those who work
hard and those who don't.

Women and Retirement

The official retirement age for men is 60, though
in practice some work longer. Women in "heavy" industry are eligible to retire with full benefits at 50 and
those in "light" industry and administrative posts at
55. Deborah Davis-Friedmann accounts for the differences between the sexes in terms of retirement as follows:

> The primary explanation for these male-female
> differences was the failure of women to achieve
> economic parity with men prior to retirement.
> This "failing" on the part of women workers can
> in turn be attributed to educational restric-
> tions placed on girls in the 1930s and 40s and
> to the traditional expectations that childcare
> and housework are female jobs that require no
> financial payment. As a result women were not
> recruited or trained for the best paying tech-
> nical and supervisory jobs in the 1950s or 1960s.
> After their marriages they took long, unpaid
> leaves of absence to raise their children and

State enterprises are defined as "grassroots units of
business management under ownership by the whole people."[1]

thereby limited their ability to complete 20 years of continuous employment. And finally, in recent years, adult children have routinely turned to their retired mothers, not their fathers, to provide full-time childcare and housework services. As a result, even vigorous, well trained female workers and staff are not encouraged to postpone retirement or find new post-retirement employment. Instead they move immediately from the position of full time worker in the paid labor force to full time, *unpaid* laborer in the home.

Among newly retired professionals I interviewed in 1978, there was overt criticism of the expectation that retired mothers and mothers-in-law take primary responsibility for the children and housework of their working sons and daughters. Several younger women who planned on retirement within the next ten years were especially critical and told me that after they retired they would definitely not care for their grandchildren. This attitude was in sharp contrast with the opinions of women from working class or peasant backgrounds who regardless of their past work history of paid employment voiced approval, or even pleasure with their household responsibilities.

From the perspective of an outsider, it appears that women who have achieved educational and occupational parity with their male peers do not expect to duplicate the current differences between men and women pensioners. As of 1980, male-female differences in educational achievement and average wages among urban residents under 35 are slight. Therefore unless policy toward female students and workers shifts drastically, it would seem likely that by the end of the 20th century, the clear cut advantages of retired men will fade. However, for the next 10 or 15 years significant inequalities will persist and any overview of the retired population must recognize these important generational and gender differences.[3]

A provincial level psychologist, a male, had a different interpretation: "Due to their physiology, men *can* work longer. The fact that women retire earlier shows the position of Chinese women in our society. We think they deserve special treatment and the government shows special concern for them."[4]

How do women view this situation? Let's let a sample of women leaders speak for themselves.

Lei Jieqiong (chairperson of the following: the Law Committee of the National People's Congress, the

All-China Women's Federation, and the China Association
for Promoting Democracy--one of China's several democratic parties) argues that:

> Sex discrimination and female infanticide are
> only visible manifestations of the invisible
> patriarchal partiality that persists despite
> all the rules and laws written since liberation
> on political and economic equality.[5]

Zhang Wenyun (Women's Federation of Fuzhou City,
Fujian Province) says:

> I think that in China, women's role in develop-
> ment and their status have improved enormously
> compared with the old days. However, the tra-
> ditional concept of male superiority still
> lingers on, and discriminatory practices against
> women continue to exist. Last year, among the
> nine speakers at the meeting in honor of model
> workers of Fuzhou, six were women. But when it
> comes to appointment of model workers to leading
> posts, few females are selected.[6]

Ma Wenrong (Women's Federation of Tianjin Municipality) notes:

> It is true that Chinese women's rights and sta-
> tus have been considerably raised over the past
> 30-odd years, and women with outstanding talent
> are generally recognized and some are put in
> important positions. Nonetheless, in training
> and promoting women *cadres*, there is still a
> tendency to discriminate against women, and the
> view that women are not as intelligent as men
> still prevails in many of these situations. Ob-
> viously, feudal ideas which dominated China for
> thousands of years, have still not thoroughly
> been done away with.[7]

And finally, Mei Shaoling (Women's Federation of
Guangzhou City, Guangdong Province) points out that:

> Some women, still influenced by old concepts,
> under-estimate themselves and feel inferior to
> men. Lacking high ideals and effort for their
> work and studies, it is not unusual for some
> women to sacrifice themselves for the sake of
> their husbands when a strain occurs between work
> and family.[8]

Non-Chinese observers often reach the same conclusions. Concurring with Davis-Friedmann, U.S. anthropologist Margery Wolf states: "Women remain the second

sex. They are found more often in the service sector basically because the male leadership is unwilling to change things. Women in the work force are men's helpers." Her research in urban factories showed starting salaries to be the same, but after five years, the women made much less. As Wolf explains: "The State paved the way for equal access to opportunities, but society places different demands and expectations."[9]

Still the effort to break down traditional discriminatory attitudes and behaviors toward women continues. The ideology of socialism demands no less than genuine equality for women, even though the culture is deeply rooted in a paternal (and paternalistic) mentality. Breaking down ancient cultural traditions (like sexism) may be even more difficult to accomplish than preserving those traditions (like respect for the elderly) deemed appropriate to be carried over into the new China. Nevertheless, as a 1983 issue of China Reconstructs points out:

> The legal system and organizations such as the Women's Federation have stepped in to offer protection and assistance to mothers giving birth to daughters who are harassed by their families. Some places now award additional benefits to parents of first-born girls (such as special bonuses and longer maternity leaves for mothers). But in the long run the preference for boy babies will not disappear without changes in women's status.
> Dr. Qian Xinzhong has proposed that for a time women should be given priority in education and job opportunities, and the Women's Federation has recently called for a concerted effort to eliminate the discrimination against women still sometimes practiced by colleges and work units. Patient public education can help break down old prejudices--such as that brides should always join their husbands' families, and never the other way around.[10]

The Rewards of Retirement

Typically, someone with twenty years' experience in a State-run unit received 70 to 80 percent of their final monthly pay each month after retirement; someone with fifteen years' experience draws an approximate monthly benefit of 60 percent; and someone with ten years of work 40 percent. Yet, there is still a degree of variation across China. Model Workers[11] and those who worked for the revolutionary effort, for example, receive at least 100 percent of their final pay as pensions. According to the All-China Federation of Trade

Unions, the government appropriated 7.3 billion yuan
for pensions in 1982, an average of 64.5 yuan a month
for each retired person.[12]

The retirement benefits, according to those interviewed in Shenyang, are sufficient not to cause major
compromises in lifestyle after retirement. In addition
to the guarantee of a lifetime pension, there are other
benefits available to the retired workers of the State
sector and, increasingly, to the peasants. For example, "Labor Insurance Regulations" which legislate pensions also provide full coverage of workers' or retirees' medical expenses and partial (50 percent) coverage for their dependents.

Pension insurance schemes were offered for the
first time in 1982 in a dozen cities and provinces by
the People's Insurance Company of China for those in
collectively-run, as opposed to State-run, units. In
Shenyang, 453 collectively-run enterprises have started
pension plans for their workers with varying contributions from employers and employees.

Davis-Friedmann and Bonavia both report that if a
retiree relocates to a small city or rural area, he or
she receives a monetary reward.[13] My own experience in
Shenyang was in line with the following observations:

> The retired worker retains his pre-retirement
> housing. If he or she is living in a private
> home or renting from the municipal real estate
> bureau, this continuity provides no particular
> advantage. But if the worker and his family
> live in subsidized enterprise "dormitories"
> there is considerable value in the retention
> of previous housing. Not only do they qualify
> for relatively high quality housing at low cost
> but more importantly other members of the house-
> holds currently living with a retiree who do not
> work in the same enterprise may also remain in
> the apartment. In this way, many retirees pass
> to their children one of the most sought after
> goods in contemporary China—a single family
> apartment of two or more rooms.[14]

Retirement is seen, though not always experienced, as a
reward and the resulting good feeling promotes a beneficence on the part of the retired worker as well. An
example from the countryside makes the point:

> Now that the peasants' income is rising under
> the new responsibility system, the collective
> is also providing a better life for the old.
> For example, Song Yongmao, 82, of production
> team No. 4, prefers to stay in the countryside
> alone in spite of the fact that his son and
> daughter-in-law have asked him to live with

them in the city. "I have my pension, 22 yuan
a month, plus a subsidy from the team. Last
year the team gave 200 yuan extra because the
peasants' income had increased greatly. Since
1980 the team has provided all the needs of our
21 retired people, men over 65 and women over
60. I hate being idle so I asked to look after
the team's office."[15]

Effects of the Work Assignment System on Family Structure

A recent change in the retirement system has to do
with the substitution of a son or daughter in a parent's position within a State enterprise or in State
service, a practice known as the *ding ti*. Under the
old system, the cadre or employee could retire early
and be replaced by one of his/her offspring. This
practice came under criticism because it was felt that
guaranteed employment, regardless of talent, effort or
professional qualifications, stifled both initiative
and the desire to work hard and produce on the part of
students. Under the new system, adopted in September
1983, young adults can still replace their parents but
they must not only wait for their parents to retire at
the usual ages, but also pass examinations to qualify
for employment in these enterprises. Shenyang No. 1
Machine Tool Works is a good example. Every effort is
made to hire the children of employees and to assign
them a position according to both their skills and the
needs of the factory. An employment opportunity in a
desirable State enterprise is highly prized for, with
the "iron rice bowl" system referred to above, the employee is economically secure within the Chinese economy for life.

Early retirement in order to step aside for one's
offspring (so the family unit can benefit from a pension plus a salary) will continue to be allowed in
cases where more than one family member is living in
the countryside or if the family has financial problems. In an attempt to circumvent these new regulations, the night they were announced by the State Council, 700 workers of the Wuhan Railway Station with 700
matching sons and daughters hastily requested early retirement before the new law went into effect. This was
publicly declared to be an impropriety and the Hubei
Provincial Government demanded that the error be re-
dressed and the situation rectified.[16] Other "retirement sprees" and their rectifications have been reported in the press as well.[17]

At the subdistrict level, a labor service committee works with State-owned enterprises and institutions

to place unemployed young people.* Using exams again
as a basis for selection, everyone is believed to have
equal chance, if not equal luck. Both temporary and
permanent assignments are made this way. People who
refuse assignments are considered not only unpatriotic
but also foolish, because they go to the bottom of the
"waiting for jobs" list and it may take years for another opportunity to present itself.[18]
     Labor service committees have also been setting up
training classes to enable some of the young the State
can't currently absorb into the workforce to set up
their own businesses. Watch and camera repair services
are currently popular. 1983 figures show approximately
1,500,000 self-employed workers in China and the numbers are growing.[19] Business streets are lined with
vendors. Such enterprise is now promoted by the government to cut down on unemployment. Many middle
school graduates are "waiting for jobs" and resort to
selling goods on the street or taking temporary positions until an official assignment is received or the
"back door" provides another entrance. Some 9,000
retirees in Shanghai have been helping young people in
their neighborhoods earn livings while waiting for job
assignments from the State through the sponsorship of
over 3,000 business cooperatives.
     In addition to the employment routes cited above,
more technical positions requiring college-trained personnel are filled upon graduation through an assignment
made by the State Planning Commission and the Ministries of Education and Labor and Personnel. Kyna Rubin
offers a very apt analogy for this system: "Some people have likened the graduate-prospective employer relationship to that between bride and groom in traditional China. Neither is permitted to get acquainted
with the other before the irreversible bond has been
sealed."[20]
     Knowing few graduates would volunteer to go to re-
mote or underdeveloped areas if given the choice, the
central control of all job assignments randomized the
placements. People conform both for patriotic reasons
and because there are very few practical alternatives
to conformity. In Beijing last year four students who
turned down assignments were officially blacklisted and
barred from working for five years. In addition, their
families received fewer food rationing coupons.[21]
     As stated in the education section, higher educa-
tion opportunities exist only for a very small percentage of the population; yet, even this opportunity

---

*The Hujialou Subdistrict, for example, under the ju-
risdiction of the Chaoyang District in Eastern Beijing,
consists of 24 neighborhood committees and has a population of 56,671--"a small community in Chinese eyes."

proves to be a double-edged sword. The more qualified a student becomes, the less likely it is that his job assignment will be near his parents or extended family. In fact, it is reported that many potential college students are being discouraged from pursuing advanced studies by parents who fear permanent separation.[22]

A week before the beginning of the 1983-84 academic year, the personnel office of the Northeast Institute of Technology was very busy placing the 100 new graduates who had been assigned to them by the State. They figured about 80 of the 100 would remain at NEIT throughout their careers and eventually retire there under the auspices of their departments. Only an extenuating circumstance, such as being requested by another unit, would alter the permanent assignment made by the central government. Each year there are graduates to place and former assignments are rarely open to revision. The units to which these newcomers come will largely shape their life situations. For example, they become eligible for housing assignments for the duration of their careers and subsequent retirement. (The lack of a housing assignment is one of the impediments to retiring to the Sun Belt of China!)

Although for the vast majority of graduates the present system of job placement will continue, some innovations are beginning to take place amidst the criticism that many graduates are given jobs that have little to do with their training. The implication is that they are not being used to their, or the State's, best advantage.

A survey of those who graduated from Shanghai University in 1981, for example, found that 20 percent had been assigned jobs totally unrelated to their studies,[23] which, though a common occurrence in the United States, does not seem to be in line ideologically with the needs of the modernization movement. Some of the reforms being tried for the first time in 1983-84 include making job assignments a year in advance with direct negotiation between work units and universities to match graduates with openings. In some cases individual units are being given the right to interview and test potential employees for greater choice in whom they accept, and universities are being allowed to make placement decisions on a trial basis. In Beijing, two percent of the students are being allowed, on an experimental basis, to select their own positions subject to the approval of the Government.[24]

Another innovation allows graduates to work on a probationary basis for a year to make sure their training is appropriate and job requirements can be met before a permanent assignment is made. If not, available options include transfer, extended probation or dismissal. Those given "hardship posts" in underdeveloped areas will receive higher pay and be allowed to transfer

after eight years. All these changes point toward
greater flexibility and a better blend of sense of purpose, productivity, and personal preference.[25]

Postgraduates are sent mainly to staff colleges,
research institutes and key sectors of the national
economy once they've finished their training. Possibilities currently exist for study abroad for this echelon and for transfers at this level depending on the
needs of modernization--not those of the individual.

In essence, education, while it assures access to
the "iron rice bowl," has mitigated against the three-
generation family during the modernization drive. As
schooling becomes more pervasive though, with the development of self- and distance-education structures,
and as the bureaucratized employment system decentral-
izes further and becomes more personal, individual
choice will undoubtedly enter the picture. Perhaps it
is no more than trying to fill in for the missing
grandparents, but well-educated Chinese are known to be
more open to equality between the sexes, and educated
males share much more in child care, household administration, cooking and domestic chores.

Position of the Elderly in Relation to the Workforce

The economic sector is in the midst of combining
private initiatives and collective responsibilities.
The economic structures are experiencing an historic
change--going from a production framework based upon
collective responsibility, collective will, and collective sharing of benefits to one based on a personal and
familial responsibility system, expanded entrepreneur-
ship and taxation by (rather than profit-sharing with)
the State.

Before 1979, when anything was needed--equipment,
repairs, housing for workers, etc.--it had to be requested from the State. Now, even inside the "iron
rice bowl," incomes are becoming more closely tied to
management efficiency and to worker productivity. It
is a time of initiative and economic growth. A look at
the tumultuous transformations industries, enterprises
and individual workers have experienced gives a clearer
perspective on what is becoming a market-influenced, if
not a market-oriented, socialist economy.

Many experiments are being tried that use wage incentives to promote increased production, i.e., "to encourage the diligent and punish the slack."[26] Income
incentives (e.g., bonuses or raises) are, at least
theoretically, an amount in addition to a baseline salary that covers "minimum living expenses; appropriate
increases to match years of service so that middle-age
and elderly employees are not penalized due to

weakening physical strength; a family allowance; and an appropriate sum to match qualifications of formal and self-education."[27]

The more individualistic/entrepreneurial/motivational practices being promoted are seen as necessary for the socialist economy. The similarity to capitalism is denied, but Occidental observers regard this denial as a semantic, rather than as an economic, distinction. Whatever the label, the perceived danger in China is that independence in economic matters will adversely affect the collective spirit and the ideal of collective security and interdependence. The fear is that private groups might be less likely to look after non-family members in terms of their social and financial support and their health and education expenses.

An opinion column in the China Daily reads like a Maslow text: "And when relative material abundance has been achieved, peasants' desire for psychological security must be stronger. Only a collective system can afford an expensive welfare and pension program that can satisfy that desire."[28] The columnist is speaking of a rural/agricultural situation, but the same can be said for an industrialized urban setting as well. Although the State, through its Labor Insurance Regulations, pays the pensions of retired workers, the work unit continues to be responsible for the overall welfare and well-being of its former employees. This practice takes time and effort and is not based upon an expected material return.

In Shenyang, retirement status in a State enterprise, factory, or institution (where work and residence have been combined) frees the individual from his workload, but allows him all the amenities and friendships that have been part of his worklife. The retired individual picks up his pension the way he used to pick up his salary; he's called upon when needed; visited by the leaders during holidays; cared for when sick or disabled; and helped financially when in need. In other words, although retired, the individual is still a recognized and respected part of the unit.

Already in Beijing, because of the increasing number of retired persons, an experiment in aggregating the care of retired workers through a central administrative unit is being tried. The rationale for the project is typical of more developed countries: the retired are thought to be served more efficiently (and thus, in a "better" way) by centralizing their care under a coordinated administration. Three similar pilot projects have been set up in Shanghai, in Mudanjiang (Heilongjiang Province) and in Anyang (Henan Province). Nationwide implementation is expected if the experiment is judged to be successful.[29]

The Role of the Elderly in the Family Economy

Although the involvement of the work unit and the government in the lives of Chinese elderly is signifi- cant, familial care and support remain paramount. Be- cause of both cultural traditions and scarce housing, the aged in the PRC do not normally live alone. Those old people living in three-generational family units are rarely "hidden in the attic"--and not simply be- cause there are so few attics! Rather, the elderly usually play a vital economic and social role within the extended family.

In pre-revolutionary China, one reason the elderly commanded deferential treatment was because of their control of the family's purse strings. Even posthu- mously, their economic influence was felt through an- cestor worship and the inheritance system. To be less than obedient to the wishes of the elderly was not only disrespectful, but also economically disadvantageous. There may not have been much wealth to control, but whatever there was remained in the hands of the fami- ly's patriarch.

The profound redistribution of power and wealth occurring across Chinese society in the wake of the 1949 Revolution echoed within ordinary families as well. The elimination of major private holdings dimin- ished the impact of inheritance practices and the ide- ology of egalitarianism translated into far more equal family relationships than had ever been experienced in pre-Mao China.

Today it is common for there to be more than one income source within each family. The pensions of the elderly are pooled with the wages of the working adults (and occasionally employed youth as well). How money is distributed is most often a family decision. The spirit of mutual support among generations is consis- tently reinforced by the government--both as a means of fostering self-sufficiency instead of reliance upon the government directly and as a mechanism of socialization into the communal, egalitarian economic/social rela- tions advocated for the nation's work and living units.

Although rarely the decisive factor, the income of elderly members does serve to tie families together and encourage intergenerational cooperation. Monthly pay in my sample group of 109 adults from Shenyang and Anshan was as follows:

12%	50 yuan or less
60%	50-75 yuan
24%	76-100 yuan
3%	over 100 yuan

At the time the survey was taken the yuan was worth about 50 cents. As government employees, everyone in

the sample expected a pension. In no conversation did
I hear the slightest doubt that money would be available for them when it came time to retire. Given the
immense changes these individuals have seen in the political world, such faith came as quite a surprise to
me. Even a discussion of demography, Occidental experience and increasing life spans did not shake their
expressed confidence. More specifically:

   5% expected pensions ranging from 65-74%
      of their last wage
  32% expected the range of 75-84%
  17% projected 85-94%
  47% anticipated 95-100%

   The grandparents, through their pensions, sometimes bring more income to the household than the working second generation. The usual pattern in three-gen-
eration households is that the grandparents take care
of the children and do much of the shopping, cooking
and household administration. Nurseries and kindergartens are increasingly available, but there are still
not enough. Since the available institutional child
care is not free, this imposes an additional obstacle
to low-income families. The grandparents thus become
invaluable, not only for the care they provide, but
also for the economic and employment opportunities thus
made possible for the second generation to pursue--the
benefits of which accrue to the unit. In addition, the
old people engage in unofficial work that increases
family income even more. They sprout seeds, sell ice
sticks, weigh and measure people on the street, and
make and sell handicrafts. What is given by the older
family members brings them a physical and psychological
return (i.e., a sense both of productivity and of being
needed).
   Dependency, a negative word in Occidental cultures, seems to promote very satisfying, harmonious,
non-competitive relationships in urban China today.
Families tend to be very close units. Even if not living under the same roof, they are usually close by for
mutual assistance. Thus, the realities of housing,
employment, pensions and income distribution in post-
Mao China all serve (at least in part by design) to
maintain the social importance and familial status of
the elderly.
   Chinese law also reinforces the economic interdependence of family members. For example, Article 49 of
the New Constitution states that "Children who have
come of age have the duty to support and assist their
parents." Moreover, the tradition seems so strong and
the notion of duty towards the old so pervasive, that
even when the second generation is responsible for the
bulk of the family income, they are not accorded the

dominant position within the family.

Respect for the elderly seems to exist regardless
of the presence, absence or pursuit of money and is
supported by all the structures of the society. The
societal mores of respect for the elderly are upheld by
law, encouraged by public opinion and criticism, and
rewarded by opportunities for advancement. With no
sizable property to be inherited (the basis for patrilineal and patrilocal systems*), the solidarity and
household arrangements of the family are based upon
choice, affection and mutual benefit.

POLITICAL/LEGAL CONTEXT

Susan Shirk states that the moral of her book,
Competitive Comrades: Career Incentives and Student
Strategies in China, is that "political designs for
social change must continually take into account the
way individuals pursue their own objectives. These designs should take into account people's real-life concerns rather than stubbornly denying them."1

Shirk's political principle parallels the principle of the "mass line" upon which the People's Republic
of China was founded. The present chairman of both the
State and Party Military Commissions and the "paramount" leader today, Deng Xiaoping, is also an advocate
of the mass line (a concept the Party uses to explain
its seemingly contradictory ideal of a "democratic dictatorship"). Understanding the mass line is the key to
understanding the functioning and operation of the Chinese government and Party system today. As Livingston
and Lowinger explain:

> The mass line, which embodies both the Marxist
> theory of knowledge and the Leninist theory of
> organization, may be defined as learning from
> the masses of ordinary people, taking their
> knowledge of the world and systematizing it,
> and giving it back to them in a more structured
> way so that their ideas about what needs changing
> in the real world can be used to make the
> changes. Mao Tse-tung, in the classic statement
> of how the mass line works in practice, put it
> this way in 1943:

---

*A *patrilineal* system traces kinship through the fathers' family ties. *Patrilocal* refers to the residence
of a married couple with the husband's parents. A
patriarchal family system is one where the males take
precedence over the females, other things being equal,
and the family head is ideally expected to be male.

> In all the practical work of the Party,
> all correct leadership is necessarily
> "from the masses, to the masses." This
> means: take the ideas of the masses
> (scattered and unsystematic ideas) and
> concentrate them (through study turn them
> into concentrated and systematic ideas),
> then go to the masses and propagate and
> explain these ideas until the masses em-
> brace them as their own, hold fast to
> them and translate them into action, and
> test the correctness of these ideas in
> such action. Then once again concentrate
> ideas from the masses and once again to
> the masses so that the ideas are perse-
> vered in and carried through. And so on,
> over and over again in an endless spiral,
> with the ideas becoming more correct,
> more vital and richer each time. Such is
> the Marxist theory of knowledge.[2]

Given this ideological touchstone, the People's
Republic of China's political self-definition, as expressed in the New Constitution, becomes understandable.
The Constitution describes the PRC as: "A socialist
state under the people's democratic dictatorship led by
the working class and based on the alliance of workers
and peasants."[3]

This political philosophy carries within it two
major objectives: first, to lay the foundation for the
desired relationship between the Party and the people;
and second, to put the bureaucrats and intellectuals in
"the second line"--secondary to, and actively serving,
the people. There is currently a major push to reform
and consolidate the Party and to support intellectuals
--but it is being done in the context of achieving socialist modernization for the benefit of all the people.
A November 1983 issue of China Daily, for example, carried the warning that:

> If we abandon the purpose of serving the people
> wholeheartedly, our Communist Party will be
> unworthy of its name and will lose the support
> of the people. And without the support of the
> people, nothing can be achieved.[4]

Since "the people" includes a significant and
ever-growing number of old people, how are these principles applied to the elderly? Broadly speaking, the
central government has made--and enforced--a strong political commitment to the well-being and centrality of
the aged in Chinese society. It has consistently supported and encouraged local initiatives undertaken by
the elderly and has sought to uphold their status.

Self-reliance is a key value of the society and the roles accorded to, and assumed by, senior citizens exemplify this virtue.

In China, retirement represents a transition from one socially and economically useful role to another, equally valuable one. A quick comparison of the legal systems in the U.S. and the PRC illustrates this point. For example, the U.S. has approximately 450 lawyers for every one in China. Although the legal profession is presently being built up, there are only approximately 8,500 full-time and 2,300 part-time lawyers in 2,200 offices in all of China.[5] It is the elderly who investigate complaints and arbitrate civil disputes. What counts is not a technical knowledge of the law, but rather the wisdom and experience older people are presumed to have in finding appropriate solutions to local problems. Their status in society, not the possession of official authority, is the secret of their successful arbitration and mediation activities.

The elderly are politically involved and influential from the corridors of power in Beijing to the most humble work or residential unit in Shenyang. This political stature is reflected in the nation's laws as well. For instance, children who have the capacity to bear the relevant costs are bound by law to take care of their parents and to support and assist their grandparents if their parents are deceased.

The New Constitution broadens the scope of the former Article 50 which stated that "Working people have the right to material assistance in old age." The new Article 45 states:

> Citizens of the People's Republic of China have the right to material assistance from the state and society when they are old, ill or disabled. The state develops the social insurance, social relief and medical and health services that are required to enable citizens to enjoy this right.
>
> The state and society ensure the livelihood of disabled members of the armed forces, provide pensions to the families of martyrs and give preferential treatment to the families of military personnel.

Similarly, the new Article 49 declares:

> Marriage, the family and mother and child are protected by the state.
> Both husband and wife have the duty to practice family planning.
> Parents have the duty to rear and educate their minor children and children who have come of age have the duty to support and assist

their parents.
        Violation of the freedom of marriage is
prohibited. Maltreatment of old people, women
and children is prohibited.

The Marriage Law prohibits maltreatment or abandonment
of family members which of course, by definition, includes parents and grandparents (when the parents are
unable to care for them). The Criminal Law dictates a
range of punishments for such "crimes" from public criticism to seven years' imprisonment. An editorial in
the China Daily was indicative of the mores articulated
in Shenyang:

        Being a socialist country, China has its own
        social behavior and customs. As the family is
        only a small component of society, anyone who
        violates the law and does not follow accepted
        social behavior should be criticized, disci-
        plined or dealt with by law.[6]

        The political imperative to respect and support
the elderly--as embodied in the Constitution and related laws--is widely known and heeded by the Chinese pop-
ulace. It is also a classic example of the mass line
in action.
        The government derived its position on the elderly
from the ethical heritage and the common practices/at-
titudes of the people. Had the government *not* adopted
this stance, and instead promulgated laws to belittle
or abandon the elderly, it would have violated the people's shared values and undercut its own legitimacy and
ability to govern (as eventually happened in the Cultural Revolution).
        Having taken its fundamental direction from the
people, the government then created a set of constitutional and other legal mandates to operationalize this
dimension of the nation's socio-economic policies.
Then, through intensive dissemination and discussion of
the laws and concrete examples of their application
across the country, the people continually are reminded
of their obligations to the elderly. From the masses
to the masses "and so on, over and over again . . . ."
        Although America's China watchers offer a variety
of different interpretations (based largely upon their
own political convictions), there is no disputing the
fact that the government is an explicit and important
presence in the daily lives of ordinary people to an
extent far beyond that experienced by the average U.S.
citizen. From the unashamedly political propaganda of
China's newspapers, chalkboards and billboards, to the
half-day each week that most Chinese still devote to
political study groups, the central government's messages and the Party line permeate every corner of

Chinese society.

As a result, China's population is politicized to a degree quite unimaginable in America. Ignorance of what the government wants and expects of each person is almost unknown. Similarly, indifference toward shifts in the country's political tides is a luxury few Chinese can afford. Whether out of a genuine zeal for the government's missions and objectives, or out of a more dispassionate calculation of self-interest, the ordinary individual's sensitivity to political affairs is quite remarkable--at least to the American observer. In conversation after conversation (even those of a largely personal nature or those occurring out of the sight and sound of other Chinese), factory workers, students, old people in the park, as well as cadres, would refer to the Constitution, to specific laws and to Party precepts on a regular basis and with considerable accuracy.

Currently, the government espouses an international spirit--a position 180 degrees from the extreme nationalism of the Cultural Revolution. This is accompanied by a headlong "Race to the Year 2000," "Health for All by the Year 2000" and a desire for rapid economic modernization and technological development. The priority now given to the ideology of world peace and international brotherhood is exemplified by the following excerpt from a speech given by China's President Li Xiannian to the First Session of the Sixth National People's Congress in June 1983:

> The Chinese people love peace. The maintenance of a peaceful international environment is the common desire of the people of China and the rest of the world. We shall steadfastly pursue an independent foreign policy, continue to develop our relations with other countries on the basis of the Five Principles of Peaceful Coexistence and expand our economic co-operation, cultural exchange and friendly people-to-people contacts with them. We shall continue our efforts to strengthen our solidarity and co-operation with other Third World countries. Together with the people of other parts of the world, we are determined to contribute to the struggle against hegemonism and for world peace and human progress.[7]

American presidents make similarly lofty statements. The difference I found is in the degree to which ordinary Chinese take these messages to heart and reflect them in their words and in their deeds. I suspect that if one asked a random group of industrial engineers, technicians and assembly workers in

Pittsburgh to talk about their hopes and dreams of the future the responses would be individualistic and diverse--and the likelihood of an international, or otherwise explicitly political, emphasis would be quite low.

This is not so among these workers' counterparts in Anshan. The penetration of the current Party line and the potency of the mass line both were revealed through an assignment I gave to my worker/students at the Northeast Institute of Technology. Six weeks into my course I read Martin Luther King Jr.'s "I Have a Dream" speech to the class. Then, they were asked to independently write their own "dream." As the following sample of their essays reveals, there was a strong similarity among their individual "dreams."[8] These statements are also persuasive evidence of their common political socialization. In reading the following brief essays, the adherence of the workers/students to the political philosophy expressed in President Li Xiannian's above-quoted speech should be noted.

The point of including them in this section on the "political" context is to underline the fact that in China today everything *has* an explicit political context. Whether the issue is treatment of the elderly, space travel or international relations, the mass line system ensures that virtually everyone understands the political context and, thereby, has the "opportunity" to adopt it as his own. The last essay perhaps presages what will shortly become a more predominant "dream."

I Have a Dream

Through thirty years of hard work, our country
          has made progress,
But today she is still a developing country.
I have a dream.
The four modernizations will have been accomplished.
The Chinese people's life will have gotten better
                              and better.

Look over history, kindhearted people suffer
          the invader's devastation.
Today the flame of war and smoke of gunpowder
          often rise over the horizon.
I have a dream.
          Finally justice will triumph over the wicked.
          Finally the good intentions of peace will wipe
          out the disgrace of war.

Even though the exploitation and unfairness seem
                              deep-rooted,
Today the ramparts rise like woods.

I still have a dream.
Abolish the exploitation and oppression.
A world, in which there is not war and not nations,
    will appear on earth.
Abolish the boundaries among all nations.

A world, in which there is not the U.S., the U.K.,
    Germany, France, the P.R.C., Japan,
    and other countries, will appear on earth.
All of the people in the world will be brothers
    and sisters.
For our later generations, perhaps it isn't
    a dream.

                    Qiu Li

                I Have a Dream

    Thirty years ago, the Anshan Iron and Steel Com-
plex was completely under Japanese rule. Then Guomindang government had controlled it for over three years.
At last, the complex belonged to the Chinese people in
1949.
    The fact is that all of the plants of the Anshan
Iron and Steel Complex were almost destroyed by the
Guomindang government when the Chinese people took
over. Workers and technicians, under the leadership of
the Community Party of China and the Chinese government, rebuilt and began to produce various kinds of
products. Compared with the advanced plants in the
world, all the plants of the complex, however, are
still backward in equipment and technology. We came
here to learn the English language so that we could
learn the advanced technology of developed countries
and change our complex situation.
    All of us come from the Anshan Iron and Steel Com-
plex, but we come from different units or plants of the
complex. Some of us come from the ore workshop. Some
of us come from the research institute. Some of us
come from the automatic research institute. Some of us
come from the design institute. Let's go back to the
ore workshop, go back to the making iron plant, go back
to the making steel plants, go back to the rolling
steel plants. The fact of the workshop and plants'
situation affects us to study and work harder than
ever.
    Facing the exciting situation of the policies and
economy of our nation, I have a dream today.
    I have a dream today that one day our complex will
have a brilliant future--that the production of iron
and steel will rise up and the consumption of coke,
power, fuel and water will fall down.

I have a dream that one day our complex will have
a group of workers that will be very accomplished and
will have a group of technicians that will have steady
essential theory and technical skills.

I have a dream that one day lots of modern machines and equipment will take the place of the old-
time machines in our workshop and plants, and computers
will control the entire production process of the workshop and plants.

I have a dream that one day lots of kinds of products of our complex will be exported to other countries
in the world and some of our inventions will be exported, too.

I have a dream that one day our complex will indeed become the largest and most modern enterprise in
our nation, and it will make more contributions to the
four modernizations than ever.

This is my hope, and this is our hope, too. I believe that the target is great, but it is hard, too.
In order to reach this goal, we must set up a principle
--to take courage, to work hard. One day we will see
the brilliant future of the Anshan Iron and Steel Complex. Let's celebrate that day when it comes.

Guo Huey-jeou

I Have a Dream

One day I read an article in a newspaper which
said that both the USA and the Soviet Union had ample
nuclear weapons to destroy the Earth and they were
still competing with each other for developing new nuclear weapons.

I thought a lot. What a pity that scientific development has brought such a result that the Earth has
become so small and the human has become so cruel that
something which could destroy the Earth several times
was being made. I had a dream that night:

In the dream, equality and friendship became the
basic principles for the whole world. People never
fought each other and never needed weapons. The energy, such as atomic energy, which was used for weapons,
was being used to solve the energy crisis. The money
which was spent for military purposes was being used to
help less developed countries. In developing science,
no country kept secrets from other countries and so the
same research work which other countries had already
finished did not need to be repeated. An international
space agency had been founded. The astronauts and pas-
sengers from different countries took the same spaceship as representatives of Earth to go to other planets. I was among them. When we set off and enjoyed

the scenic view of the Earth, I was so excited that I
dropped down from the window of the spaceship. Suddenly I woke up.
It was nothing but a dream!

Yu Tai

I Have a Dream

I had a nice dream of becoming an astronaut. In
my childhood, while I was sitting outside to enjoy the
cool of a summer evening, I raised my head to look at
the dark blue sky. Stars twinkled in it. The moon
moved slowly. "How far is it to the moon?" "How can I
go to the moon?" "Are there men on the moon?" I asked
a lot of questions of my grandmother. "It is very,
very far from here. You could go to the moon if you
had a scaling ladder. There is not a man on the moon,
but a beautiful white rabbit with a pair of red eyes,"
my grandmother answered. I looked at the moon carefully again. It seemed that rabbit was moving in the
moon. How mysterious it was!
The next day, when I told my father what I had
heard, he told me it was a fairy tale. There was no
scaling ladder leading to the moon, but astronauts
driving spacecraft could go to the moon to explore in
the future. "I want to be an astronaut," I said loud-
ly. "I hope you can," he answered, "but you must study
hard." I moved my head up and down. From that time
on, I not only studied hard, but also read some children's literature about space exploration. I took part
in a group making model airplanes and won the prize in
a model airplane competition. It was an interesting
book named We Love Science. The cover of the book
showed a boy riding on a spacecraft flying to the moon
and beckoning us to follow him. I liked it very much.
I would have followed him if I could. But I couldn't.
When I was a pupil studying hard in the fourth grade,
the Great Proletarian Cultural Revolution happened. I
couldn't go to school. Education was stopped. My family had to go to the countryside and I had no opportunity to go to a university to study science. I had
only a chance to take part in a "July 21" college.
Even during hard times, my dream was still in my mind.
I dreamed that man lived in outer space peacefully with
no war, no fighting, no sorrow and no sadness.
I was thrilled with the news that American astronauts had landed on the moon in 1969. It was the first
time for man on the moon and one of the most exciting
adventures in history. I hailed the astronauts in my
heart and admired their spring of dedication. The road
of science erects a "scaling ladder" leading to the moon

Facing the facts, I knew I couldn't drive a space-craft and land on the moon in person. But I hope and dream that our country will become a powerful and mod-ern nation and Chinese astronauts will land on the moon someday, too. They will also go to Mars, to Venus, and to planets beyond the solar system.
It is my dream now.

Zhao Wei Li

I Have a Dream

I have a happy dream in my mind. In the dream, a new world emerges. In that world, there will be no boundaries, no racial discrimination, no war, no inva-sion, no oppression and no exploitation. In that world no matter what color the man has, he will have the same right with the others to share equally in liberty and in the pursuit of happiness. In that society, science, technology and all the property will belong to the whole of mankind. At that time, humanity will use atom-power and new energies to create happiness in the world, not to make weapons. Money will be spent on space science, on the public utilities necessary to meet the coming needs of people, and on any projects which will benefit the whole of humanity. In this new world people will live a marvelous life never seen be-fore. The nations all over the world will unite as firm as one family. Maybe people will live on a new planet in the future. During that period, an historian will be able to say: "Humanity has entered a 'Paradise Era.'"
Well, someone may say that my dream is a fond one, but I am sure such a paradise world will approach soon-er or later as it is what the whole of mankind wants.

Yang Songlin

I Have a Dream

I have a dream. Oppressed and exploited people in the world will be set free. Everyone in the world will have a right to say what he wants, to do what he likes and to do what he loves for the whole society. Oppres-sed and exploited people are also people. But they are suffering a lot now in the capitalist countries. They need freedom. They must gain freedom. This is my dream.
There are still slaves and poor people who can't support themselves in the world. They must be liberated

by the revolutionary people. In my dream they are
freed from what they are now.

There are still colour distinctions in the world.
The big race bullies the small one. The developed
countries bully the poor and small ones. The whole
world is unpeaceful. There should be no colour distinctions in the world. I have a dream that one day
the racialism will be gone for ever.

I have a dream that one day everyone in the world
will be free. A Communist society will come into being
finally.

Wang Chin-shan

I Have a Dream

In the world today there is still chaos caused by
war, starvation, pestilence and natural calamity. In
spite of this, I still have a dream about the world,
science and our country.

I have a dream that one day the source of war is
extirpated when differences do not exist. The world
will become one of peace, freedom and equality. No one
will be out of work. No one will suffer hunger or cold
and no one will struggle to save his life. All countries, whether big or small, and all nations, whether
black, yellow or white, will be harmonious and friendly.

I have another dream about science as a force to
change the world and resist nature. One day human beings will be able to control nature for the benefit of
mankind. Arid desert will be changed into oases. The
ice which covers the whole continent of Antarctica will
be used to provide fresh water. The snowdrifts on high
mountains will be melted to irrigate the fields. The
hot water and steam under the ground will be drawn to
generate electricity and heat. There is no limit to
the development of science. Space travel will be as
common as airplane flights. The marvel of the electronic age, the computer, will make man's life more and
more comfortable and "wonder" or "miracle" drugs will
be able to exterminate various pestilences and disease.

I still have a dream about my country that one day
a strong, thriving and prosperous China will appear in
the world. She will forever extricate herself from
poverty and weakness. The four modernizations will be
realized, and people's lives will be filled with peace
and happiness. Then China will contribute her bit to
the advancement of the world.

Today these are my dreams, but tomorrow they will
be facts.

An Yun pei

My Dream

I always sleep very well, so I never have any dreams.

Yesterday evening, I stayed up late. It was nearly midnight when I went to bed. I had a beautiful dream.

Now I'm very happy. I have a new house. The house is very modern. In the kitchen, there is an electric fire, a washing machine and a refrigerator. In the bedroom, there is a color TV. And in the garage, there is a motorcar. My wife, my daughter and I are having dinner in the kitchen. There are a lot of foods on the table: fish, beef, pork, vegetables and wine. My daughter wants to swim. I drive the car to the beach. We swim in the sea. I feel the sea water cool. Suddenly there is a rainstorm. I feel very cold; my daughter is crying.

I woke up. I looked outside. It was raining heavily. The cold wind blew into the open window. I closed the window and soon I slept again.

Zhang Kai

HEALTH CONTEXT

Physical Health

Mention "health" and "China" in the same sentence to most Westerners and the word that immediately springs to mind is "acupuncture."

Acupuncture is certainly utilized in the PRC, not only as treatment for a myriad of ailments, but also as an anesthetic in some surgical procedures. Indeed, one of my most vivid memories of China is of sitting in an operating theater in Shanghai's Hua Shan Teaching Hospital and witnessing the removal of a golfball-sized malignant brain tumor--using three acupuncture needles for anesthesia. The patient was awake and answering questions throughout the operation; even smiling and waving as he was wheeled out after the surgery. Yet, for all its fascination and occasional drama, to emphasize acupuncture is to miss the point of what is really special about China's health system today.

The unique and noteworthy features of the Chinese system have been documented in the writings of Drs. Victor and Ruth Sidel--especially their 1982 volume entitled The Health of China.[1] My own knowledge in this field was deepened by accompanying the Sidels for a health study tour of the PRC during the summer of 1982 sponsored by the American Medical Student Association. Their work has had a marked influence on my own --although we may emphasize different dimensions of the

Chinese experience.

While many health issues are dealt with from an "emic" perspective in other sections of this volume, what is presented here is an "etic" framework, i.e., an overview of health-related statistics intended to orient the reader to the realities experienced by today's Chinese elderly during the course of their lifetimes.

Historical Development

Prior to 1949, China was quite literally a society on its deathbed. Malnutrition, poor health, crippling conditions and serious diseases were rampant. If it's true that the good die young, then one can only conclude that China suffered from an excess of "goodness"; in 1949 the Chinese accounted for 25 percent of the world's infant mortality and life expectancy across the country then was only 35 years.[2] As Livingston and Lowinger remind us:

> Apart from the lack of medical facilities, sanitation was nonexistent, and many serious diseases were spread because of the lack of sanitation. Between 5 and 10 percent of the urban population of China had venereal disease, and in some rural areas this figure was as high as 48 percent. Thirty-three percent of the population was afflicted with trachoma, an eye infection that often leads to blindness. Entire areas were wiped out by schistosomiasis (snail fever), a disease carried by snails and spread through the use of untreated human excrement as fertilizer; the disease was endemic in some areas of the country. The crude death rate in peacetime was about twenty-five per thousand; the infant mortality rate (before one year of age) was two hundred per thousand live births—one in five. In addition, millions of people died in famines, and additional millions were so weakened by starvation that their resistance to any disease was nil. This is, of course, the briefest of sketches of the health situation before the Liberation in 1949, but it serves to give us an idea of the enormity of the task that faced the Chinese people at Liberation.[3]

From the Long March forward, Mao envisioned a new society in which the eradication of the causes of disease and the promotion of the elements of good health would be a top priority. It was an active vision in which the Army participated by caring for the sick and disabled Chinese they would encounter. The inclusion of health care and health promotion at the forefront of the Revolution was not simply a humanitarian gesture.

It was, in fact, a thoroughly practical investment on Mao's part.

Three of Mao's purposes were served through an emphasis on health. First, it was necessary to build the physical strength of those engaged in the struggle against the Japanese and the Guomindang. Second, it was powerful and tangible evidence of the Communists' concern for the masses--and thus an invaluable organizing and propaganda tool through which to capture the hearts and minds of the people. And third, Mao knew that the vital new society he hoped to create could not be built upon the backs of a sick, starving, infirm and weak people.

Thus, along with political mobilization of the masses and land reform, health-promotion continued to be a primary mission for Mao's forces. As the Sidels note:

> With Liberation--the assumption of state power by the Chinese Communist Party in 1949--health care retained its high priority and visibility. A combination of directives from Chairman Mao and principles adopted at a National Health Congress in Peking in the early 1950s resulted in a set of precepts which to this day form the widely quoted ideologic basis for the development of health services.
> 1. Medicine must serve the working people --in the Chinese idiom (*gong-nong-bing*) "workers, peasants, and soldiers."
> 2. Preventive medicine must be given priority over curative medicine.
> 3. Practitioners of Chinese traditional medicine (*zhongyi*) must be "united" with practitioners of Western medicine (*xiyi*).
> 4. Health work must be integrated with mass movements.[4]

Over the past 30 years, the aforementioned principles were put into practice with a zeal unmatched by any other country. Public health measures (from mass immunizations, to popular campaigns against pests, to vastly improved water systems and sanitation practices) were implemented throughout China, and health personnel at all levels (including the famous "barefoot doctors") were trained in record numbers. In addition, the government launched enormous propaganda drives to promote better hygiene and an ethic of self-care and self-reliance among the Chinese.

The accomplishments of this 30-year struggle are nothing short of stunning. Two key indicators of health status--infant mortality and life expectancy-- reveal the magnitude of success attained. Before 1949,

China's infant mortality rate was 200 per 1000. Today, it is 10 to 20 per 1000 in the developed urban areas and 20 to 30 per 1000 in the countryside.[5] Whereas China used to account for 25 percent of the world's infant mortality, it now has dropped to 9 percent--and this occurred during a period in which China's total population doubled.[6] This decline of more than 90 percent in the infant mortality rate in approximately 30 years is an unparalleled achievement.

The story in terms of life expectancy is perhaps even more impressive, for, as Grosse argues:

> . . . analysis of life expectancy and the specific causes of low expectation of survival will tend to paint a generally accurate picture of the major health problems in developing areas. Furthermore, population averages for life expectancy may be closely related to the *quality* of life in less developed countries. In developing countries, levels of income, sanitation, literacy, education, and disease are all closely related to life expectancy: all manner of social "goods" seem to go hand in hand.[7]

As noted earlier, the average Chinese could anticipate a life span of only 35 years in the pre-revolutionary society. Today, it has virtually doubled. According to the 1982 Census data, national life expectancy in 1982 was 67.0 for men and 69.5 for women. Projections for 1985 show a rise nationally to 68.5 years for men and 71.1 years for women.[8] (Figures are higher in the cities: in Shanghai life expectancy is now 71.3 for men and 75.5 for women,[9] and in Beijing, 71.8 for men and 74.2 for women.[10])

The most obvious implication of this change is that there are now far more old people in China than ever before--and both the absolute numbers and relative proportion of the elderly are expected to rise dramatically well into the 21st century. For example, according to U.N. figures,[11] the number of Chinese over 60 doubled between 1950 and 1980 (from 42.4 million to 83.7 million). Moreover, demographers predict that this age group will double again (to 169.5 million) by 2010.

The anticipated increase is even higher for the upper ranges of the "elderly" category. In 1950, there were only 6.5 million Chinese over the age of 75. In 1980, there were 16.7 million in this cohort. By 2010, the expectation is that more than 40 million Chinese will be over 75.

The Connection between Health and Development

As the World Bank reported in its World Development Report 1981:

> . . . China's most remarkable achievement during the past three decades has been to make low-income groups far better off in terms of basic needs than their counterparts in most other poor countries. They all have work; their food supply is guaranteed through a mixture of state rationing and collective self-insurance; most of their children are not only at school but are also being comparatively well taught; and the great majority have access to basic health care and family planning services. Life expectancy--whose dependence on many other economic and social variables makes it probably the best single indicator of the extent of real poverty in a country-- is outstandingly high for a country at China's per capita income level . . . .[12]

What China has done is to collapse into three decades a process that took centuries to accomplish in the Occidental world. Obviously, the Chinese have had the advantage of the example and the fruits of the West's progress in health care and maintenance. Yet, few non-Western countries (other than Japan and Sri Lanka) have so fully taken advantage of this knowledge --and no other has moved so far so fast.

The patterns of health and disease characteristic of countries as they modernize tend to conform to the theory of epidemiologic transition. As described by Omran, high mortality rates due to famine and infectious disease characteristically decline during the transition, and man-made and degenerative diseases take their place as principal causes of mortality. High levels of fertility also characteristically diminish as economic development takes place. The stages of transition have varied in length from centuries (in the West) to decades (as illustrated by the rapid development of Japan).[13]

The first phase, "the age of pestilence and famine," was characteristic of the situation in China through the late 1950s and into the early 1960s. In remarkable time the society passed through "the age of receding pandemics" into "the age of degenerative and man-made diseases." This change was accelerated by the push of a very determined political effort to improve the health and productive capacity of the people through a preventive model of easily accessible and equalized medical care.

The demographic transition--i.e., the change in

the population profile over time--is dominated by the epidemiology of disease and mortality patterns. For example, the primary causes of death in Beijing in 1953 were:

1. pneumonia and diseases of the respiratory system
2. tuberculosis
3. cardiovascular disease

In 1979, the top three killers there were more characteristic of developed countries:

1. cerebrovascular disease
2. cardiovascular disease
3. cancer[14]

In Shanghai in 1980, the available mortality data showed a different ranking:

1. malignant tumors (23.5%)
2. heart disease (20.1%)
3. cerebrovascular disease (19.0%)

but the transition to the developed nations' causes of death obviously still applies.[15] Although small consolation to those directly affected, this shift in causes of death is a fairly reliable correlate of economic development.

Another factor explaining the health progress made in China can be found in the development of the agricultural sector. A great deal of energy and effort has gone into ensuring that the spectre of malnutrition--indeed starvation--that plagued the country in earlier years will never haunt China again. Significant strides have been made over the past 30 years both in terms of overall agricultural productivity and, especially, in terms of creating a reasonably efficient and equitable distribution system. Consequently, the incidence of malnutrition is very low and the proportion of disease and health problems associated with poor nutrition and inadequate food supplies has declined markedly.

According to a recent survey of over 7,600 people of the Beijing Municipal Sanitation and Anti-Epidemic Station, Beijing residents are getting "nearly enough protein and calories, but too much fat and salt."[16] The survey found that urban dwellers averaged 2,371 calories and 68.2 grams of protein daily while those in the countryside consumed less: 2,512 calories and 67.1 grams of protein. "Both amounts approach normal human needs," the survey said. It added, however, that while Beijing residents were getting more meat than ever before, they were also eating too much pork fat creating

a tendency towards obesity, especially in children.
Salt was also about ten grams over the recommended daily amount.

China still must import large quantities of grain
from other nations. For instance, China recently became the largest customer for U.S. wheat in the world.
Yet, productivity is increasing and China one day may
be able to support its 22.4 percent of the world's population with what is judged to be only 7 percent of the
world's farmland.[17]

Health Problems of the Elderly

Because no current health statistics could be obtained concerning the health situation in Shenyang, I
was very lucky to have my request to meet with Dr. Xu
Huanyun accepted. I was already familiar with Dr. Xu's
pioneering work at the Xuanwu Hospital of Chinese Medicine in Beijing. In order to understand the health
patterns of the elder residents of the five neighborhoods served by the hospital and how best to serve
their needs, Dr. Xu and his staff interviewed 967 of
the 983 local people over 60 on a one-to-one basis. As
an indication of how carefully this work was undertak-
en, it took twelve doctors two and one-half months to
collect and analyze the data. Dr. Xu was kind enough
to share the results.[18]

Although the following data, then, are from
Beijing rather than Shenyang, Dr. Xu did not expect
that the results would have been different had the survey been conducted in Shenyang. Both are large cities
in the northeast and their overall health status indicators are similar.

Of the 967 aged individuals interviewed, 903 (93%)
cited "health" as their primary concern. Some 688 reported being troubled by illnesses, among them the
following (ranked in order of frequency):

hypertension	37.8%
chronic bronchitis, emphy- sema, pulmonary diseases	30.8%
chronic heart disease	18.2%
arthritis	9.7%
apoplexy (stroke)	6.1%
gastric disturbances	6.0%
cataracts	3.3%
neurasthenia*	1.5%
diabetes	2.0%
senile dementia	.3% (2 people)

*A nonspecific neurosis marked by chronic fatigue, lack
of energy, feelings of inadequacy, moderate depression,
inability to concentrate, loss of appetite, insomnia.

Other problems which concerned them were difficulties
in housing, grocery shopping and relations with their
spouses or children.

The percentage of females in the survey was 53.7.
I asked Dr. Xu if he had seen any significant differences between men and women as they aged. "Women," he
responded, "have poorer economic conditions, lower social status, and fewer hobbies."

Dr. Xu's interest in the health of the aged goes
beyond data collection. As Vice-Director of the Hospital and Chairperson of the Department of Internal Medicine, he persuaded his staff and the hospital to adopt
the following preventive measures to meet the health
concerns of the elderly. It should be noted that
Dr. Xu's work is exemplary and I am confident it will
serve as a model as expanded health services for the
elderly are developed across China. The key features
are as follows:

1. Each doctor is assigned a designated section of
the community for which he or she is responsible. Regular health check-ups are given to keep abreast of the
health situation and to detect serious illnesses at an
early stage.

2. Home visits are paid to invalids and those suffering from chronic diseases. The administrative aspects of record-keeping, case management and follow-up
work are considered important aspects of the approach.

3. If not a proverb, "Life means movement" is certainly a current slogan. Exercise is seriously encouraged. In fact, a new "exercise for life"--*e-sho-gong*--
was developed by the doctors here.

4. A senior residents' health care association has
been organized to promote mental health and social activities for its membership. The "Center for Service
for the Elderly" is supported by the government with
the subdistrict office taking charge of the organizational work. Health facilities and technical advice
are provided by the Xuanwu Hospital, the Tianqiao Hospital and the health division of the Beijing Post Bureau (located in this neighborhood). At the time of
our talk, 217 people had joined the association, and it
was hoped that eventually all the elderly residents
would find something there to enhance their lives. As
Dr. Xu stated:

> The great advantage that most old people have
> is free time. Once the association is set up,
> we hope to help them put this to good use.
>
> We can't wait for the State to do this
> for us, nor can we do it all ourselves. But
> with a concerted effort by families, society
> and the State, I think we can work out a dis-
> tinctly Chinese solution to the problems of
> growing old.

Much has been accomplished, but more remains to be done. The Chinese seem to recognize this fact and are continuing the push for better health. As the Sidels observe:

. . . although a number of statistics show startling improvements in the health of the Chinese people over the past 30 years, there are still, especially in rural areas, high rates of infectious disease, including some that are clearly preventable. Even more disturbing, the incidence of some communicable illnesses, such as infectious hepatitis, appears to be increasing. The health status of China's population appears to be far better than that of 30 years ago and of people in comparable poor countries, but further improvement--especially for rural people--appears to be needed. In urban areas--and increasingly in rural areas--the leading causes of death and disability are the degenerative diseases of older age. Prevention of these illnesses, and of the disability associated with them, requires different types of efforts, such as prevention of cigarette smoking, reduction in industrial pollution, avoidance of obesity, and early detection and treatment of hypertension and of treatable cancers. China is beginning to make notable efforts in these fields as well.[19]

In contemplating the progress China has made in raising its health status, the role of public health, better nutrition and more effective access to trained medical personnel (traditional and Western) are key explanatory variables. And yet, the emic (or cultural) dimension must not be overlooked. Cultural forces are central to the psycho-social experience of health and disease.

Donald Ardell, in High Level Wellness, argues that "the precondition for health is the integration of the physiological, psychological and spiritual dimensions of the individual."[20] One of my students in Shenyang, Mr. Sun, was more specific. He said that in China good health was believed to be 70 percent attitudinal and 30 percent physiological. Both Dr. Ardell and Mr. Sun would agree that a sense of well-being is a predictable correlate of a healthy individual.

However, in order to explore the issues of attitude and self-perception, one must make the subtle transition from a discussion of physical health to a brief description of the factors of mental well-being.

Mental Well-Being

If anything in Chinese culture and society remains "inscrutable" to the Occidental observer, it is the pattern of mental illness and mental health. Occidental and Oriental observers routinely remark upon the high spirits, optimistic attitudes and positive social and interpersonal behaviors of the Chinese. Compared to Occidental nations, the incidence of mental illness among the population in general, and the elderly in particular, appears to be startlingly low. The Sidels report that surveys undertaken by the Ministry of Health show a rate of "mental illness" of 5 to 7 per 1000 and a rate of "serious mental illness"--of which schizophrenia occupies first place--of 2 to 4 per 1000.[21] The World Health Organization documented rates of schizophrenia at 1 to 2 per 1000 in the PRC as compared to 10 per 1000 in the U.S.[22] Depression, as well, according to Dr. Wu Chenyi, chairperson of the Department of Medical Psychology (started in 1980, the first of its kind in China), has been found to be much less common in China than in the U.S., with a rate of psychosis of 5 to 7 per 1000. He made the point that, in general, only very serious mental illnesses are considered psychiatric problems. Most common minor illnesses, such as the neuroses, are considered social problems, and are dealt with by the family and the community, by peer counseling and other supportive activities.[23]

A contrast is often drawn between the Chinese and the Russians (who are portrayed as a grim and dispirited people with high rates of suicide and alcoholism). Even critics of the Chinese government come away from their experiences in China with an admiration (however grudging) for the Chinese people. Anecdotal evidence is not proof of Chinese mental health, but it certainly serves to create a kind of consensus that an extraordinarily high proportion of the population cope with the circumstances of their lives in socially acceptable and personally satisfying ways.

Given the obvious relationship between one's mental state and one's "sense of well-being," the cultural context of mental health and mental illness in China will be discussed here. The broad background this section provides is supplemented by more specific information gathered through my interviews in Shenyang and described in the next chapter.

The underlying question is how the Chinese have managed to cope so well with a set of conditions and circumstances that would fully justify far more negative reactions. This is especially true for the elderly who have witnessed--and often been adversely affected by--a continual history of upheaval and suffering. The society into which today's elderly were born was one in which unrelenting poverty, misery and oppression were the way of life for all but a tiny elite. Mass starvation and widespread disease claimed many infants and kept the average life expectancy low.[24]

Throughout this century, the earth of China has absorbed the blood and sweat of untold millions. It's no wonder that in Chinese landscapes, people have always been so minute. They've rarely been treated as if they've mattered at all. Their very numbers seem to have obscured their individuality and rendered them inconsequential other than as faceless statistics or as pawns in the power struggles of foreign (or domestic) rulers.

Chapter 3 presents a more detailed chronology of major events in 20th century history of the people of Shenyang and other sections of Northeast China. "Bound feet" may be an apt metaphor for what life was like when today's elderly were young. Similarly, "the ravages of war" describes what they experienced in the "prime" of their lives. The elderly are the survivors who have risen from the ashes of a society that could bear no more. Psychiatrist Ling Ming-yu, for example, reported the burdens being borne by the Chinese during the anti-Japanese War of 1937-45 (a war particularly affecting the population of Northeast China):

> Millions have been killed or wounded, hundreds of thousands of homes have been broken up, and a vast amount of property has been destroyed. There has also been mass migration of people from the eastern to the western part of the country in the face of almost unbelievable difficulties. In many communities scattered throughout China the normal social structure has been uprooted to such an extent that not a single native soul was left. City inhabitants had to stand the terror of aerial bombing for years. Millions of soldiers had to fight under even more unfavorable conditions. The amount of emotional shock sustained by the whole nation therefore is almost beyond imagination.[25]

Even after Liberation, when Mao Zedong stood in Beijing's Tian An Men Square and declared that "the Chinese people have stood up!" life for the Chinese was neither easy nor free from continued turmoil. The Cultural Revolution was another protracted period in which careers, families and lives were severely strained, if not shattered. And yet, the spirit of the Chinese people was not broken and the psychiatric disorders to which their history entitled them are rarely in evidence.

Why? Occidental observers might be inclined to

think that this phenomenon is explained more by under-diagnosis than by any other factor. Psychologists are literally one in a million in China (1,100 out of over one billion inhabitants) and most of these are in educational psychology or management posts rather than serving as clinicians.[26] Fully trained psychiatrists are estimated to be about 3,600.[27]

There is a certain logic to the "underdiagnosis" theory. An analogy would be for an outsider to come back from a remote mountain region and remark upon how few people wore glasses. Is the low incidence a function of unusually good eyesight or unusually poor access to opticians and optometrists? Similarly, it is impossible to say for sure whether a dramatic increase in the number of specialists capable of (and willing to) label people along a psychological continuum would lead to an equally dramatic increase in the number of Chinese identified as having mental disorders.

Even more to the point, it is difficult to be sure what a build-up of psychiatric and psychological services would actually mean. Many people having mental problems might be correctly identified and made eligible for treatment. Or, it could happen that specialists would just view and label people through the lens of their specialized training. As Mark Twain once noted: "When your only tool is a hammer, every problem looks like a nail."

A second explanation for the small proportion of people thought to have mental health difficulties in China is that the Chinese have a different definition of mental illness. In Occidental nations, mental illness is usually divided into three categories: organic disorders, functional disturbances and life crisis adjustment problems. Mental illness, the Chinese believe, is caused by biological, constitutional and psychogenic factors--defined as difficulties in handling "contradictions." These contradictions usually have a political context and nature, and their resolution comes, with help, through attitudinal change.

Another Chinese explanation of mental health and mental illness is based upon a classic Chinese belief that still informs current attitudes. As Ruth and Victor Sidel note:

> Ancient Chinese medical writings attributed all disease, including mental illness, to an imbalance of two forces: the *yin* and the *yang*. This imbalance was thought to be caused by deviation from the *dao*, the "way," which provided the guide for all morality and human conduct. The *dao* can be further thought of as being an "ethical superstructure"; once transgression against this ethical superstructure

occurred, return to health was through a
return to *dao*.28

The more modern concept of mental illness has been
political in nature. In a sense, socialist/revolution-
ary thought was raised to the position traditionally
reserved for the *dao*. Deviation from the proper political attitude has been seen as a cause of mental problems and emotional stress. The basic "cure" is a return to "revolutionary optimism." As one might expect,
this highly politicized perspective reached its apex
during the Cultural Revolution. The following excerpt
from a statement of this period about Chinese psychotherapy summarizes this line of thought:

> Help the patient to regard his illness with a
> correct attitude, and to establish a spirit
> of revolution and optimism. Help the patient
> to be cheerful, lively and spirited. Help
> the patient to dispel fears and worries about
> his illness, and establish his confidence in
> complete recovery and his determination to
> fight against the disease. In order to in-
> spire the patient's will to struggle against
> his illness, we must solve the problem of
> motivation. We think the sense of responsi-
> bility toward socialism is the only unlimited
> source of motivating power.29

The reasoning that flows from such a political interpretation is fascinating. If mental illness is
largely political, i.e., a matter of bad attitudes and
a counter-revolutionary spirit, then the extent of political dissent also becomes the measure of mental disorders. Since the Chinese have long since discovered
that deviating from or expressing opposition to the political norms of the moment is bad not only for their
mental health, but also for their physical health,
there are few people who externally espouse or exhibit
anything other than revolutionary optimism.

The third explanation for the low incidence of
mental illness in China is a cultural/anthropological
one. The basic thesis is that in Chinese culture the
manifestations of mental illness are different from
those found in Occidental cultures. The implication is
that mental and emotional upsets may occur as frequent-
ly among the Chinese as among Westerners, but the manner in which the Chinese deal with these upsets make
them less susceptible to psychiatric diagnoses.

The most extensive work in this area has been done
by psychiatrist and medical anthropologist Arthur
Kleinman. In his book, Patients and Healers in the
Context of Culture, Kleinman compares cognitive coping

processes in Chinese and American cultures. In China, Kleinman argues:

> Dysphoric affective states are initially rec-
> ognized by using the non-specific term *hsin-
> ching pu-hao*, which connotes general emotional
> upset. This label is used with family and
> close friends and by the subject to identify
> and think about his inner state. Usually he
> does not further define the emotion, but uses
> the vagueness of this general term to cope
> with various distressing effects. That is,
> Chinese reduce the intensity of anxiety, de-
> pressive feelings, fears, and the like by keep-
> ing them undifferentiated, which helps both to
> distance them and to focus concern elsewhere.
> Other related coping strategies are: (1) mini-
> mization or denial, (2) dissociation, and
> (3) somatization (i.e., the substitution of
> somatic preoccupation for dysphoric effect in
> the form of complaints of physical symptoms
> and even illness).[30]

Kleinman makes a variety of intriguing observations about what is considered stressful and how stress
is handled in Chinese and American cultures. In the
diagram reproduced on the following page,[31] he attempts
to demonstrate the cultural differences in the way Chinese and Americans label, perceive and cope with somatic and psychological symptoms of illness. While they
may vary in type, pattern and intensity across various
groups, his generalized differences in coping strategy
give a clue to the answer to how the Chinese have managed to survive their tumultuous history.

A key point is the extent to which the Chinese *ex-
ternalize* stress and see the cause, consequence and
cure as all being either physical (somatic) or social
(situational). Americans, by contrast, *internalize*
stress and attempt to deal with it accordingly. The
distinction here can be seen in the Occidental preoccupation with guilt (i.e., an internal negative self-
assessment) and the Oriental preoccupation with shame
(i.e., an external negative assessment).

The fourth, and final, explanation for the apparent rarity of mental illness in China is that Chinese
society is structured in ways that either prevent its
occurrence or restrict its manifestations to a significant degree. Both historically and currently, the Chinese way of life emphasizes interdependence and mutual
support. It is a country in which one is said never to
be out of earshot of another person and where one's
family, work unit and country are judged to be more
significant than the needs of the individual. Indeed,
the kind of rugged individualism American society

Cognitive Coping Processes in Chinese and American Cultures

Cultural influences on:	Chinese	Americans*
1. Perception of stimuli as stressors, and relative ranking of stressors	Primary concern with inter-personal stimuli	Primary concern with intra-personal stimuli
2. Perception, labeling and valuation of affects	Recognition and expression of strong or dysphoric affects are disvalued. As a result, there is lack of experience in precisely defining, labeling, and communicating about affects.	Recognition and expression of strong or dysphoric affects are valued. As a result, there is greater experience and skill in precisely defining, labeling, and communicating about affects.
3. Chief cognitive coping strategies used to manage affective experience	Suppression, somatization, undifferentiation, minimization, externalization, situation-orientation	Expression, psychologization, differentiation, overemphasis, internalization, focusing on intrapsychic self
4. Pattern of affective experience and of experience of affective disorders	Vegetative idiom	Psychological-existential idiom
5. Lay and indigenous folk treatment approaches	Family-based, externally oriented clinical reality (somatic and interpersonal)	Individual, internally oriented clinical reality (psychological)
6. Evaluation of therapeutic efficacy	Interpersonal and somatic criteria	Personal-existential criteria

*Middle-class, college-educated Caucasians

promotes as its ideal is antithetic to the Chinese
world view.

Joan Hinton, the brilliant nuclear physicist who
helped develop the atomic bomb, left "the science of
destruction" as an act of conscience, choosing instead
to promote and improve life by becoming a farm machine-
ry technician in rural China. She recently answered an
interview question about personal freedom in the following manner: "It is more important to eat. But most
of all, it's more important to be a part of a system
that is working for everybody's good. I believe that
the good of the community is more important than that
of a single individual."[32] She offered the key to understanding the road to mental health in China. Her
answer compares to the goals of psychotherapy as delin-
eated by one of China's most outstanding psychiatrists:

> The goals are: to help the patient understand
> the disease and to help the patient have a
> proper attitude toward the disease. The "prop-
> er attitude" includes the understanding that
> you don't belong to yourself, you belong to
> your community and your country. Everyone de-
> pends on everyone else, and you are responsible
> for not wallowing in your sorrows.

Dr. Wu believes that patients can be taught not to be
selfish, to think of others first. He gave himself as
an example. Educated by missionaries and in universities in the West, he had strong feelings about the importance of the individual, but the revolution in China
proved to him that the community is more important.[33]

In China, an individual's mental or emotional
problems are neither unknown to, nor ignored by, the
family and the unit. There are always people, especially elderly people, with whom one can have "heart to
heart talks"--a favorite Chinese therapeutic technique.
Social organization in China is geared to solving most
of the people's everyday problems within the extended
family, rather than turning them over to outside specialists. This problem-solving mechanism does not just
work in reaction to whatever difficulties may arise.
Rather, the effort hinges on establishing and applying
strict behavioral codes intended to prevent trouble--or
at least to nip it in the bud. In such a system, mental and emotional upsets are rarely allowed to fester
or otherwise get out of hand.

The other critical factor here is that each family, unit and commune is explicitly tied to the larger
society and its collective goals. The kinds of special
interest, or single issue, politics so common today in
the United States have no counterpart in China. Instead, there is a more or less unified and coordinated
effort to integrate everyone's lives in the pursuit of

the Great Leap Forward, the Four Modernizations, the Race to the Year 2000, or whatever other political campaign is in progress. Many observers from Occidental nations--used to the aggrandizement of the individual--view these collective drives with disdain or disbelief and regard them as dehumanizing. By contrast, many Chinese seem to derive an overarching sense of purpose and commitment that, in turn, positively affects their attitudes and mental health. As one Chinese observed:

> We think that mental health is far more than the absence of mental illness, and the reason the Chinese are so mentally healthy must therefore go beyond the absence of bad things. We think that the life of the Chinese people, owning their own country, poor though they may be, and with the opportunity for each person to contribute to the building of the whole country, produces mental health. Everyone can belong and have a sense of purpose; everyone can feel that he or she is helping to build China. Participation, purpose, belonging: This is why people in China are mentally healthy, despite the fact that they live lives which are very hard in many ways.[34]

The power of these bonds must not be underestimated if one is to understand the Chinese. Even under the most adverse circumstances, when overt resentment or alienation would be typical Occidental responses, the Chinese tend to "keep the knife in the heart" and find their means of coping through identification with their group. One poignant example of this pattern can be found in the words of Yang Jiang, an intellectual and cadre who was "sent down" to the countryside during the Cultural Revolution:

> I was truly a part of the team, going out with everyone else before dawn and returning to base camp only after dark. Though you couldn't say what I did was manual labor in the strict sense of the word, just being with everyone else and doing light jobs around the site made me feel part of it all. I gradually developed a sense of group or team spirit, a fellowship in which I was part of the whole. There was a satisfying feeling of belonging. I had never had this feeling when I worked on short term community labor projects in the past; with those once the assigned work or construction was completed, everyone had gone their separate ways. Intellectual work is even less conducive to a team spirit. Even when you collaborate with other people, you tend to regard your own

individual contribution as the most important.
If you write an article with someone else,
the person in charge of collecting and col-
lating the material and the person who writes
it up very rarely manage to work as one. In
the cadre school it was different: the pros-
pect of an indefinite future of working together
with little or no hope of ever going back
brought about a strong feeling of community, of
"us-ness."[35]

This sense of participation and of belonging has
particular force when applied to the elderly. Zavarine
underlines the relationships between social supports
and a sense of well-being among the elderly in China:

Chinese elders have a greater chance of maintaining mental health in old age than do
elders in the United States. They continue
to have societally sanctioned roles within a
setting of continuous group membership and
respect, whereas in this country there is no
generally accepted and respected role for
people who are past the stage of productive
work and childrearing. Retirement usually
signals loss of significant work, social and
interpersonal contacts and finally loss of
self-esteem.
    According to Irving Rosow, writing about
aging in America, "Loss of roles excludes the
aged from significant participation and de-
values them . . . . Old people show unmistak-
able signs of strain, with higher rates of
suicide and mental illness than any other age
group." Rosow points out that findings of
extensive research substantiate Durkheim's
classic study of suicide, that is, that "people effectively withstand stress to the extent
that they have strong group supports." Unlike
the Chinese, whose family and work unit both
supply constant group identification, elders
in the U.S.A. are too often reduced to isolation and loss of identity.[36]

The support structures provided by the family and
the work unit are also central to the treatment of mental disorders. Most cases of dementia or senility
among the elderly are taken care of within the family.
When help is needed beyond the home environment, it is
provided by the same people in the same local factory
or commune clinics that handle the full range of health
problems. Little differentiation is made at this level
between physical and mental disorders. Only in rare,
severe instances are elderly people suffering from

mental illnesses sent for treatment or long-term care to the few mental hospitals in existence across China.

Several contrasting--but perhaps complementary-- explanations have been given in this section for the low reported incidence of mental illness in China. It seems likely that no one of them tells the whole story. Instead, the various factors cited probably all apply to different degrees in different circumstances for different individuals. The essential point is that whatever the "correct" explanation may be, the fact is that the Chinese people have been able to bear extra-ordinary burdens without breaking under the strain. There is much to admire in this fact and, as discussed in the final chapter, there may be something we can learn from it as well.

NOTES

1. Definition quoted from a lecture given at Duke University, October 12, 1983, for the Society for Culture, Illness, and Healing by Arthur M. Kleinman, entitled "Illness Meanings: The Role of Culture in the Experience of Illness and Medical Practice in the United States and China." Dr. Kleinman is Professor of Medical Anthropology in both the Departments of Social Medicine and Anthropology at Harvard and concurrently a Professor of Psychiatry in the Medical School. He is editor-in-chief of Culture, Medicine and Psychiatry: An International Journal of Comparative Cross Cultural Research, serves on the editorial board of additional journals and publishers, has edited six books on Medical Anthropology, and has written or co-authored over 70 articles in his chosen field. His best known work is Patients and Healers in the Context of Culture: An Exploration of the Borderland between Anthropology, Medicine, and Psychiatry and his work in Medical Anthropology is considered seminal in the establishment of a theoretical framework for understanding how health care systems can be understood between cultures.

RELIGIOUS/ETHICAL CONTEXT

1. Richard C. Bush, Religion in China (Niles, IL: Argus Communications, 1977), p. vii.

2. Huang He, "A nun's search for the 'Pure Land' of Buddha . . . in China," China Daily, 3:599:6, 6/29/83.

3. Bush, Religion in China, p. 12.

4. Hugh D. R. Baker, Chinese Family and Kinship

74

(London: The Macmillan Press, Ltd., 1979), p. 11.

5. Judith Treas, "Socialist Organization and Economic Development in China: Latent Consequences for the Aged," Gerontologist, 19:1:34-43, 1979.

6. Ralph L. Cherry and Magnuson-Martinson, "Modernization and Status of the Aged in China: Decline or Equalization?" The Sociological Quarterly, 22:256, 1981.

7. John King Fairbank, "Self-Expression in China," The China Difference: A Portrait of Life Today inside the Country of One Billion, Ross Terrill, ed. (New York: Harper & Row, 1979), p. 86.

8. C. K. Yang, Chinese Communist Society: The Family and the Village (Boston: MIT Press as quoted in Cherry, "Modernization and Status of the Aged in China: Decline or Equalization?" 1965).

9. T. W. Ganshow, "The Aged in a Revolutionary Milieu: China," 1978, in S. Spicher, K. Woodward, and D. Van Tassel (eds.), Aging and the Elderly: Humanistic Perspectives in Gerontology. Atlantic Highlands, NJ: Humanistic Press. Also in Lowell Holmes, Other Cultures, Elder Years: An Introduction to Cultural Gerontology (Minneapolis, MN: Burgess Publishing Co., 1983), p. 120.

10. "Party organ calls for new better work style," China Daily, 3:601:4, 7/1/83.

11. "Commission stresses need for discipline," China Daily, 3:638:1, 8/13/83.

12. "Party consolidation," China Daily, 3:692:4, 10/15/83.

13. "Rectification goal: A stronger, purer, unified Party," China Daily, 3:695:4, 10/19/83.

14. Michael Weisskopf, "China to begin purge of party members," The Washington Post, 10/11/83, p. A7.

15. Colin M. Turnbull, The Human Cycle (New York: Simon and Schuster, 1983), pp. 229, 278 ff.

16. China Reconstructs (Ch. edition) Vol. XXXII, No. 7, July 1983.

EDUCATION CONTEXT

1. For a good historical background to Chinese society today, I highly recommend John King Fairbank, The

United States and China, 4th ed. (Cambridge: Harvard University Press, 1980) for both text and annotated references.

2. Yang Jiang, A Cadre School Life: Six Chapters (Translation by Geremie Barme) (Hong Kong: Joint Publishing Company, 1982). Also see Mao's Harvest: Voices from China's New Generation (ed. by Helen F. Siu and Zelda Stern) (New York: Oxford University Press, 1983).

3. "More investment should be made in education," China Daily 3:604:5, 7/4/83.

4. "Symposium to scan population problems," China Daily 3:790:1, 2/7/84.

5. "School enrollment rates are rising in six provinces," China Daily 3:682:4, 10/4/83, taken from reports published in Renmin Jiaoyu (People's Education).

6. "Education goals 'hard but possible,'" China Daily 3:624:3, 7/28/83.

7. "General education," China Daily 3:629:4, 8/4/83.

8. Xiao Song, "Primary schools for all can wipe out illiteracy," China Daily 3:619:5, 7/22/83.

9. "Compulsory study urged," China Daily 3:645:4, 8/9/83.

10. "General education," China Daily 3:629:4, 8/4/83.

11. John Woodruff of The Baltimore Sun in "College will be the key to a modern China," The Chapel Hill Newspaper 61:168:4A, 10/9/83.

12. "More investment should be made in education," China Daily 3:604:5, 7/14/83.

13. Zhong Hua, China Daily 3:614:1, 7/16/83.

14. "Brighter prospects for new graduates," China Daily 3:614:1, 7/16/83.

15. Personal communication with President Bi Ke-zhen, Northeast Institute of Technology, 8/23/83 (Interview).

16. Susan Shirk, Competitive Comrades: Career Incentives and Student Strategies in China, 1981.

17. "TV University enrolls 15,000," China Daily 3:604, 7/5/83.

18. "200 million Chinese at school," China Daily 3:815:1, 3/7/84.

19. "Self-taught students," China Daily 3:678:3, 9/29/83.

20. Wendy Lin, "With its colleges jammed, China plugs home study," Chronicle of Higher Education, XXVI:15:21, 6/8/83.

21. "City-run day colleges enroll 15,000 to meet local needs," China Daily, 3:675:3, 9/26/83.

22. John King Fairbank, The United States and China, 4th Ed. (Cambridge: Harvard University Press, 1980), pp. 436 ff.

23. Daily Reports (FBIS), 9 March 1982, p. K6, as quoted in Hong Yung Lee, "Deng Xiaoping's Reform of the Chinese Bureaucracy," The Limits of Reform in China, ed. Ronald A. Morse, Boulder: Westview Press, 1983, p. 33.

24. "Leadership echelons," China Daily 3:636:4, 8/11/83.

25. "Xi outlines goals of unions' 10th Congress," China Daily 3:675:1, 9/26/83 and "Leadership teams 'are the key to modernization,'" China Daily 3:620:1, 7/23/83.

ECONOMIC/EMPLOYMENT CONTEXT

1. The definition of state enterprises was given by Xue Muqiao in "The System of Economic Management in a Socialist Country," Economic Reform in the PRC, ed. and transl. by George Wang (Boulder: Westview Press, Inc., 1982), p. 24.

2. "Iron rice bowl; debate revolves around three views," China Daily 6/16/83.

3. Deborah Davis-Friedmann, "Retirement Practices in China: Recent Developments," speech given at the conference, "Aging and Retirement in Cross-Cultural Perspectives," held at the Rockefeller Study and Conference Center at Bellagio, Italy, June 22-26, 1981.

4. Personal communication with Wang Shu-mao, Associate Professor at the Academy of Social Sciences, Shenyang, Liaoning Province, PRC.

5. Ge Dewei, "Traditional values keep women in outdated roles," China Daily 3:646:1, 8/23/83.

6. "Views on Topical Women's Issues," Women of China, 9, Sept. 1983, pp. 3-7.

7. Ibid.

8. Ibid.

9. Margery Wolf, "The New China: Informed Sexism and Deformed Socialism," speech given at Duke University, Durham, NC, April 21, 1983, sponsored by the Department of Anthropology.

10. "Views on Topical Women's Issues," p. 7.

11. Selfless service is highly regarded as the status of Model Workers shows. Special insignia and certificates are awarded to them and increased benefits are theirs for the length of their retirement. The role of model workers was well-defined in an article entitled, "Don't neglect model workers' health," China Daily 3:604:4, 7/4/83:

> Many officials ask model workers to take the lead in daily and overtime work, but when there are benefits available, such as new apartments, they ask model workers to give up their turns to others. Hard work, too many social activities, poor rest and delayed treatment of illnesses have turned their health from good to bad and from bad to worse.
> Model workers, who have both a strong sense of being masters of the country and high expertise, contribute more to the country than others. Only in this respect are they different from other people.
> Like all human beings, they need food, rest, study and recreation. They have to support their parents and feed and educate their children. They also hope to improve their own lives.
> In addition, as they devote more energy to work than others, they deserve more care.
> The more model workers give and the less they ask for, the more that officials should take good care of them. This is both necessary and logical as it will encourage all the people to devote themselves to China's modernization.

(Gongren Ribao commentary)

12. "Retirement means a new life for millions of

workers," China Daily 3:706:3, 11/1/83.

13. David Bonavia, The Chinese (New York: Lippincott & Crowell, 1980), p. 16, and Davis-Friedmann, pp. 8-9.

14. Davis-Friedmann, p. 8.

15. Wang Mingzhen, "Vegetable farmers prosper under new policy," China Reconstructs (Ch. ed.), XXXII:7:50, July 1983.

16. "Shape-up call after improper retirements," China Daily 3:677:3, 9/28/83.

17. "4,000 illicit recruits lose their jobs," China Daily 3:791:3, 2/8/84.

18. "How to find jobs in China," China Daily 3:612:4, 7/14/83.

19. "Federation of private workers proposed," China Daily 6/16/83, p. 3.

20. Kyna Rubin, China Exchange News, as quoted by John Woodruff of The Baltimore Sun in The Chapel Hill Newspaper, 61:168:4A, October 9, 1983.

21. Wendy Lin, "China to let some graduates pick own jobs," The Chronicle of Higher Education, XXVII:1:25, 8/31/83.

22. Wendy Lin, "China eases job placement for college graduates," The Chronicle of Higher Education, XXVII:6:32, 10/5/83.

23. Lin, "China eases."

24. Lin, "China to let."

25. In addition to Lin's reports, articles delineating innovations in the job placement system include: "Brighter prospects for new graduates," China Daily 3:614, 7/16/83; and "Shanghai students to get 'right' jobs," China Daily 3:605, 7/6/83.

26. Qui Yang, "Semi-floating wage aids salary reform," China Daily 3:681:4, 10/3/83.

27. Ibid.

28. Huang Yasheng, "Collective system brings wealth to vegetable farmers," China Daily 3:628:4, 8/2/83.

29. Yang Yi, "Project aims to help pensioners," China Daily 3:622:3, 7/25/83.

POLITICAL/LEGAL CONTEXT

1. Susan Shirk, Competitive Comrades: Career Incentives and Student Strategies in China, p. x.

2. Martha Livingston and Paul Lowinger, The Minds of the Chinese People: Mental Health in New China (Englewood Cliffs, NJ: Prentice-Hall, Inc., 1983), p. 5.

3. Article 1, The Constitution of the PRC (Adopted and Promulgated for Implementation on December 4, 1982, by the Fifth National People's Congress at its Fifth Session). Translation can be obtained from Beijing: Foreign Language Press.

4. "Rectification goal: a stronger, purer, unified Party," China Daily 3:695:4, 11/19/82.

5. "Lawyers crucial to development--minister," China Daily 3:609:1, 7/11/83.

6. Zhang Wen, "Elderly care a social duty," China Daily 3:792:4, 2/9/84.

7. Translation of speech at the First Session of the Sixth National People's Congress of the People's Republic of China, June 21, 1983, available from Beijing: Foreign Language Press.

8. The essays included were the best written representative samples. Those excluded contained the same political themes but were more poorly written repetitions of the ones included.

HEALTH CONTEXT

Physical Health

1. Ruth Sidel and Victor W. Sidel, The Health of China: Current Conflicts in Medical and Human Services for One Billion People (Boston: Beacon Press, 1982).

2. Chen Guanfeng, "WHO's fruitful cooperation," China Daily, 3:651:2, 8/29/83.

3. Martha Livingston and Paul Lowinger, The Minds of the Chinese People: Mental Health in New China (Englewood Cliffs, NJ: Prentice-Hall, Inc., 1983), p. 31.

4. Ruth Sidel and Victor W. Sidel, Serve the People: Observations on Medicine in the People's Republic of China (Boston: Beacon Press, 1973), p. 21.

5. Background statistics on children in China from Beijing Review interview with the Secretary General of the Chinese People's National Committee for the Defense of Children (CPNCDC). "For the Healthy Growth of China's 300 Million Children," Beijing Review 25:22:19ff, 5/31/82.

6. "UNICEF head hails achievement," China Daily, 3:710:3, 11/15/83.

7. Robert N. Grosse, "Interrelation between health and population: Observations derived from Field Experiences," Social Science and Medicine, Vol. 14C (Great Britain: Pergamon Press, Ltd., 1980), p. 99.

8. U.N., 1982, Demographic Indicators of Countries: Estimates and Projections as Assessed in 1980, pp. 254-255.

9. Huang He, "Taking better care of the elderly," China Daily, 6/2/83, p. 6.

10. Figures given in a speech by Mr. Yu Guanghan, Chairman of the Chinese Delegation, at the World Assembly on Aging, Vienna, July 1982.

11. U.N., Demographic Indicators of Countries, 1982.

12. The World Bank, World Development Report, 1981 (New York: Oxford University Press, 1981).

13. Abdel R. Omran (ed.), Community Medicine in Developing Countries (New York: Springer, 1974), pp. 108, 259-274.

14. Huang, op. cit.

15. Gu Xing-yuan and Chen Mai-ling, "Vital Statistics," American Journal of Public Health, September 1982 Supplement, Vol. 72, No. 9, "Health Services in Shanghai County," p. 20.

16. "Improved diet for Beijing residents," China Daily, 3:721:1, 11/18/83.

17. Xiao Song, "Grain Shops in Beijing," China Daily, 3:708:6, 11/3/83. Surveys continually report advances in nutrition being made, but rationing still existed in the summer of 1983. In northeast China, coupons get used along with money when buying a piece

of fried bread along the street, when eating in a res-
taurant or buying food in stores. Coupons for grain
are a surplus item at the present time and often just
waved away. My experience in Shenyang corroborated the
following excerpts from the above-cited article.

The ration system was established in 1954.
A newborn baby is alloted 3.3 kilograms grain
per month in its first year and then the ration
increases at an average rate of one kilogram a
year until the child reaches the age of 12.
Middle school children from 13 to 18 years old
get a monthly ration of 14.8 kilograms for female and 16 kilograms for male students.
The fixed allowance of grain for adults is
divided into three groups according to their
work.
Teachers, office employees and shop assistants get 14 kilograms for women and 16 kilograms for men each month. Construction workers,
equipment operators and truck drivers are alloted about 25 kilograms. People doing heavy
industrial labour are provided with 25 to 30
kilograms of grain each month.
In Beijing, there are still three kinds of
grain coupons. It is part of the long history
of grain shops to provide citizens with a basic
diet summarized as "two whites and one yellow"--
rice, flour and cornmeal. Red beans, mung
beans and millet are sold irregularly.

Surplus Grain

The prices per kilogram are 0.30 yuan for
rice, 0.36 for flour and 0.22 for cornmeal. In
the past 30 years, only the price of flour was
raised by 0.001 yuan in 1966.
As people take in more than staple food like
meat, eggs, fish and vegetables, nearly every
family has a grain surplus. A family of four
is alloted about 50 kilograms grain each month,
but they usually buy only 30 kilograms.
The present average monthly income in Beijing
is 40 yuan per person. If a family of four earns
160 yuan and buys 50 kilograms grain with their
monthly grainbooks which cost 20 yuan, the
grain expenditure takes 12 per cent of their
income. . . .
In the negotiated-price grain shops, ration
coupons are not necessary and customers can
buy as much as they like. The prices, though,
are about double those in the common grain
shops.

18. Dr. Xu reported some of the survey results in the following month's Women of China, "Measures to Protect the Elderly," Vol. 9, Sept. 1983, pp. 18-20. His sample was well described there:

1. Family status: The 967 interviewees were in 703 households with an average family size of 3.7 members. Altogether 285 households (40.6 per cent) have five or more members. 343 had lost their spouses and 86 of those live alone. Most are living with their children and 95.1 per cent said they were on good terms with their family members.

2. Source of income: These elderly interviewees who were mostly rickshaw-pullers, street cleaners, and handicraftsmen in old China, found regular jobs in factories and other state enterprises after liberation. Today, in spite of their age, 56 are still active, earning a regular income. 567 are retired pensioners and 344, mostly housewives, have never worked outside their home. Of those interviewed, 555 are able to support themselves, 79 claim to be partially self-supporting and the other 333 are dependent on their children. 80.5 per cent of the total said they feel quite at ease about their personal welfare.

19. Sidel, The Health of China, p. 98.

20. Donald B. Ardell, High Level Wellness (Emmaus, PA: Rodale Press, 1977).

Mental Well-Being

21. Sidel, The Health of China, p. 117.

22. Arthur Kleinman, Presentation at Duke University, October 12, 1983.

23. Interview with the American Medical Students' Association Delegation to the PRC, June 1982.

24. Belden, Jack. China Shakes the World. New York: Monthly Review Press, 1949 (Reprint ed., paperback, 1970).
    Hinton, William. Fanshen: A Documentary of Revolution in a Chinese Village. New York: Random House, Vintage Books, paperback, 1966.
    Hinton, William. Shenfan: The Continuing Revolution in a Chinese Village. New York: Random House, 1983.
    Horn, Joshua S. Away with All Pests . . . An

English Surgeon in People's China, 1954-1969. New York: Monthly Review Press, 1969 (Reprint ed., paperback, 1971).

Myrdal, Jan. Report from a Chinese Village. New York: Pantheon, 1965.

Parish, W. L. and Whyte, M. K. "Health, Education, and Welfare Policies." Chapter 6, Village and Family in Contemporary China. Chicago: University of Chicago Press, 1978.

Pruitt, Ida. A Daughter of Han: The Autobiography of a Chinese Working Woman. New Haven: Yale University Press, 1945.

Snow, Edgar. Red China Today. New York: Vintage Books, 1971.

Snow, Edgar. Red Star Over China. New York: Random House, 1938.

Spencer, Jonathan D. The Gate of Heavenly Peace: The Chinese and Their Revolution 1895-1980. New York: Viking Press, 1981.

White, Theodore H. and Jacoby, Annalee. Thunder Out of China. New York: William Sloan, 1946 (Reprint ed., 1973).

Yang, C. K. Chinese Communist Society: The Family and the Village. Boston: MIT Press, 1959.

25. Ling Ming-yu, "Psychiatry in China Today," National Reconstruction Journal, Vol. 6, No. 3 (1946), pp. 20-30. This article provides a historical setting for the period just before Liberation, and an understanding of traditional Chinese values, by a Chinese psychiatrist, as quoted in its entirety in Livingston and Lowinger, pp. 138-154.

26. Martha Livingston and Paul Lowinger. The Minds of the Chinese People: Mental Health in New China. Englewood Cliffs, NJ: Prentice-Hall, Inc., 1983, p. 127. The biographical sketch of Wang Shu-mao, a psychologist with the Liaoning Province Academy of Social Sciences in the footnotes to Appendix A may also be of interest.

27. Livingston and Lowinger, p. 120. Estimation of psychiatrists by Dr. Xia Zhenyi, President of the Chinese Society of Neurology and Psychiatry.

28. Sidel, The Health of China, p. 114.

29. Li Ch'ung-p'ei et al., "Some Problems Concerning the Cause of Psychasthenia and Attempts to Find Quick Treatments," Collection of Theses on Achievements in the Medical Sciences in Commemoration of the 10th National Foundation Day of China, Vol. II, Beijing, 1959. Translated by U.S. Joint Publications Research Service No. 14829, pp. 652-670. As cited in Livingston

and Lowinger.

30. Arthur Kleinman, Patients and Healers in the Context of Culture. Berkeley: University of California Press, 1980, p. 148.

31. Ibid., pp. 174-175.

32. Marie Ridder, "Leaving the Science of Destruction Behind," The Washington Post, March 12, 1978, pp. G1-4.

33. Livingston and Lowinger, pp. 192 ff.

34. Livingston and Lowinger, p. 28.

35. Yang Jiang, A Cadre School Life: Six Chapters, trans. Geremie Barme (Hong Kong: Joint Publishing Co., 1982), p. 36.

36. J. Carolyn Zavarine, "Post-Retirement Role of Elders and Mental Health in the PRC," Paper given at the American Public Health Association Annual Meeting, Nov. 16, 1982, Montreal. Dr. Zavarine can be reached at the Boston University School of Medicine.

III
The Manifestations of Well-Being Among the Elderly in Shenyang

THE SETTING

Of course, there is a complex and rich world
that shimmers just on the other side of our
abstractions. There is a world of inner conflicts and personal strivings, nasty ambitions,
lusts and melancholias, frustrations and dis-
satisfactions that belong to the individuals
who comprise China. That may seem obvious;
yet, these things have been missing from the
"luminous portraits," in Simon Leys's aptly
sarcastic phrase, that have been done of China.
And inevitably so, given the energetic strivings
of the regime to present the individual as little more than an enthusiastic participant in
its grand national schemes. Often missing also
from these portraits is the nature of that regime itself, as a still intrusive, controlling,
terrifying, and irresistible force. When we
in the West examine the Soviet Union or Eastern
Europe, we are appropriately obsessed with the
plight of the puny individual in his confronta-
tion with the awesome clumsiness of totalitarian
power. For some reason, when we look at China,
the challenges of courage that the individual
faces are rarely considered. Yet, they exist.[1]

Shenyang, the capital of Liaoning Province, is the
largest city in the industrial Northeast and the fifth
most heavily populated in China* with a city population
of 3.033 million and a municipality (five districts,
four suburbs and two counties) population of 5.142 million in 1983. The majority population is Han,** but 27

---

*Shanghai--11.9 million; Beijing--9.2 million; Tianjin--
7.8 million; Guanzhou--5.4 million.
**China as a whole is 93 percent Han.

minority nationalities are also represented (Hui, Man, Korean, Mongol, etc.).

It was in this part of the world that Peking Man walked erect and used tools and fire 400,000 to 500,000 years ago. A complete skull and other fossils judged to be over 10,000 years old were recently found by quarry workers in a Liaoning Province cave and during the summer of 1983 archeologists discovered foundations for nineteen buildings in the northern outskirts of Shenyang dating back approximately 7,200 years. Such relics as utensils, pottery, jade and wood carvings are a testament to the fact that a relatively advanced civilization existed here prior to 5,000 B.C. The city assumed its present outline 2,100 to 2,200 years ago and today one still gets the feeling of time advancing slowly.

Shenyang is the ancestral home of the Qing (Ch'ing) Dynasty emperors. The founder of the Qing, Nurhachi, united the tribes of this nomadic nationality and established his capital at Shenyang from 1625 to 1644. He then conquered the central Chinese capital of Beijing and the Qing Dynasty began. The dynasty prospered in the 1700s, declined in the 1800s and ended in 1911 when the Chinese overthrew their Manchu rulers.

The area seems to embody many ages at once. Remnants of the past are present all over Shenyang. One sees the high walls, narrow streets and ancient buildings from the Middle Ages, the Russian and Japanese architecture built in the first half of this century (reminiscent of domination and occupation) and the beautiful carving of Mao Zedong that still stands in the middle of Red Flag Square.

The transportation system also reflects Shenyang's characteristic blending of old and new. Vegetables are delivered to the market areas by horsedrawn wagons and unloaded onto the ground. Trolley buses come every two to three minutes so packed no one fears falling. The conductor knows who has paid and very efficiently gives change and receipts for fares based upon the number of stops. Full concentration is needed to find pathways through the incredible traffic of bikes, trucks (filled with workers), buses, motorcycles, army vehicles, Shanghais (taxis), and even children on tricycles. There are specially adapted sidecars for small children in winter, custom designed bicycles for the handicapped and bikes pulling or pushing carts of people, produce or both. Sometimes it sounds as though every one is honking a horn or ringing a bell!

A complex municipality with heavy and light industry (e.g., machine tool, electrical, textile, metallurgical and chemical factories), agriculture, scientific and technical research, arts and handicrafts, Shenyang is also the center for provincial and interprovincial railway lines. Statistics about the city reveal the existence of:

- 3,342 enterprises
- 25 state farms
- 104 people's communes
- 1,465 production brigades
- 8,618 production teams
- 113 independent research institutes
- 19 colleges and universities
- 26 technical schools training technicians
- 112 technical schools training skilled workers
- 12 agricultural schools
- 332 middle schools
- 1,559 primary schools
- 39 theatres and movies
- 18 special teams (units) for opera, drama and plays
- 13 libraries
- 1,475 health units
- 38,000 medical personnel (doctors and nurses)
- 19,000 hospital beds[2]

Zhou Enlai went to middle school in what is now Primary School Number Six in Shenyang from the autumn of 1910 to July 1913. A visit may be arranged to the small museum there honoring his memory and leadership. Liu Shaoqi was sent by the Central Committee of the Chinese Communist Party to work as Party Secretary in the Northeast from July 1929 to March 1930 and from there led the workers' movement against the counter-revolutionary forces--the Japanese and the local government under Japanese rule. ("Counter-revolutionary" is defined as whichever power is oppressing the people.) Zhang Xueliang, son of the famous Shenyang warlord Zhang Zuolin, joined forces with Yang Hu Shen to capture Chiang Kaishek in Xian in a still famous incident.

Shenyang is the site of the Cemetery for Martyrs of the Korean War--a memorial containing graves of 128 national heroes. (The rest of the Chinese killed, including Mao Zedong's own son, were buried in Korea.) A historical museum containing photographs and personal artifacts of the soldiers also has been created there.

Clothes are hung all over the free market stands bordering the main shopping streets. The co-mingling of State and free market enterprises demonstrates the new pragmatism of Chinese socialism and its concern that everyone have the chance to eat and support himself. "Have you had your breakfast?" and "Have you had your dinner?" are still common salutations in Shenyang.

Underneath this view of "so many people" and "so much action" are a people of grace, depth, generosity and intensity. In an essay one of my students wrote: "Music is like power. When I hear it I get more force

to do everything . . . ." The pulse of life in Shenyang is like that for me. Serious work feels good to
do, not for material reward, but for the chance to exercise your mental powers, expand your knowledge and
express your feelings in appropriate ways.
    Shenyang is very crowded, but the people are now
healthier, living longer and continuing what appear to
be positive interpersonal relationships. Feudalistic
practices have, for the most part, been done away with
and the modern family seems to be based on cooperation
and adjustment. That is not to say that conflict does
not exist between the old and the young, between mothers and daughters-in-law and between old and new ideas.
It's a part of life everywhere, but in Occidental history tyranny gave birth to independence. In the Orient, harmony was conceived. Accommodation to others
has been characteristic of the people of the Northeast,
but not always by choice. There have been many times
in this century of domination when conformity made the
difference between life and death.
    An 84-year-old resident of a commune retirement
home began his talk with me by emphasizing that many
people there had very sad stories to tell:

        During the Japanese occupation, people were
        forced to work in the mines and factories and
        then killed. I saw people buried alive in
        the mines and in the earth. Then the reaction-
        aries came and treated us not as people but as
        animals.

The earth has opened up many times to prematurely receive the dead. The older the cohort, the more suffering that has been known.
    A chronology of political and military events that
have affected life in Shenyang this century[3] suggests
some of the trauma through which the Shenyangese have
lived and for which they have sacrificed their loved
ones. I have tried to include events to which references were made in my interviews and those I know affected the lives of those about whom I am writing:

    1898   Russia leased land on Liaoting Penin-
                    sula (the area south of Shenyang) and
                    built a naval base at Fort Arthur and
                    a port at Dalian.

    Early 1900s   Russians occupied Shenyang and con-
                    structed a Russian Quarter.

    1904-1905   Russo-Japanese War--one of the causes
                    of which was control of the Liaoting
                    Peninsula. The Russian forces were
                    defeated at the Battle of Mukden

(another name for Shenyang).

1911-1912	The Revolution of 1911 overthrew the Manchu Qing (Ch'ing) Dynasty which had ruled for 267 years. The 3,000-year-old feudal monarchical system was replaced by a short-lived Republic with Sun Yat-sen (Zhong Shan in Mandarin) as Provisional President.
1912-1927	Period of rule by the Northern warlords. Shenyang was under the control of Zhang Zuolin.
1914-1918	World War I. When China joined the Allies and declared war on Germany in 1917, the Japanese had an excuse to invade North China. They defeated the small German army stationed there and began to colonize China. The Versailles Treaty, rather than returning the German "possessions" to China, gave them to Japan.
May 4, 1919	Anti-imperialist and anti-feudal strikes and protest demonstrations.
1920s	Japan remained protective of her interests in Manchuria. A number of ardent and courageous young Chinese used literature as a weapon to attack the old society.
1921	Founding of the Chinese Communist Party.
July 1929-March 1930	Liu Shaoqi sent to Shenyang by the Chinese Communist Party to work as Provincial Party Secretary. He attempted to lead the workers' movement against the counter-revolutionary forces.
Late 1920s	Massacre of communists by Chiang Kai-shek resulted in the deaths of tens of thousands. Following this, Mao assumed leadership of the CCP.
Sept. 18, 1931	The Mukden Incident (Shenyang was also known as Mukden): the Japanese invasion of Manchuria began with a clash between Chinese and Japanese forces near Shenyang. Invading and colonizing the city by armed force, this began the first large-scale Japanese occupation of Chinese territory. Japan gradually

took control of Northeast China and established the puppet state of Manchukuo with the last Qing emperor as its nominal leader. The Japanese occupation provoked great feeling, but Chiang was unwilling to commit his forces to resist the aggression.

1934-1935   The Long March (6,000 miles)

1935   The Japanese military forced the end of the formal Nationalist presence in North China.

1936   In the midst of gradual preparations to challenge Japan, Chiang was kidnapped in Sian by Zhang Xueliang, the son of the famous Northeast warlord Zhang Zuolin. Stalin convinced the Communists to spare Chiang's life and form a United Front with a policy of resistance against the Japanese.

1937-1945   War of Resistance Against Japan (also known as Sino-Japanese War, War of Japanese Aggression and anti-Japanese War).

1939-1944   The Nationalist-CCP United Front gradually dissolved as the Communists extended their influence throughout North China.

1939-1945   Manchuria served as an important industrial base for Japan. In the last days of World War II, Russia declared war on Japan, occupied Manchuria, and helped the CCP gain power. They blocked the Nationalists' advance into Manchuria stripping the region of many industrial and military supplies.

Sept. 7, 1945   Japan surrendered to China. The name Mukden changed to Shenyang Shi (Shenyang City).

1946   Soviet troops withdraw.

Nov. 2, 1948   Shenyang liberated.

1946-1949   The War of Liberation with the Communist Red Army defeating the Nationalists, ended with the establishment

of the People's Republic of China on
October 1, 1949.

1950   Sino-Soviet Treaty of Friendship,
Alliance and Mutual Assistance signed.
During the 1950s, 10,000 technical
advisors were sent from Russia to
assist in China's economic development.
China entered the Korean War. The
Marriage Law providing freedom of
marriage and divorce went into effect.

1952   Basic land reform completed after a
five-year campaign. All land deeds
were destroyed and land redistributed
(roughly two million landlords executed).

1953   Korean War armistice. Inauguration of
PRC's First Five-Year Plan, relying on
Soviet model of industrial development.

1954-1955   First constitution of the PRC promulgated and collectivization of agriculture stepped up.

1956-1957   In the wake of Krushchev's denunciation
of Stalin and political explosions in
Poland and Hungary, Mao called for a
"Hundred Flowers Movement" to improve
the relationship between the CCP and
the people. Critics attacked the legitimacy of CCP rule and the Party
responded with an "anti-rightist" campaign suppressing the opposition.

1958-1959   Mao undertook the "Great Leap Forward"
in economic development, relying on
mass mobilization, the commune system
and indigenous ingenuity. The effort
failed for the most part because of
administrative weakness and natural
disasters such as floods and droughts.
Many people, in fact, starved to death.

Late 1950s   Beginnings of Sino-Soviet split.

1960-1963   Full-scale split. Soviet technical
advisors withdraw in 1960.

1960-1962   In the wake of the Great Leap Forward
and the withdrawal of Soviet technical
aid, China turned to Japan as an economic alternative and trade began.

1965-1976   Mao led the "Great Proletarian Cultur-
            al Revolution" attacking the Party
            bureaucracy (which has been frustrating
            his initiatives) and reviving revolu-
            tionary commitment. Millions of stu-
            dents (the Red Guards) were mobilized
            and many Party veterans were purged--
            most notably Liu Shaoqi and Deng
            Xiaoping. From 1971 on, Mao suffered
            from increasing senility and the Gang
            of Four usurped power, ruled with excess
            and put the country in even greater
            chaos.

1976   Zhou Enlai died in January; Mao in
            September. Four weeks later Premier
            Hua Guofeng arrested the Gang of Four
            and the following month instigated
            the "Four Modernizations Program."
            Sinologist William Hinton concludes
            Shenfan with this observation:

            Even though Mao-inspired mass
            movements fell far short of their
            goals, even though they failed to
            create institutional alternatives
            that could nourish the new social-
            ist relations of production, the
            socialist culture and the continuing
            socialist development that Mao deemed
            essential, they nevertheless pro-
            pelled hundreds of millions into
            unprecedented political action, set
            them to examining every facet of
            Chinese civilization, and drasti-
            cally altered the set of their minds.
            Now when pronouncements come down
            from on high, ordinary people, espe-
            cially the young, no longer accept
            them at face value. They want to
            know *why?* Asking *why* has created a
            new climate of opinion that will
            surely unsettle and may even unlock
            the future.

1984   Leadership:

            Hu Yaobang--Party Chairman--General
              Secretary of the CCP
            Li Xiannian--First President since the
              Cultural Revolution
            Zhao Ziyang--Premier, State Council
            Deng Xiaoping--Chairman of both the
              State and Party Military Commissions

> Hua Guofeng--Chairman of the Chinese
> Communist Party Central Committee
>
> The basic principles set out by the
> Party Central Committee are adherence
> to:
> --the socialist road
> --the people's democratic dictator-
> ship
> --leadership by the Chinese Communist
> Party
> --Marxism-Leninism and Mao Zedong
> Thought[4]

GETTING DOWN TO CASES

In reporting my findings, I will discuss each unit
I visited and what was learned in order to show both
what was unique about each situation and what seemed to
be characteristic of being old in Shenyang. I have
tried to convey what was communicated to me in words as
close as possible to what was translated. I am fully
cognizant of the fact that even in my native tongue so
much as a missing comma can completely change the meaning of what was intended. (Take, for example, "Woman
without her man is a savage!" and see what a difference
punctuation makes!) Nevertheless, everyone seemed to
recognize this limitation and gave me ample opportunity
to repeat and clarify. There is no need to use ficti-
tious names for the interviewees because their remarks
were neither private in nature, nor offered in confidence. (See Appendix A.)

Once again, it is worth noting that my largely
positive portrayal of the people and sites discussed
below is not meant to imply that life for China's elderly is perpetually carefree and blissful. Rather,
the positive characterization offered here is a function of three realities. First, while my Chinese hosts
arranged a cross-section of sites, they doubtless chose
to exclude the "worst case" situations from my investi-
gation. Second, the lessons to be learned from the
failings of China's care of its old people are less vital to bring before an international audience than the
lessons one can garner from China's success. After
all, there is a dearth of positive models of well-being
among the world's aged people. Third, and most important, everything I've been able to learn from sources
inside and outside the PRC has left me convinced that,
on balance, China's policies and practices regarding
the elderly *do* represent a genuine success story well
worth telling. It would be a shame if the current fad
of "investigative journalism" about the PRC precluded a
willingness to give the Chinese their due when they

have succeeded in a particular area.

Jing Lao Yuan--Shenyang City Aging People's Home

The first site to be discussed is a home for old people.[5] There are presently 11,000 such homes across China.[6] In 1983 alone, there was a 20 percent increase in these institutions.[7]

Jing Lao Yuan was set up in September 1957 as a "Home for Social Well-Being" by the municipal government. It is located 22 km south of Shenyang City, covers 12,800 sq. meters and has 21 buildings.

The home has presently adopted 159 aging people: 78 males and 81 females. The oldest resident is 98; the youngest is 61; 53 are over 80; and 11 are over 90. The average age is 77.5. Some are original residents and have been there for over 25 years. There are:

2 veterans (former mobilized soldiers)
23 family members of "martyrs"
47 retired workers from enterprises and factories
87 people supported by the social system

This last group had been unemployed or had worked without an adequate pension scheme. The 47 retirees pay only for their food; their living expenses, like the food and living expenses of the others, are paid for by the State. The veterans and family members of martyrs are especially honored. As a symbol of their high status, they are given a sofa in their rooms and receive other forms of special consideration. The mandate for the Home comes from the Constitution: "We must protect the old," meaning that those without family, social or financial support should be taken care of by the government.

The Home is being expanded to accommodate 240 persons, so new construction is occurring. "To protect the good health of the old people," there is a hospital with 25 beds and a health care ward (clinic) for regular check-ups. A small grocery store, a barber shop/hair salon, sewing room, bathing facilities and laundry are all on the premises. Each building, designed to house 24 people, has an entertainment room with a television set, games and magazines. The residents go to Shenyang City to see films or to attend the theatre and exhibitions. The Civil Administration Bureau arranges for troupes to perform at the Home and for films to be shown. Especially during the holidays, leaders of the province, municipality and army visit the old people. Throughout the year, people from various administrative units, army groups, schools and universities go there "to serve."

The Home provides young students and army members

with a concrete opportunity to promote the Five Points (hygiene, civilization, discipline/order, responsibility and courtesy/virtue) and to manifest the Four Beautifuls (a kind heart, action/behavior, language and environment).[8] Accordingly, Jing Lao Yuan is an important venue for properly socializing the young to venerate their elders. In this political education, the leaders teach the workers "to act as relatives to the old people--to be as sons and daughters" and "to work heart and soul" for the old people.

I asked Mr. Gao, the Vice-Director of Jing Lao Yuan, what differences socialism had made, given that respect for the aged had always been a part of Chinese culture and tradition. He replied:

> About two years ago, the government began a campaign stressing the Five Points and the Four Beautifuls and encouraged the people to translate these words into actions and these actions into goals. They're sometimes discussed during political study and encouraging slogans appear on blackboards. [In China, blackboards, widely used and read, are a very important method of communication.] A Five-Good Family Campaign was also mounted to protect the old traditions in developing the new socialism. A Five-Good Family educates their children well; maintains a good relationship between husband and wife, with the neighbors, and with parents and in-laws; and provides a beautiful environment and good hygiene within the family (including the use of birth control). Honor cards began to be awarded to such families after the Third Session of the National Party Congress which stressed the importance of Spiritual and Mental Civilization.[9]

Addressing the Model Family Campaign, I asked what sorts of conflicts arose in a family situation:

> In a family situation, the old people have the high position and try to arrange everything. Yet the second generation wife can have her own opinions and a conflict or contradiction can arise . . . so the most important point becomes maintaining good relationships in the family.

Moving on to the issue of health, Gao Zinyan noted that:

> The biggest health problem among the residents is painful joints, followed by tracheitis. Many people get this inflammation.

Out of the 159 old people, only one has
senile dementia.

The medical equipment in the home hospital includes X-ray and electrocardiogram machines. There are
four doctors and thirteen nurses on the staff. Examinations are given daily and care given according to the
health condition. There is a special house for those
over 80 and in the same building a special care clinic
for the sick. If the condition can't be treated on the
premises, the patient is taken to the hospital downtown. As Mr. Gao noted:

> The Medical Research Society, the Chinese
> Medical University in Shenyang and the Army
> Hospital all send special personnel to give
> general health check-ups without charge.
> The number one doctors and the number one
> hospitals serve our people here. Two of the
> doctors studied both Western and traditional
> medicine. We also offer physiotherapy.

Healthy old people share common buildings. One
attendant serves each building of 300 sq. meters. The
attendant cleans the rooms, washes the clothes and
changes the sheets.

> The living standard is very high. The people
> get enough sunshine and have steam heat and
> toilets inside the building. In summer
> they're given a straw mat for coolness and in
> winter, an electric blanket. A big effort is
> made to beautify the surroundings, to make a
> fresh environment for the old people and to
> protect against pollution.
>   The old people themselves are the masters
> of the home. They elect a management committee
> democratically from amongst themselves. The
> committee has many functions: they make plans
> and arrangements--for example, organizing
> "ecology work" to improve conditions; they
> discuss problems and possible solutions; they
> represent and convey the feelings and ideas
> of the residents to the leaders of the home;
> they pass on criticisms and make recommenda-
> tions for improvement. Each week, as in most
> units, half a day is spent in the study of
> political issues. The meetings are arranged
> and conducted by the residents themselves.
> To improve their health and broaden their
> interests, the old people participate in the
> work of the home in any way they want. There's
> no special time or task for this. If they
> would like to do something, they can. Everyone

gets some spending money, but those who work
(for example, by raising vegetables or flowers
or by contributing in a special way) get a
little more as a reward.

The old people maintain contact with the
outside world through their radios and papers.
The staff reads newspapers to those who need
help. The 59 staff members and workers, from
the director to the attendants and cooks, try
to serve the needs of the old people.

Three meals are served each day which include rice,
bread and cakes. For lunch and supper a main dish and
a soup are served. Other dishes are added for festivals and vacations. Birthdays are celebrated with very
special care. According to custom, *shou*, special long
noodles symbolizing longevity, and a lotus egg (an egg
broken into boiling water resembles a lotus), a symbol
of life, are served. The two favorite dishes of the
person whose birthday is being celebrated are prepared
and the director pours their wine and makes a special
toast to wish them long life.

Those over 80 are given a glass of milk every
morning according to the regulations of the government
which state that special care must be given to those
over 80. It is believed that giving special care encourages people to live longer. The milk is taken as a
symbol of their status, not because of the increased
calcium needs of the old--though that is a side benefit.
Like the sofas in the rooms of veterans and family members of martyrs, it adds a measure of pride and respect.
A glass of milk is a luxury and as such is to serve as
a reminder of the progress of the new society.

How does one come to live here? One of Jing Lao
Yuan's administrators described the process as follows:

> In the city the street committees make recom-
> mendations to the civil administration organ
> as to who needs this kind of care. All those
> who apply get to come; yet, of course, those
> who want to remain in their communities can do
> so. A place here is not based upon economic
> need, but on the situation of having no chil-
> dren or close relatives to care for them. The
> Ministry of Civil Administration at the State
> level allocates money to the Civil Administra-
> tion Bureau for Liaoning Province which then
> rations out the money to the various substruc-
> tures under their care.

On a tour of the home and the grounds, it was ob-
vious everyone and everything were well taken care of.
I was used to the very clean personal habits of the
Chinese, but the external environment is rarely as

fastidiously kept as here. The walls and floors were
well washed; there was no smell of urine. A couple of
women burned incense. There were three or four to a
room, though those who were deaf and those with conta-
gious diseases were given private accommodations. Married couples also had their own rooms (with the beds
pushed together). Visiting the rooms and talking informally was a wonderful treat for Mrs. Sun, one of the
translators, and me. We felt as though we had been
pampered by multiple grandmothers and grandfathers.

The following excerpts from interviews with four
of the residents of Jing Lao Yuan are illustrative of
the life stories, concerns and attitudes shared with me.
The intention here is to highlight those portions of
the interviews that either speak to these old people's
sense of well-being or describe their impressions of
the situation of the elderly in the pre- and post-revolutionary periods. The final chapter will provide an
analysis to complement these descriptive statements. I
have tried to retain to the best of my ability the
words and feelings communicated to me.

Mr. Chang Jiemin--Age 61

Born in the "old society," Mr. Chang worked in a
factory. He was considered "hard labor"--not a "worker"--and was often beaten. He pointed out that he had
to accept this treatment or starve altogether. His
face was deformed and fingers were missing due to an
industrial accident. When the Chinese Communist Party
liberated the poor, workers became masters of the factory. He was given safety protection equipment. In
the old society, they ate flour made from cotton; in
the new society, they eat rice, wheat flour, fish, meat
and good steamed bread. He says his happiest day was
being liberated by the CCP. Each month he receives 100
percent of his former pay having worked in the foundry
of the same factory for over twenty years. He also receives free medical treatment.

> Every morning at 4 a.m., I walk outside in the
> fresh morning air with the two birds I have as
> pets. When they were in the same cage, they
> didn't sing. I separated them and now they
> each sing beautifully. . . . If I feel alone,
> I can always be with my roommates.

His health has improved since he came here. His
tracheitis has disappeared and his body weight is up
2 *jin*.* For many old people in China, gaining weight
is seen as a measure of good health. Telling me his

---

*1 *jin* - 1.1 lbs.

body weight had gone up from 160 to 162 *jin* was something he did with pride. The university professors were the only ones who expressed the idea that keeping one's weight *down* was important.

Mr. Chang had been here two years. During holidays and festivals the factory leaders come out to visit him bringing gifts of oranges and vegetables.

He says he has no fear of dying.

Mr. Ho Gishen--Age 77

Mr. Ho, a former teacher and principal of a school for orphans, lived through the changes of two societies and retired at 64. In the old society, the position of education and the status of teachers were very low. Mr. Ho remembers that:

> Conditions were terrible during the Civil War.
> Often we didn't get our salary for three or
> four months. I couldn't support my family.
> All they could get to eat were potatoes and,
> to grind into flour, the bitter seeds of the
> rubber tree flower. The students and teachers
> would strike and the police would come and
> arrest the leaders, but after liberation the
> situation was different. I became the princi-
> pal of an orphan school. We stood up and be-
> came masters of our country.

In 1974 his wife died. In the fall of 1982 he developed a very bad case of arthritis and couldn't walk or take care of himself. The government arranged for him to come to Jing Lao Yuan. He recalls:

> In the beginning (of the arthritic condition)
> I felt desperate, lonesome and hopeless because
> I had no child to take care of me, but when I
> entered this home my situation became very
> different. To paraphrase a Chinese poem:
> "There is no road to the mountain. I can't
> see through the water. I feel despair. But
> when I go close the situation is very different.
> The flower blooms, the water falls, and the
> surroundings are very, very beautiful."

He had been troubled by what he might find in an old people's home, but after he got there, he felt very happy about his living environment:

> The government is concerned about the position
> of old people. "To serve the people" is the
> slogan of the staff. They often have "heart-
> to-heart" talks and follow the spirit of re-
> specting the old and nurturing the young.

Much is done to help wipe out loneliness.
Many people come to see us, singing and dance
troupes perform, soldiers come out to volunteer their services and help clean the courtyards. In the old society, no one took care
of the old people if they had no children.

Mr. Ho stayed in the hospital of the home for two
months with his arthritis. It was impossible for him
even to go to the toilet. He cooperated with the treatment prescribed by the doctors and the condition went
away quickly. Presently he feels happy, well cared for
and healthy. He attributes his good life to the following:

The government and the people take care of the
aged. The staff serves the old like they are
our children. I never had a child. Every
person who serves us does so carefully, atten-
tively, like my own child would have.
Young people and soldiers often visit
our home and clean it. Teachers sometimes
visit us and give us gifts (such as picture
magazines). The cinema sends us tickets even
though in the city it is very crowded and people wait in line to get in. The commercial
bureau of the city often arranges for stores
to bring some things to the home to sell.
Young artistic troupes come to entertain.
Famous Shenyang restaurants send their best
chefs to prepare meals for us. Children from
the Railway Elementary School come and sing
and dance so we won't feel alone.
In Chinese society, aged people are very
happy. Pride is felt for the young. When you
feel alone, you find a young person here and
you feel like you have a grandson. The situation is much different now than before Liberation. Children from the orphan school where I
worked in Shenyang also come here to take care
of the old people.

Mr. Ho retired at 64, whereas most men in a similar position retire at 60. It was his choice to work
longer and he wasn't restricted from doing so. He sees
his present good health as a miracle and says he has no
worries.

Mrs. Zhang Songyu--Age 85

Mrs. Zhang came from a poor family and her parents
arranged a marriage for her at 16. She referred to
herself as "a victim of feudal sacrifice." Her husband
contracted TB and died before they ever lived together.

Still she was considered a widow and never married.[10]

Before Liberation, conditions were very bad. She remembers eating wild vegetables in order to survive. No work was available to her.

Mrs. Zhang was one of the earliest residents here. She saw the home get better and better:

> As an aged person in the old society with no one to tend to my needs, I would have died. But now, the staff receives me just like my child would have so I feel very happy. I don't worry about anything. There are people I care about here and who care about me. Being content makes me healthy.
>
> The home offers us three meals a day, shoes and clothes and gives us everything we need. Even when my birthday comes, I eat longevity noodles and get a gift put at my table. Special dishes are served at birthdays and festivals, especially during Spring Festival. At the Chinese New Year, a round moon pie is served. It signifies "reunion of the family." Even though I live in this home, I also eat moon pie. I feel I have a big family here.
>
> I listen to the radio, watch TV, have general health checkups and any illness which comes along gets treated in time. Before, I had mental trouble, but now it's disappeared. We have a happy feeling here. We don't worry about anything and this will allow me to live very long. Sometimes a member of the staff washes my hair and my feet just as my own daughter would . . .

No one there has relatives so they consider the staff as family and are well taken care of by them. She says the key to her long life is this personal attention. When she has an illness she stays in the sickroom and is well cared for . . . She's not afraid of getting old or dying.

Mr. Wang Chunshan--Age 70

> The first day after my birth, I began what became a bitter life. I was born into a peasant family--farmers--and we were very poor. When I was young, my mother often took me outside as a beggar. There were 40 in our family. My father had five brothers. My grandfather and grandmother were also farmers and worked for the landlord. Living conditions were very bad, miserable. When my grandfathers and uncles were still alive, their lives were like that of the horse and cow--no food to eat or clothes to wear.

> When I was 18, I left my family and
> joined the army--the Anti-Japanese Red Army
> in the Northeast. My first commander was
> killed by the Kuomintang. I joined a unit
> led by Yang Ching-yu but he was killed by the
> Japanese army in 1940. After the Japanese
> surrendered, I joined the Eighth Route Army
> and in the Black Mountain Battle I was wounded
> six times, four times seriously and twice
> minor. My stomach was shot full of holes. My
> intestines fell out of my stomach. My ribs
> were broken. I was treated in a hospital and
> when I recovered I went back to the countryside.
> After twenty years service in the army, I re-
> tired. Because I didn't get an education the
> only work I could do was farm in the country-
> side.

When Mr. Wang went back to the countryside, he
found that he was the only survivor of his 40-member
family. "Four had been killed by Kuomintang reactionaries, the rest by the Japanese invaders." Forty peo-
ple--his family--all his family--died before Liberation.

> I don't want to talk about this; I won't be
> able to sleep . . . When I came back to my
> home, there wasn't anyone . . .

Mr. Wang was crying very hard at this point. (He wasn't
alone for it was the saddest story I'd ever heard.)
     Mr. Wang took an active part in organizing cooper-
atives in the collective movement, but he came down
with myelitis and had to enter a hospital. After his
cure, he entered the home which at that time was for
members of martyrs' families. Later it expanded to include others.
     Since 1980 he has had two major operations which,
he said, cost the old age home 2,000 yuan.

> They spent money to buy me life. The Party
> has saved my life many times. When I was in
> the hospital everyone in the home cared about
> me and was concerned about me. When I was
> operated on in Shenyang Third People's Hospi-
> tal, the nurse--her name was Shen Shao-hua--
> cared for me and paid attention to me. She
> cooked good food for her family and brought
> it to the hospital to also give me. She was
> not my relative, but she cared for me like my
> daughter so I got better soon. It's like I
> died and got a second life. The workers spoon-
> fed me and the leaders of the home called upon
> me.

When he recovered he was determined to work hard
for the Party which "gave him life." "I do my best to
contribute to our society--to repay the government and
the people who served me." And, each day, the director
said, Mr. Wang works very hard doing whatever is needed
at the home.

$$* \qquad * \qquad * \qquad * \qquad *$$

The time I spent at Jing Lao Yuan was extremely
rewarding. The love among the people was very evident
and I felt privileged to be able to experience it. The
elderly here are respected; in fact, they're treated
like VIPs in a hotel. Leaders, staff and workers are
here to serve the elderly: the focus is on the old
people's needs and desires, as well as giving them the
honor to which they are believed to be due. Just as
important, the people who work and live here are family
for one another. People were put together in rooms not
just because there was space, but because their person-
alities and personal habits meshed well.

Everyone seemed to appreciate the interview situation. People listened very intently to one another.
Rather than getting bored, everyone got more and more
into the discussions. Perhaps they didn't have that
kind of personal, philosophical conversation very often
or perhaps they just really cared and were there for
one another as a matter of course.

What I was able to give back to them was an outsider's validation that the elderly in China *are* respected compared to other countries, and that special
care really *is* taken of them; that the kind of caring
and the kind of love I experienced there didn't exist
many places and I explained that that was what I wanted
to write about. To this group of people--who contributed so much of their life's energy to their nation's
progress and to the ideal of socialism--it felt very
good to hear from a foreigner that their work and what
they had created together at Jing Lao Yuan were worthy
of being viewed as a model.

On the way home I asked Mrs. Sun how people dealt
with grief in China--for the residents of the home certainly had experienced more than their fair share of
suffering. Was it considered better to just suppress
sorrow and set your mind on something else or to let
all the tears flow to try to dissolve the pain? She
answered in terms of the old age home. "In that home
people live in the company of others and they're free
to do whatever is right for the situation. Sometimes
grief should be let out. Other times, it should be
managed. The people there have to sense what is right
for the individual and help them through it." My observation is that the staff and residents acted upon--
indeed embodied--that principle.

A long-time resident of Jing Lao Yuan

Shenyang Electric Cable Plant

The entranceway to this "model factory" is like a botanical garden with beautiful flowering plants everywhere in view. The factory employs 6,000 workers and staff members (of whom 1,700 are women). In addition, approximately 1,000 retired workers are looked after by the plant. Built in 1938 by the Japanese, the plant was rebuilt in 1949 and expanded in 1956. Today more than 200 types of cables are manufactured--from thick copper line, electric and mining cables, cables for use on ships and high voltage electric cables (which can carry 500,000 volts) to ones thinner than a piece of hair.

Services for the workers include a kindergarten, nursery school, clinic and bathing station. There are three libraries--in the hospital, in the plant itself and in the dormitories for single people--and a "cultural palace" which includes a cinema and stage for

amateur productions. Classes are offered for workers
in technical fields and design and many enroll in TV
University classes. Some workers, like one of the basketball stars, attend a night university sponsored by
the municipality. There is a dining room for those who
are alone and three cafeterias have been set up outside
the plant for the convenience of other workers. Four
buses transport mothers and children back and forth and
a car picks up workers who live far away from the factory.

Sports were especially emphasized by everyone.
There are organized teams in basketball, ping-pong,
weight-lifting and volleyball. The Electric Cable
Plant is third in the municipality for basketball and
their weight-lifting team has won sixteen gold medals
and one bronze. One of their weight-lifters broke the
record for Shenyang. All the work production areas
have amateur teams and a different kind of competition
is held monthly in which four teams from each workshop
compete. To mark International Women's Day each March
a running competition is held. Every two years there
is a factory-wide Sports Day. Fifty people also participate regularly in song and dance troupes.

Concerning the elderly, Mr. Zhang Jiun (Secretary
of the Director's Office) pointed out that, outside of
work responsibilities, there are no differences between
workers and the retired in the life of the unit. He
described some of the ways in which the plant cared for
the old. For example, the retired are invited to take
part in the major meetings of the factory and in all
sports meetings. To reflect their status, they're invited to sit with the Chairman of the event. Special
meetings are also held to ask the opinions of the retired regarding their requirements and needs. The
housing regulations specify that rooms must be kept for
retired workers to hold meetings.

Within each unit, the leader or his emissary is
sent to help the retired worker if he has a problem.
Special care is taken of those without children.
They're given help in buying food, doing their laundry
and getting to the doctor. Wood for heat and special
tickets for plays and entertainment are sent to the
homes of all retired workers and, when necessary, their
pensions are home delivered as well. As occurs elsewhere, the leaders bring gifts during Spring Festival.
There is a health treatment house for "women with female diseases" and an ambulance that belongs to the
plant. The retired are assured that they will spend
the rest of their lives free of material needs or loneliness.

If there is a problem in production, the retired
are asked to come back and help out. If there's a
problem in technique, their advice is sought. "The
plant and the retired workers think of each other!" I

was told repeatedly.

Pensions are determined by the length of time worked. Those who worked prior to 1949 and Model Workers (of which there are 1,000 at this factory!) receive 100 percent of their final pay as their pension. The average pension is 55 yuan--75 percent of the final salary.

I asked if there were any unique problems for the elderly in the unit. Mr. Zhang replied that:

> Sometimes their children have an illness and the old people are left needing help. Home repairs can be a problem. Sometimes the elderly need a special place to get together for activities--for cards, for instance. We can give them help in getting special identification for free entrance to the park. The old people like to go to the sanitarium for chronic disease treatments and we can help them get there. There's starting to be a numbers problem, though, for it takes a lot of people to care for the retired workers the way we do. We take them to the hospital when they need to go. We deliver their pension when they live far away. We keep track of everyone. If they go back to their home town to live, we still try to send letters and visit. If they don't receive their pension, we have to track it down. They send us their medical expenses and when they have a problem with living expenses, they can apply for an allowance and we try to help them.

The following interview excerpts and summaries show how these services actually affect the well-being of their intended beneficiaries.

Mr. Zhao Yanhe

Mr. Zhao retired last year at 56 because he had high blood pressure and couldn't work. Although he continues to smoke, his blood pressure went down due, he felt, both to his physical training with *t'ai-ji* and to the use of Western medicine. He loves to raise flowers, especially jasmine. He manages to get 30 flowers on the same branch and as many as 45 flowers on his fuchsia. In the back of his home he has 25 kinds of flowers including five kinds of climbing tigers and morning glories. In the evening he likes to play chess with the other old people and then walks in the park.

Before retirement he was the attendant at the plant's Cultural Palace. He often goes back now and works without pay because he enjoys it so much. With 6,000 people in the unit a film is shown six times in order to give everyone a chance to see it.

He had served as a mobilized soldier and married at 30 (respecting the Party's call for late marriages). He has a son in high school who intends to be an artist and a daughter in middle school who is both a top student and a long-distance runner. I asked him if he had any worries and indeed, like many a parent, he identified his children's quarrels as troubling him. I asked him how he handled the situation:

> I try to stop and educate them. It's a tradition to respect the old and take care of the young. Through mutual assistance and mutual respect, a happy family can be achieved. When I quarrel with my wife, usually over a small matter, the children educate us! Generally speaking, I have a very happy late life.
>
> I do worry too, though, about my children's studying, and about how to promote their unity with other children. I hope my children will be qualified people. I'm very involved in their education. Teachers come to our home and we exchange ideas about how to bring up children and what's best for them.

Mrs. Shen Sulan

Mrs. Shen retired a year ago at the age of 50. A very beautiful woman, she has a son and three daughters --all of whom live at home and work at the Shenyang Electric Cable Plant. Her son and second daughter graduated from the technical school of this plant and her eldest daughter studies through the TV University. Her husband, who's also 51, will retire in nine years.

Mrs. Shen worked in the production team responsible for melting copper. Those who work in extreme temperatures, as did she, are eligible to retire five years earlier than the customary age for women of 55. She says that she really enjoys being home taking care of her big family and doing the housework and cooking. Times are good now, and she finally has the chance to minister to their needs. Outside the home, Mrs. Shen does family planning work for her Street Committee each day. As do most of those interviewed, she seeks Western medicine for acute problems and traditional care for chronic conditions.

Mr. Chang Xincai

A former crane operator, Mr. Chang retired in 1982 at 58. Most workers who do such work retire at 55 but in 1978 many young people came to the factory in need of training. He stayed for four more years until his eyes started to fail and his body was no longer limber enough to do such heavy work. Mr. Chang described his current circumstances in the following terms:

> I have a very big family--eleven people:
> three sons, two daughters, two daughters-in-
> law, two grandchildren and a wife. We all
> live together. Nine of the eleven work here.
> We have three rooms--our living area is 60
> square meters. . . . Each day, my wife packs
> food for me and I buy soda water. Then I
> walk to the park and fish. Each month, I
> receive 90 yuan pension.

I pointed out that the age of mandatory retirement
had just been changed to 70 in the United States. Did
he think that would happen here as people lived longer
and the number of retirees expanded? He responded that
one of the advantages of socialism is that the time you
retire is based upon the needs of the unit. In his
case, he was able to work and contribute four more
years and managed to train lots of young people.

I asked him how he managed having so many people
in his home. He responded:

> When I say something, they all do it. I treat
> them all equally, so they respect me. You have
> to begin it that way at the beginning and per-
> sist day-to-day to lay a good foundation in a
> family. I have to be very careful to do this
> with my grandsons.

Mr. Chen Tie

A car and truck mechanic, Mr. Chen has been retired for three years. There are three in his household: his wife, his 22-year-old daughter and himself.
He has two married sons. The elder works for the Shenyang Municipal Government and the younger is in Tsing-
dao. Both have their own homes. His elder daughter
lives in Beiling (about a 30-minute bus ride). To an
inquiry, Mr. Chen said:

> My health is good. I raise flowers. Before I
> had high blood pressure, but I studied Chinese
> traditional medicine, treated myself and now I
> feel very well. I'm learning how to prevent
> disease and lead a very long life. I read
> everything I can from the bookstore on how to
> prevent "old age disease."

I asked him what he'd learned and he answered:

> There is a law for old people. They shouldn't
> have the habits of the young. They should get
> up early, not eat much, get proper nutrition--

not over, and exercise often. They should do
physical labor, but not too much.

He feels much better having taken this advice and in
fact lowered his high blood pressure. With a small
family and a maximal salary he's been able to buy books
and read. He often goes to the park and he's lived
very happily, he says, "due to the policy of the State
to protect workers' lives." When he had problems with
high blood pressure, for example, he would call the
factory and a car would be sent to take him to the
clinic.
     I asked him if he ever talked about death with
anyone. His response got everyone laughing. "You
think that's what I talk about when I meet other old
people in the park?" Big laugh. "Chinese don't talk
about it. We don't worry because our children are
qualified." Suddenly serious, he continued, "In my
heart, though, I'll tell you, I don't want to die. I
want to see the results of the nation's development."

Mr. Li Hongjun

     Mr. Li retired in 1978. He says he's not bored
because he has a five-person family: himself, his wife,
son, daughter-in-law and grandchild. He receives 80
yuan per month and his wife 50. He likes to stay very
active. He exercises every morning in the park at 4:30
while his wife takes care of the grandchild and buys
what they need. He works with the Street Committee every day but Sunday. He repairs roads, plants trees to
beautify the city and helps prepare propaganda to encourage people to have only one child. He feels he is
very representative of the common old people.

Mr. He Jikui

     Mr. He considers himself happily retired. He
likes to research mechanical manufacturing and is busy
every day. He's often invited to small factories to
advise. He's not paid for this, but sometimes receives
presents. (He's trying to educate his son in the same
specialty--innovation in mechanical techniques.) When
there's nothing else to do, he plays chess.
     In response to a question about the source of his
obvious sense of well-being, Mr. He explained:

     It's due to both the plant's policies and the
     Party's leadership. The workers in the factory
     help each other and the plant helps them all
     because they have the same interests at heart.
     We unite and help each other. If someone's
     home catches fire, people donate money to help
     the suffering family. The plant gives money

too. Though we're old, we're still members
of this big family. In the factory if someone dies, the family gets a subsidy and fu-
neral allowance. It's the policy of the
State.

I asked for some clarification--were pensions dependent
on the company's profit? He replied:

No, money is given by the State through the
Labor Insurance Regulations--not according
to profits, according to regulations, and so,
no matter what happens, we'll be secure. The
socialist system ensures all of this.

Shenyang Number One Machine Tool Works

The following introduction was given by Mr. Zhao
Zhuofu, a worker at the plant since 1949 and now Chairperson of the Director's Office. I have included it to
convey the special history and feeling of the setting.
The situation at the factory is considered a "good"
one.

The factory was built in 1935 by the Japanese
imperialists who employed 1,000 people in a
mining repair operation. During the Second
World War, a light tank was produced by the
company with Chinese labor. These tanks were
then used by the Japanese to kill Chinese people.
When the Nationalists occupied the area,
the tank factory was dismantled and the site
set up as a military post (camp and stable).
The workers were displaced and had to find a
way to make a living themselves. Under the
leadership of the Chinese Communist Party and
Mao Zedong, Shenyang was liberated in November
1948 and the factory put into the hands of the
people.
Many workers returned under the management of the government and the call of the
Party. In order to resume production, people
were asked to reequip the factory. Enough
tools and equipment were obtained to make
possible the first production of machine tools
in September 1949. The factory played an important part in the reconstruction of the
country. To meet the economic demands for
large-scale recovery, the factory enlarged its
production capability. Support came from all
parts of the country and, in 1956, the reconstruction and expansion were complete.

The factory was able to fill its quota
according to the First Five Year Plan (1953-
1957) ahead of time. The lathes made through
1957 were of a foreign design, but in 1958,
the first year of the Great Leap Forward, the
factory was transformed and new models designed
and produced through the innovations of the
Chinese workers themselves. More lathes were
created to benefit agricultural production and
transportation development. The production
rate during the Second Five Year Plan increased
50 percent over that of the First Five Year
Plan.

After the smashing of the Gang of Four,
during the period of national economic adjustment, output increased rapidly. The Party and
the government reinstated useful rules and regulations that had been dismantled during the
Cultural Revolution and the factory went through
a time of restructuring, readjustment and improvement.

An incentive pay system was put into effect
to mobilize and encourage the activities of the
workers and staff. Production again rose stead-
ily. Pay is now determined on the basis of
labor (in other words, workers are paid by the
piece) and the administrators (directors, section leaders, office staffs, etc.) become eligible for a 10-15 percent bonus (reward) in
addition to their salary as do those in management (chairman of the workshop, quality examiner,
designers, group leaders) depending upon increased output of their units. With this system, the production requirements of the State
have been met for several years running. In
fact, the plant can presently "overfulfill" the
target set by the State and do so ahead of time.

Workers are obtained from three sources:
work assignments by the State, graduates of
technical schools and children of employees.
People are hired according to the needs of the
factory. About 10 percent of the elderly continue in their positions after they are eligible
to retire. The determination as to who works
beyond retirement age is made on the basis of
the needs of the unit. Many people would like
to work for longer periods than they are needed
on the first line, but they must step aside
when asked.

The factory produces crankshafts for farm-
ing tools and tractors, lathes for automotive
parts, high tension pipes for the oil industry,
control lathes for digital equipment, computers
for national defense purposes, high precision

lathes for the electronic industry and lip-
screw lathes for basic industry. Given specifications, the factory can produce whatever is
requested.
A large amount of what is produced goes
into the foreign market. The quality and price
are both competitive and customers are drawn
from 38 countries and regions of the world
(West Germany, Australia, Japan, U.S., Hong-
kong, Singapore and Macao, to name a few).

As factory production has improved, living standards have increased. There are now 120,000 sq. meters
for housing 6,800 employees. Ten thousand sq. meters
are added annually for living space and 75 percent of
the workers have their own flat. There is a 100-bed
hospital and a clinic in each workshop. Yearly physi-
cals are given to all employees. There are nurseries
and kindergartens and bus transportation is provided
for the women to go back and forth to visit/nurse their
young children. There are libraries, a cinema (for
films and dancing), organized basketball and volleyball
games, and traditional Chinese gymnastics. To enhance
worker literacy, cultural and political life, a college, a technical school and other specialized schools
within the factory grounds offer 150-200 classes per
year. In fact, in order to realize the modernization
of factories, workers have been called upon to learn
technology, culture and politics.

Mr. Jiao Bai-Shun

Mr. Jiao is 69 years old. He retired eight years
ago from his work in the foundry (where liquid iron is
molded). Although he has a bad eye (due to an industrial accident, after which he was fired by the Japanese who occupied the plant), poor hearing and bad
teeth, he has a happy spirit. He says that mentally he
doesn't feel old at all, but he does physically. He's
much slower now than he used to be. He never goes to a
doctor, but when he's ill, he exercises and feels better. His work required full concentration; now he can
relax and be happy. Mr. Jiao lives with his wife. He
has a son who lives outside Shenyang.
Old age is no problem, according to Mr. Jiao, because the trade union, the Party and the government all
dictate that elderly people be respected. On holidays,
especially Spring Festival, the factory leaders call
upon him. He receives 100 yuan per month pension, 100
percent of his former salary; his wife receives 30. He
carefully budgets his money and uses 80 yuan to cover
his living expenses, gives some to his son and deposits
the rest in the bank for his grandson. He wanted to
work a few years longer, but the unit leader, concerned

over the possibility of an accident, said that due to
his eye disability, he needed rest. Should Mr. Jiao
need medical care, it would be free and according to
the regulations concerning retirement benefits, should
his family need medical care they would only pay one-
half the cost of their medical expenses.

He wanted to do something special after retirement
and so goes often to the park to help build up the
flower garden there. He does so without pay. He feels
he has enough money on which to live, given his pension, and he really enjoys working with his hands and
letting people see what he can do.

Mr. Jiao says you can't fear death--it's a natural
thing!

Mrs. Liu Zhen

At 56, Mrs. Liu, formerly the Chief of the Nursery
for children of workers, has been retired a year. Because she felt her country's development and modernization hadn't yet been realized, Mrs. Liu didn't want to
leave the work force. The regulations state, however,
that a woman of 55 should retire and, since she trusts
the system, she complied. Still, she often goes back
to the nursery to visit and lend a helping hand.

The happiest moment of her life was Liberation.
"It was miserable before that with war and not enough
to eat or wear." As long as she has the ability, she'd
like to work for her family by taking care of her
grandchildren, doing the housework and participating in
Street affairs. When she's sick she goes to the Western doctor for fevers, infections and injections, and
to the traditional doctor for chronic disease problems.

Mr. Li Xiang

Mr. Li Xiang, the husband of Liu Zhen, is 63 and
has been retired for three years. In pre-Liberation
days he had been part of the Eighth Route Army, the
main force in ousting the Japanese. At Shenyang Number
One Machine Tool Works, Mr. Li was Chief of the Guard.
Like his wife, he didn't seek retirement, but the State
asks the people to follow the system and he did so. In
his heart, however, he didn't want to leave his post.
He feels everyone does what he can for modernization--
he himself volunteers his time to an active residents'
committee. He has a large family with whom he lives
and says his grandchildren give him more joy than anything. He can't do some things as easily as he used
to, such as carrying groceries, but the young people
help him. Only a minority of the young are ill-man-
nered, he says, and when they act so, they are publicly
criticized. Like his wife, he chooses Western medicine
for acute needs, traditional care for chronic conditions.

Philosophically, Mr. Li stated that:

The affection among working people goes deep
in Chinese society. The old people created
the motherland for the young. In turn, the
State asked the young people to give respect
to the older generation. The task now is for
the old to continue to help the young build
up the country--and to do it beautifully--so
they will be able to enjoy it together. The
old place their faith and hope in the young
because the future of the country is in their
hands.

Mrs. Huang Yunni

At 54, Mrs. Huang has been retired four years from
her post as an administrative accountant. Due to a
health problem she retired early, but subsequently,
through exercise, recovered. She has a full pension of
71.5 yuan per month, 100 percent of her former pay, and
in addition currently has a contract to work five to
six hours a day as an accountant for her residents'
committee (for which she receives a small salary). She
is also involved with the young who live in her community for not only does she care about them personally,
but she also feels that helping the young helps her
country. If she needed medical care, she would prefer
Western medicine, but she hardly ever goes to a doctor
now. Her health has gotten better and better since her
retirement--a fact she attributes to her daily exercise
routine.

Mr. Liu Junsheng

Mr. Liu is 64. He's officially been retired for
three years from a position in housing management, but
he continues to work half a day installing gas systems
in the workers' living quarters. Like many others at
the Shenyang Number One Machine Tool Works, Mr. Liu
didn't like the "ideology of retirement," but had to
retire "because it was time."
As far as medical care is concerned, Mr. Liu
doesn't like to take chances and goes to both Western
and traditional doctors for the same complaint. He attributes longevity to activity, health and nutrition.
He walks every morning and evening and eats a huge bowl
of rice every day. His wife cooks delicious meals, he
says, and he accompanies them with two cups of wine
each evening. He believes that he can live to be over
80.

I have an unburdened, hopeful heart and a big
bowl of rice each night. I don't worry about

anything. When I'm sick I can phone the factory and they'll arrange everything I need.
I don't even need to pay for my medical care.

      *   *   *   *   *

In addition to conducting interviews, I toured the
plant workshops with the retired workers. A nice, informal atmosphere existed and the retirees especially
seemed to enjoy themselves. I appreciated the easy-
going spirit between the retirees and plant directors.
The fact that the people were obviously content,
happy and well-exercised shows that this was a sample
of people who had been successful at aging. They've
witnessed incredible advances in their homeland during
their lifetimes; they've been a part of the development;
they've had a purpose to their lives. They've been active all their days and they continue to be active in
retirement.
They do all this in spite of the trauma they've
experienced as their city and factory changed hands and
policies. They experienced famine but never feast.
They all believe activity and exercise make good health
possible and postpone disability. Pensions seem to be
sufficiently high and they feel they can depend on the
plant to help them in times of need. For example, if
Jiao Bai-Shun died and his wife needed more than her 30
yuan pension, she would ask the plant for help. As is
the usual case in State factories and enterprises, medical expenses are free for the retired worker and the
family receives care at half the cost.
In sum, the people seemed well-adjusted and in
good health. Their avowed commitment to their families
and to the ideals of socialism was the factor to which
they attributed their individual and collective sense
of well-being. In fact, the reluctance they expressed
to retire was indicative of the depth of commitment
felt by the workers rather than an expression of dis-
content with their lives as retirees. They simply
wanted to contribute as much as they could for as long
as they could. Unlike some other factories, the Shenyang Number One Machine Tool Works has a sufficiently
large and well-trained group of younger workers so that
the overwhelming majority (90 percent) of older workers
retire on schedule.
Mr. Zhao Zhuofu (who had worked here since 1949
and is now Chairman of the Director's Office) felt the
attitude toward the elderly showed the superiority of
the socialist system, the government and the Party.
"The people who worked in the Liberation movement are
now old and must be respected. Whether as workers or
retirees, the elderly continue to participate in the
modernization movement. If they are not in the factory, they are training, educating or laboring at home."

A Chinese elder with his grandson

Zeng Yang Street Retirement Committee

Just as the formal pose the Chinese strike in
front of cameras masks the animation of the people being photographed, so too the high walls and storefronts
on either side of long alleyways give little hint of
the mass of life which resides within. A "Street" is a
poor Anglicization of the total neighborhood structure
to which it refers. It is too cold a term to convey to
Occidentals the living, breathing organism of individuals, families and organizations to which it refers and
that comprise a social unit in pursuit of common goals.
As one enters Zeng Yang Street community, he or
she is immediately struck by the mass of color, the organization and the order. Even on rainy days, Zeng
Yang Street was cozy. The blackboards were filled with
colorful messages; directions and pictures were painted
on the walls; and the winding maze of walkways made me
feel I was experiencing what Maria Montessori would
have lauded as a wonderful learning environment.
The Street Office has a distinct role in the hierarchy of the municipal government. It administers government programs and campaigns, oversees Street factories and health facilities and, probably most impor-
tantly, activates the citizenry to creatively solve
problems and design solutions appropriate to both central government directives and local conditions. Under
the jurisdiction of the Street Office are residents'
committees defined at the Sixth National People's

Congress in June 1983 as:

> . . . grass-roots mass organizations of self-
> management with distinctive Chinese character-
> istics. As organizations through which the
> people educate and serve themselves and man-
> age their own affairs, they handle public
> affairs, administer collective welfare, me-
> diate civil disputes and help maintain public
> order and security. It is more appropriate
> for them, rather than institutions of political
> power, to perform much of this work, and they
> can do it more effectively. We should conscien-
> tiously analyze their experience and disseminate
> it and encourage them to act.[11]

Often those at home during the day--housewives and
the elderly--form the core, first, of residents' small
groups and then, representatively, of residents' committees. (Those working, of course, belong to a work
unit, which, having its own political structure, com-
pletes the opportunity for everyone to be politically
involved.) These residential organizations take care
of local needs--child care, sanitation, health education, maintenance, household services and cultural en-
richment.

Mr. Yang Dung-ming, the first Director of the Zeng
Yang Street Retirement Committee, very carefully gave
me the ups and downs of the short history of the committee. Mr. Yang, born in the Year of the Tiger, is 70
years old and has spent the last 30 years here. He
volunteers his time organizing activities to answer the
call of Hu Yaobang, Chairman of the Chinese Communist
Party, "to make a good life for the elderly." In April
of 1982 he was elected to his post as director. Initially 400 retirees were involved. The number has
grown to 800 in the sixteen months they've been organizing and Mr. Yang thinks they have accomplished a
great deal.

The committee feels a strong commitment to do social work for the local community. They've organized,
as a preventive measure, teams to patrol the streets
and keep the neighborhood safe. (The government is
very concerned about the rising rates of crime and has
embarked on an anti-corruption campaign.)

Other teams have been organized to check prices in
the free market and State Department Stores to make
sure each seller is charging the prices set by the
State. The committee originated this community service
and received the backing of the municipal government
through special cards signifying their official right
to investigate. Although their authority extends to
the whole of Liaoning Province, they mostly patrol
their own area. If prices are found to be unfair, they

"first, re-educate the seller, then punish by demanding a fine."

Members of the retirement committee try to make friends with young criminals to help them not do "unsocialist things." Families quarrel, and as is the custom, the old try to help "adjust and unite them." Director Yang feels that as the society has developed, family fighting has declined. The period is better, so family life is better. (Put this in perspective of the scars suffered during the Cultural Revolution and the Great Leap Forward Depression.)

The retired workers have been given another card enabling them to receive immediate attention when they need to see a doctor. This is in accordance with the respect and privilege extended to the elderly and helps them avoid the long lines that can be very difficult to handle for an aged person in need of immediate care. The Retirement Committee has opened a lovely senior citizen center as well, rebuilding an old structure. One room is for cards, chess, reading, etc., another for meetings, and a third set up for arts and handicrafts. Adjoining this center for the aged is one for young people.

When this committee got started in 1982, the district level was unable to offer any financial support. The committee members went to small stores, workshops and factories on the street to ask for donations and thus they were able to buy some entertainment supplies. In 1983, however, the new economic policy of the State had a negative effect. To be in line with the principles of the new responsibility system, factories and workshops reorganized and no longer wanted to help (even those who had originally supported the committee). The committee soon lost its limited funding. "We didn't even have money to buy a newspaper . . . . This was a very serious concern and threatened the very existence of our organization."

Mr. Yang thought of collecting a little money from each old person, but extra money is very limited and he thought better of the idea. He was very worried and unable to sleep. When the district leader came to inspect the Street, Mr. Yang approached him with the committee's need for money. The leader backed Mr. Yang and gave him the encouragement and emotional support he needed: "You are old workers. You have cadres, teachers and many others here. Get together, think of the financial answer and I'll support you." Mr. Yang explained to me that the motto of the Chinese is "self-reliance and hard struggle" and they went to work with renewed strength.

They first thought of opening a small factory given their skills, but they didn't have the money to set it up. Next they came up with the idea of giving classes in English and Japanese using an old house as a

classroom. The district firmly supported the idea and
directed the Bureau of Education to help the committee
every way they could. (I feel this is a good example
of how the political system supports grass-roots ideas
and how an activated citizenry is encouraged.) The Bureau of Education suggested they charge one and a half
to three yuan per student for a month's worth of
classes, but the Retirement Committee decided on two
yuan--some of the money going to the retired teachers
responsible for the classes and the rest to the old
people for their group activities. Happily two hundred
twenty students enrolled. There are four classes, each
meeting three times per week. After four months, the
committee has realized 1,000 yuan for their own use.

Another project the Retirement Committee has in
mind is to rebuild an old house and turn it into a retirement home for those who need it.

Participation in the committee is voluntary. As
one resident reminded me:

Some old people want to continue working and
earn money; others have grandchildren to care
for and have no opportunity to take part.
Poor health doesn't allow others to participate.
We try to visit these homebound at least once
a month to make sure they don't have any problems or difficulties.

Mr. Yang was a very tall, thin man with beautiful
hands he used to gently emphasize his points. His
clear dark eyes were sunken into a face of dignity and
concern. He was a model community leader both sensitive to local needs and creative in helping people find
their own solutions to the problems and concerns arising
in their later years. His dedication and determination
to make the Street Retirement Committee a success for
the old people reminded me of the quotation from The
Family of Man: "We two form a multitude."

It should be noted that Liaoning Province has established 2,300 such committees to take care of 900,000
retirees. In addition, more than 170 recreation centers have been set up for Liaoning's elderly.[12]

Mrs. Bao Cheun-yi

Mrs. Bao has lived all her 75 years in the Zeng
Yang Street neighborhood. She is squarish in build
with grey hair brushed straight back and rectangular
"granny glasses." Her handshake was very firm and
strong, her skin wrinkle-free. Mrs. Bao's parents arranged for her to be married at the age of 22 and she
went, as was the custom, to her husband's family home
to live. She had seven children, three of whom now
live in Shenyang and three outside the area. Her first

daughter, the one to whom she was closest and in whom
she confided, died in 1977 of bone cancer. Mrs. Bao is
now raising that child's daughter. Caring for her
granddaughter, she says, makes her have courage and
keeps her in a happy and optimistic frame of mind.

"Old people in China have a reputation for being
wise," I said. Mrs. Bao retorted: "What old people
have is experience. Young people think more quickly
and old people have more experience." The translator,
a man in his mid-thirties, in English so the woman
wouldn't understand, offered his opinion that he didn't
think old people were wise. Did I?

I asked what made people age well. "Being happy,
optimistic and secure," was her answer. In her case
she felt the basis for her security was her large family.

Her happiest years had been when she was in school.
She had attended a women's high school which, at the
time, was the highest institution of learning in Shenyang. After a year or two she had had to stop because
of poor health. She had been born into a rich family
in the old society, the younger of two girls. The
hardest years of her life came during the Cultural Revolution, not only because of her own background, but
because her husband was a high intellectual. "The Cultural Revolution was the whole nation's sad story," she
emphasized, "not just ours."

She and her husband are the same age and both have
remained quite busy during their retirement. She cooks,
takes care of her granddaughter and does voluntary labor for the Street Retirement Committee. Her husband
sees a film or two a day and does the shopping. She
thinks more about the meaning of life as she ages, but:

> . . . there is an old saying in China, "There
> is birth and there is death." I'm not afraid.
> Finally, I'll die. Now I have a happy family
> and I don't want to leave them. When I die
> my husband will live with one of our children
> because he can wash, but not cook. If he dies
> first, I'm independent, and will continue to
> live by myself. The main scare of old age,
> though, is trouble with your legs--loss of
> mobility.

Mrs. Chang Su-ren

Mrs. Chang, a beautiful woman, has lived on Zeng
Yang Street for more than 50 years. She's now 70 and
still leads a very active life. She's in charge of
family planning for 120 families and oversees the
cleaning and maintenance work to keep the neighborhood
attractive. Her work has been an apparent success.
There are beautiful signs and lovely little flowered

courtyards. Zeng Yang Street has the feeling of being protected from the outside world--delicate interiors tucked behind drab storefronts that line the street.

Mrs. Chang often accompanies a group of students to the park for the day. As she notes:

> An active life feeds my spirit and keeps me from unnecessary worry. . . . After the smashing of the Gang of Four, things have been especially good for old people. With the new economic policy there seems to be enough money, enough jobs, and a good pension system.

She and her husband, for example, together receive 150 yuan per month. A retired worker from a watch factory, her husband, who is 74, does *t'ai ji* every morning, shops, raises goldfish, plants and flowers, and shares the cooking. She does the housework, some cooking and shopping herself, and the home administration work. As of yet, her youngest son and his wife (who live with them) have no children. She has two other sons, four grandsons and two granddaughters and feels she's very fortunate.

Retiring can be hard for some people. It certainly was for Mrs. Chang's husband. He still goes back as often as he can to help out or advise.

"Times are better," she says. Her health is better than her mother's was at the same age. She's very involved in the present and plays a vital role within both her family and her community. Working for them is very important to her. Even though she's getting on in years, she doesn't think about death. "I'm willing to put it off as long as possible!" she laughs.

Mr. He Zing-chi

Mr. He, now 71, worked 50 years: first in a bank, then as an accountant in a factory. When he returned from his "countryside stint" during the Cultural Revolution, he was past the age of retirement, but the administration asked him to stay on and train young people in accounting. He retired in 1978 at the age of 66.

Since then his health has improved. He used to need "sticks" for help in walking, but not any more. Mr. He says he's in good spirits most of the time and volunteers to help the Street Committee whenever there's something to be done.

Mr. He has seven daughters and a son. His son, daughter-in-law and their two children live with his wife and him. His wife takes care of the home administration and if he has a health problem he talks it over with his son who teaches chemistry at the Institute of

Chinese Traditional Medicine.

His happiest years were between Liberation and the Cultural Revolution. Prior to that he worked under the Japanese during the Occupation and endured the oppression of that period. When the Chinese themselves became "masters of the country," he found good work as a banker. "Life is again good," he believes. "People are working hard for the benefit of each other and society as a whole."

He attributes his good health to exercising morning and night (*t'ai ji*) and keeping his mind active. He reads newspapers and Chairman Deng's writings, and tries to follow Premier Zhou's example in his attitudes and actions.

Shenyang Number One Woolen Textile Factory

The Shenyang Number One Woolen Textile Factory was first set up in 1920 and produced woolen underwear, blankets and clothes. Sixty percent of the 6,000 workers are women and 600 retired workers are part of the unit.

A factory in China is nothing if not a triumph of function over form. People labor in shifts for long hours in often unpleasant (and certainly spartan) conditions. Even where environmental safety precautions are taken, the amount of noise, poor illumination, heat (or lack of it), dust and fumes can probably make a working career seem incredibly long. Jacobson's work has shown that working conditions have a measurable impact on older workers' attitudes towards and readiness and willingness to retire.[13] The more difficult the working conditions and the more physically demanding the job, the higher the proportion of workers who thought that the retirement age in their jobs ought to be below the pensionable age.

The retired workers interviewed ranged in age from 48 to 58. As most Chinese look younger to me than their actual ages, I complained that these people were not old; they appeared middle-aged. With Jacobson's work in mind, though, I began wondering about the impact of the nature of their work and working conditions upon their health and subsequent decision to retire.

When asked about the changes that accompanied retirement, it was expressed by one woman that:

> Retirement is a very honored thing, but for my personal view, I worked here 33 years and wasn't willing to go home and leave my work to others. For the first six months, I felt a real sense of loss. I felt I'd lost friends, work, and colleagues and I missed seeing the students who often came to the factory.

According to the regulations, retirement is
at 55 unless you have a special skill in the
work. Then the manager asks you to remain two
more years. Now I'm not sad though; I have a
good feeling about the factory.

Yu Chuen Xinong, who at 48 just retired, did so
because of heart trouble. The factory asked her to retire ahead of time. She still comes to the plant to
volunteer her time teaching others how to use the
equipment and to visit the other workers. What became
apparent here at the Woolen Textile Plant was the importance of the factory in the lives of its retired
workers. They go there to bathe, visit, advise and
recreate. Mrs. Yu said the factory gave her many advantages: seeing the doctor for free; facilities for
bathing every other day; tickets for entertainment and
visits from the leaders at Festival time. She feels
free to bring up any problem with which she may need
help.

Forty percent of the workers have been employed at
this factory twenty years or more, making them eligible
for a pension of 75 percent of their last pay. If
they've been injured or designated a Model Worker, they
receive an additional five percent and workers who have
been there since before 1949 continue to receive their
former salaries after they retire.

Each of the five retired workers had remained productive. They objected to being treated as if they
were old. "It's always good to be respected, but bad
to be treated as old when you feel good." Mr. Liu, a
former foreman of a painting workshop, now continues to
train students. "He's always been good at management,"
reported the others. He begins his days, as do many,
with t'ai ji at four a.m.

Mrs. Cheng Yuyeng, for example, at 56 just retired.
She lives with her mother of 82 and four other family
members on 300 yuan per month combined income. She
sees life as coming from physical movement and values
exercise for that reason.

Mrs. Suen is very active in her Street Residents'
Committee. She looks after the families of workers, is
a watchperson in charge of security within her neighborhood and a recognized arbitrator. The neighbors
come to her when they're not getting along and she
seeks them out as well if she thinks they're having
problems. Each Street has a "social work organization/
foundation" run by several retired workers. These retirees are not only respected, but expected to solve
community problems in a just manner. Primary health
care, public health work, family planning and home security all have been placed under their purview. Under
the direction of the elders, the Residents' Committee
chooses Model Families and runs social welfare campaigns.

I asked if old people were ever considered a burden. If it happened, I was told, the Street Committee
would help the young people correct their uncivilized
spirit, wrong thinking and incorrect behavior. They
are assisted in this effort by newspapers whose function it is to criticize, propagandize and educate.

Besides a high level of community involvement,
these retirees at the Woolen Textile Factory pursued
their personal hobbies and took very active roles within their families. In many respects, these individuals
embody the Chinese model of workers who retire not to a
life of inactivity or social marginality, but rather to
another form of socially productive work.

Da Ching (Big Green) People's Commune Retirement Home

Da Ching People's Commune is composed of 2,500
families and has a total population of 10,900. There
are ten brigades and 48 production teams. Due to innovative planning and an irrigation system, 90 percent of
the land is used for rice production. Other crops,
such as peanuts, do well in the commune's sandy soil.

At Da Ching there are approximately 800 people
over retirement age. The 24 aged people who have no
one to care for them live in the Retirement Home. The
buildings and homes look new--a reflection of the present prosperity of the commune. One can see a higher
standard of living emerging out of poverty. To the Occidental eye, it looks like a new neighborhood where
the buildings seem to interrupt the landscape, not yet
being an integrated part of it.

Before Liberation, the land where Da Ching People's Commune stands was largely infertile and inhospi-
table. Depending on that land made life very hard.
Nor did history treat the people kindly. An 84-year-
old resident of the commune retirement home emphasized
that many people there had very sad stories. "During
the Japanese occupation people were forced to work in
the mines and factories and then killed. I saw people
buried alive in the earth. Then the reactionaries came
and treated us not as people but as animals."

Power came to a worn and battered people with Liberation. "Mao gave us a good life!" the old man continued. With the "socialist road," simple production
teams were organized in 1952 followed by collectivization in 1954. Da Ching People's Commune was then firmly established in 1958 as part of the Great Leap Forward Movement. Mr. Li Shuen Xiang, the Party Secretary
and Head of Da Ching elaborated:

We were able to use our two hands to make a
life for ourselves. The people became masters.

Everything is collectively owned by the commune. Members can use all the equipment.
Activity is stimulated this way and people
work very hard.

The commune is doing very well with a
well-developed irrigation system and wise
use of the agricultural areas. Presently
there is an account of 100,200 Renminbi contributed by the brigades for use by the commune. There are 43 trucks, 84 tractors, 150
cars, 8,000 pigs and 40,000 other animals; 48
different factories employ 1,500 workers and
make an annual profit of 600,000 yuan. Since
the new economic policy of 1978, there has
been a 38 percent increase in production.
The average production of each family is
5,000 *jin* (1 *jin* = 1.1 lbs.). A certain
amount is required from each *mu* (1 *mu* = .165
acres). The surplus may be kept or sold.

The commune members themselves share in
the success. The average per capita income
for commune members (and here each child,
adult and retired person is included) is
600 yuan. Some farm workers earn 1,200 and
highly skilled farmers 2,000 yuan. The people's salary is roughly 1.5 times what it was
prior to the new economic policy. Most of
the homes are new and owned by the peasants.
Every family has a radio and its members have
watches. Eighty percent of the families have
TV; ten percent have a motorized vehicle (gas
is given by the State). Things are better
here than for leaders of medium status in the
government.

Along with the development of better living conditions, other advances have also occurred. Children now
study without tuition or book charges. There is a middle school and (in each brigade) a primary school and
kindergarten. As well, there is a department store
(like a small town general store) in the commune center
and a branch in each brigade. Plays and entertainment
are organized by the people themselves.

Pensions are now given to agricultural workers at
Da Ching People's Commune according to the length of
time worked. One yuan is given per year worked per
month, i.e., for twenty years service, twenty yuan per
month is received. Age requirements for retirement are
65 for men and 55 for women. If health conditions are
not good, retirement can be advanced, but work cannot
be extended past the age of mandatory retirement.

For factory workers here, retirement is possible
at 60, but mandatory at 65. Factory workers receive
70-75 percent of their final paycheck as a pension.

Some would like to keep working, but are not allowed to do so.

Old Age at Da Ching People's Commune

The "well-being home" was begun in 1959 under the direct leadership of the commune. There are now 24 residents who, according to one, consider it their personal home. If old people have a son or daughter, preference is almost always given to staying with them; however, those without family or from a family with major conflicts can ask for a home here. The locally-generated resources of the commune are used to take care of the aged, children, and those with disease as part of the new economic policy. In the same way, everyone is responsible for the improvement of the People's Commune.

Because many of the residents are retired farm workers, they have been able to develop a model garden. The old people raise animals, collect fertilizer, and take advantage of the recently implemented "responsibility system." Some of the experienced farm workers also set up classes and receive a modest compensation for their training efforts.

Life in the retirement home was explained by Mr. Chi, a tall, dignified man who had lived here for nine years. Mr. Chi had come from a poor family, which, like many, had toiled year after year for a landlord. By age 25, the lack of food and hard living conditions had resulted in his having very poor health and cataracts.

Liberation occurred and his life began anew. The Party sent him to the Chinese University of Medicine in Shenyang where an operation made it possible for him to experience light and five colors where before he could only distinguish light from darkness. A problem with his nervous system was also discovered. Mr. Chi's health had kept him single and the early production team system took him in and gave him "the five supports."[14] Then, in 1974, a commune committee invited him to come to the retirement home. He considers this his "personal home" and lives accordingly.

Mr. Chi had the air of a leader and assumed that position in our group situations. Although blind and missing his front teeth, he had a strong, deep voice and conveyed an aura of dignity and seriousness. Mr. Chi's overview of life at the Da Ching Retirement Home included the following comments:

We're 24 people here; our average age is 74. If our health permits, we get up around four in the morning, walk, then work in the garden and take care of the animals. We have rice and flour every day by exchanging the rice we

grow for the flour we need. We all raised
vegetables as farmers. Now we're all getting
on in years, but we remember how to do it,
and still produce our own beans, cabbage,
tomatoes, carrots, cucumbers, peanuts, turnips
and eggplant.

We have good medical care; our spirits
are high. In winter when the days are short
we have two meals and then three in the summer
months. Every Sunday we have a special dinner
with dumplings and for Spring Festival and the
first of October we slaughter one of our 400
jin pigs and have a very special celebration.

I asked if there were any special problems or
needs. Mr. Chi responded, "No, every month we're given
five dollars and can buy anything we need. Every summer we receive new clothes; every two years new underwear. Cotton uniforms we receive when we need them."
Their lives have seen such economic contrasts that it's
no wonder they answered this question materialistically.
In the old society, I heard over and over, many had no
food and no houses, so they appreciate their current
situation very much. Another resident noted:

In the old society, people died at 40 or 50
because of poor medical and living conditions.
There is good health now and people are living
longer. No one here is educated--because we
are from the old society. All of these changes
have come to us through the Party.

And another added:

I have been here six years and not only is life
comfortable and our needs provided for by the
People's Commune and the Party, but everyone
here cares for one another. I had no way to
support myself. Without Mao and without the
Party, I'd be begging door to door.

Other aspects of the situation elicited comments
from a variety of residents. For example: "This living situation has kept us active and healthy and keeps
loneliness away. Everyday I feed the chickens. It's
my job, my duty, and makes me happy." "We appreciate
this situation very much. Worry shortens life; having
a job you're responsible for lengthens it." "We want
to live to see the four modernizations--to see with our
own eyes the development of our country."

When I asked about attitudes towards death, I
didn't get the usual response of death being a natural
law with nothing to be done. There was a real desire
to live. Death wasn't rationalized as a natural law;

it was seen as something against which to fight.

Who says you have to be educated to understand life? A tiny 78-year-old woman, her hunched-over body supporting a beautiful face, reminded me that "Old people like us would be dead in the old society. Here I expect to live at least another ten years." What makes her so healthy? "Good food, exercise, and thinking widely, not narrowly!"

According to Party Secretary Li, the factors contributing to the good physical and mental health of Da Ching's elderly members are:

1. *A good spirit.* Everyone has the same rights as everyone else, which was not so in the old society. Society is now balanced.
2. *A good economic situation.* People get good salaries; living standards are good; there's enough food; and people have no monetary burdens. In the old society, after breakfast people had to start searching for greens for lunch.
3. *Activity.* Old people like to continue to be productive. They can work as they like and can organize their days as they like.

One of the commune's resident physicians, another Dr. Li, provided further details on the health status of his older patients:

The government says it's very important now to pay attention to the elderly population. The main health problems at Da Ching are: (1) heart attack; (2) stroke; (3) high blood pressure; and (4) cancer, although mortality from heart attacks is presently decreasing. Health surveys are routinely taken and yearly checkups, including electrocardiograms, given. Chronic disease is a problem, but I deal more with acute care. Western medicine is used in the emergency room, but traditional medicine and care are given to help the patient recover. I believe in giving patients a choice and I always get very good cooperation.

Dr. Li feels prevention is the main thing. Life expectancy in the commune is 70. He feels medical attention is better in the countryside and in communes like Da Ching than it is in the cities, largely because immediate care is available. "In the city, there may be no bed when acute hospital care is needed." Party Secretary Li feels people live longer in the rural areas due to a healthier lifestyle.

There are four doctors, 32 barefoot doctors (who have received a year of training in a medical school

setting) and nurses providing 24-hour coverage in Da
Ching's hospital and in the commune clinics in each of
the ten brigades. If needed, the doctors make house
calls. With the one-child family policy, much attention is given to medical care of children and they receive free care until the age of 18. Each week the
barefoot doctors come to the hospital to talk about the
health situation, current diseases and problems, methods of treatment and lessons to be drawn.

Finally I asked the Party Secretary what he thought
could increase the quality of life at Da Ching. He said
it was his personal opinion that "peace in the world"
was of the primary importance. The second factor would
be for his country to get rich--the key, he thought, to
strength and development. "As the State gets strong,
the people will have better conditions and better spirit
as a result." The third factor to an improved quality
of life has to do with "improved family relations: the
peaceful handling of conflict brings people together and
promotes a good family life."

Retirement at the Northeast Institute of Technology

The Northeast Institute of Technology is a national "key" university established in 1949 on the foundation of the Northeast University.[15] The campus is very
much like a compressed Occidental college town. Twenty
thousand people live within the confines of the 250-acre
walled compound. Tucked among classroom buildings and
dormitories are small stores and markets, a clinic, post
office, theatre, nurseries and an elementary school.
Wednesday afternoons are reserved for political study
and Sunday is a day of rest. On Sundays only two meals
are served in the cafeterias: a late breakfast and dinner at three in the afternoon.

The breakdown of residents is approximately as follows:

```
      41 professors
     260 associate professors
     798 lecturers
   3,800 supporting staff
   7,611 students:    264 graduate
                    6,400 undergraduates
                      947 correspondence and spare-
                          time students (non-resi-
                          dential)
     300 retired personnel (85% of whom live on
         campus)
   8,392 others (family members, etc.)
```

As stated earlier, work assignments are generally
permanent, so once assigned to NEIT, unless there is a

problem or promotion outside the university, an individual will more than likely raise his or her family
and eventually retire on campus. The top administrators and faculty live in eight-family buildings. Each
apartment has two or three rooms. In summer the space
between buildings is filled with carefully tended rows
of corn, tomatoes, beans and sunflowers. Porches are
hung with laundry--the informality is very comfortable
and appealing.

Though clothes are becoming more individualized
and one sees a lot of prints amidst the white shirts
and blouses, variation is not found between the clothing of professors and other workers. Dress is always
neat, clean, comfortable and modest. In the summer men
sometimes wear shorts or roll their pants legs up to
their knees. Sleeveless t-shirts are condoned for men
outside the classroom, but women's shoulders are always
covered.

My point in describing dress is that the distinctions among people are neither as emphasized nor as obvious as they are in Occidental societies. There is
more of an egalitarian feeling which extends to relationships as well. "Units" within the university, however, are characterized by formality. They function
somewhat autonomously, are highly bureaucratized and
are not basically collaborative. It becomes an incredible production, for example, to obtain the use of
films from a library intended for undergraduates to
show to another group of students.

Building, however, is one activity that goes on
seven days a week. One is always aware of progress and
"the race to the year 2000." In the summer ice stick
(popsicle, ice lolly) carts abound even as the early
risers return home for breakfast around six. As soon
as it's light, open and green spaces are taken for exercise, reading or recitation. Work begins at eight,
stops for lunch and a two-hour rest at midday, and then
resumes until six.

"According to Regulations": Retirement Practices
at NEIT

First of all, regulations are governmentally, not
locally, determined. The function of the Personnel Administration Office is to see that they are carried out
as well as possible. Section leaders Liu Chen Yuan and
Ja Juan very carefully explained the ins and outs of
retirement at NEIT, as summarized below:

There are no retirement stipulations for veteran
workers. Government regulations for university professors suggest retirement at 60, but given one's state of
health and the needs of his or her department, work can
be extended to 70 if desired. Presently 2 to 3 percent
of the professors and associate professors are over 60.

Decisions about retirement, such as when to reduce the
workload or change responsibilities, are group decisions made by the administrative authorities and the
older professor. The freedom exists to choose an appropriate course. If lecturing is too much, the older
professor can step back to advise students. Being able
to prolong retirement is considered special treatment--
an honor showing respect for contributions the individual made. There are over 80 retired professors at
NEIT who continue to be part of the life of the university, albeit without formal roles or titles. They can
work when and as they like once they've achieved retired status.

Administrators and nonprofessorial faculties (in-
structors, lecturers, etc.) retire at the usual ages--
60 for men and 55 for women. Those who joined the revolutionary work force before 1949 get 100 percent of
their last salary as a pension and those who joined before 1945 get one to two months' salary over and above
the 100 percent. When retired, these groups often "re-
treat to the second line," continuing to help in an ad-
visory capacity.

There are differing pensions according to the
years of work. Those who worked over twenty years receive 70 percent of their salary plus an additional 5
to 10 percent if designated as Model Workers--regard-
less of their unit or field. "Honored and fighting heroes" are given 5 to 15 percent above their final salaries in recognition of their contributions to the nation.

Top priority is given to the 5 percent of the retired who are Veteran Cadres. An Office for Veteran
Cadres at NEIT oversees the daily life of these individuals. Within each unit, there is also a leader in
charge of seeing to their needs. For example, if a
veteran cadre becomes sick or disabled, a special person is sent to look after him or her. Those without
children are assigned care-givers and, when hospital-
ized, the Office for Veteran Cadres assigns attendants.
(In Chinese hospitals the family usually stays with the
patient, feeding and caring for them.) After the veteran cadres have "left the work unit for rest," the
leaders often call upon them and try to enrich their
daily lives.

Life in retirement for the other 95 percent is also considered to be very satisfactory. A special person within the Personnel Office is assigned responsibility for the retired and tries to solve problems as
they arise. If a retired worker is short of money, for
example, the Office is in a position to help. Medical
care continues to be free, as it was when they worked,
and pensions and benefits are the same for men and wom-
en.

Each situation regarding health and retirement is

analyzed individually. Work for the disabled, for example, is reduced according to the particular disability. As a rule, people want to keep working as long as they can in a university unit. Though objectively they may be getting old, most want to continue to show their strength and capabilities--to contribute and be needed.

I asked if there was any evidence of conflict between the young and old professors--stemming, for example, from the older having the richer experience and the young having more up-to-date technical knowledge, or from the perspective that older professors do less work and get paid more money. Mrs. Ja replied:

> First of all, both sides are needed. They consult with each other. The Chinese people have a tradition. "The old help the new and the new respect the old." Within each unit the strengths are built upon and everyone helps each other. People want to keep working, feeling they should do more, yet getting old is an objective law. When they were young they did a lot--just like the young people of today. Now they should enjoy what the State gives them. Young people believe they will follow in the footsteps of the old, so they don't say anything. It will happen to them.

Faculty Interviews[16]

Mr. Zhu, Chairman of the Department of Steel Processing, lives with his wife, son, daughter-in-law and granddaughter. His son is in research here at the University. Decisions in his home are group decisions. If he has a problem, they all discuss it--as a unit. Mr. Zhu thinks this works best when people live in very close quarters. Mr. Zhu has another daughter who lives on the other side of the city. She has her mother-in-law living with her. Mr. Zhu pointed out that in most of China (contrary to the situation in his family) parents usually prefer to live with their daughter and son-in-law. The belief is that there's less conflict in this situation. He disagreed strongly with another faculty member's observation that elderly women liked to live with their daughters and elderly men liked to live with their sons. (I had also been told that the father's home is considered the formal home and the place where celebrations, such as Spring Festival, occur, regardless of the living configuration the rest of the year.)

Mr. Zhu would like to work until 70 to help make up for the loss to society caused by the policies and upheaval of the Cultural Revolution. From 1966 to 1969, with the exception of four months in the countryside, he stayed at home and studied. His wife, a teacher, was also "sent down" but to a different location.

His health at 58 is exceptionally good. "Many older people have broncho-respiratory problems and rheumatism, but my only problem is that I'm getting a little fat!" He identifies the gaining of weight as a health problem in contrast to blue collar workers I interviewed who saw it as a measure of health. He exercises in the park each morning and was, in fact, a good athlete when he was young.

He finds as he gets older, he gets more respect-- which made him uncomfortable at first.

> Old people feel angry if they are cut-off or
> considered an outcast. During the period of
> the "Gang of Four," old people were treated
> badly on the street. But these wrongs have
> been turned around. In fact, given the pres-
> ent family organization with women working,
> there is a great deal of cooperation and the
> status of the elderly is high.

In the cities, the status of old men and women is equal, but in the countryside, he believes the status of women to be lower. I asked if perhaps that wasn't an artifact of education rather than of urban/rural differences and both Mr. Zhu and his interpreter agreed. (The higher the education the more work is shared and the more equal the status and treatment.) "The social structure is more in harmony in the cities and our way is not just due to Confucius," he laughed. (Most others at least pay lip service to Confucian tradition-- some, such as the psychologist with whom I worked, take the Confucian legacy very seriously.)

In Occidental countries, productivity is considered a determinant of health. I asked Mr. Zhu if retirement in China was just as active as the work years.

> People are like machines and if not used will
> rust. My father and father-in-law declined
> after retirement. The elderly provide a lot
> of useful services, but life is not as active
> as before and it can be seen in the decline of
> health . . . Speaking of health, the population
> needs more protein. If they had more they'd
> be better off . . . The more protein, the
> better the football team!

Mr. Zhu feels the aging of the population is a distant problem for China. As he argued:

> Most of our population are in their twenties
> and thirties and working so there are more
> workers than retired persons. When the bal-
> ance starts to shift too much the other way,

people will be allowed more children. The
old people of China are the most fortunate in
the world. They have good families, no serious
problems and they're secure. It has to do with
socialism: all have work to do or at least
their sons do. There is no competition and
the old people are not worried about their future. They know they will be cared for. The
government encourages this ideology and teaches
the young to support the old--through the media,
through the Model Family Campaign, and through
praising those who are true to such socialist
ideals.

The following remarks are taken from informal
group interviews with three professors from the Mining
Department. All three agreed that working as long as
one can contributes to a high quality of life . . . and
that the definition of well-being has both spiritual
and material dimensions. As university professors,
they feel well-off materially--certainly compared to
the rest of society. They don't compare themselves to
the West. The spiritual side refers to both the psy-
chic benefits of being productive and a basic enjoyment
of life, art and philosophy.
Questioning them about the notion that the elderly
compare their lives with their counterparts in the old
society and feel satisfied, while the young compare
their lives with those of foreigners and feel dissatisfied, they all agreed that there is a problem of changing values:

The young didn't experience the old society and
are exposed to their own idea of Western development and lifestyle. The more educated the
person, the more the spiritual side of life is
valued. The government is taking a very active
role in expanding educational opportunities and
in educating the young to respect the old.
This philosophy is emphasized from primary
through high school and the social organs (Youth
Leagues, Women's Federation, and worker unions)
have been instructed to help in this reeducation
effort. This is all formulated and directed by
the Party in an effort to restore the excellent
traditional values of Chinese society which were
so brutally sabotaged by the Great Proletarian
Cultural Revolution. The Central Committee of
the Chinese Communist Party calls on the young
people to build up a powerful socialist and
Chinese-style society as opposed to importing
Western ideologies.

The three professors considered themselves to be
the decision-makers in their families, although important decisions were discussed with their wives and family members. We agreed that decision-making and independence in Occidental countries are promoted at a much
earlier age than they are in Chinese families, and they
wondered if this spawned disharmony as a side effect.

Their wives retired between 55 and 60, a little
later than usual, by choice. They now stay active with
housework, raise flowers and goldfish. Cooking three
meals a day in Shenyang means buying vegetables daily.
Contrary to the belief that the more educated the couple, the more work at home is shared, it was pretty
clear that these husbands didn't have to do much--that
they were well taken care of by their wives. If something happened to these men, no so-called "benefits"
would come to their families. Each individual receives
his or her own pension based upon the length and quality of his own work.

What kind of health education did they and their
cohorts receive? The first concern of their doctors
was smoking, followed by alcohol-induced problems.

Loneliness is not a problem. These men not only
work in the same department, they live very near one
another. They have spent most of their working years
right here at NEIT and will remain here until they die.
To move to another area would be difficult given that
most housing is publicly-owned and they would have no
right to it somewhere else. Here their families each
have three rooms and the organization of life makes
daily life relatively easy.

They feel they themselves lost ten years during
the Great Proletarian Cultural Revolution and that the
effect of this period on the society has been devastat-
ing. Scientific work came to an absolute standstill.
"Of course, we still feel angry about it, but anger is
not a productive feeling." They each want to work as
long as they can to help the Modernization Movement.

I asked if life was more satisfying in China as
old or young men. Not surprisingly, they would like to
have it all: the experience of age combined with the
vitality of youth!

As both the President of a prestigious university
and an aging Chinese, President Bi Kezhen values the
proverb, "One generation will be better than the last."
He expects (to cite another proverb) "The pupil will
surpass the master." Everyone is presently trying to
do his or her part to achieve modernization and the
generations are dependent upon each other. The old
teach the young *how* to work and then the young learn
the advanced technology. Most of the members of President Bi's Academic Committee are old people. They discuss issues together and help him make decisions on the
basis of their accumulated insight and experience. He

is working with a moral elite, of course, because to
get into the university to begin with and then advance
in the ranks, the candidate must surely be a model for
moral development as well. Otherwise, they would not
have made it through the intense ethical (as well as
technical) scrutiny that one undergoes in being considered for promotion.

President Bi plans to step down from his position
in four years when he reaches the age of 70. He is
looking forward to reading and writing and being re-
lieved of the strain that accompanies his job. He will
always be active in the university, but a younger man
will bear the responsibility. Although he tries to de-
centralize the decision-making to the appropriate levels (which he defines as "where the impact will be
felt"), he feels he bears the ultimate responsibility
for everything that happens.

"The old must withdraw as their energy wanes."
He's had a heart attack in the past and though he feels
the keys to maintaining good health are activity, the
right foods, and enough rest, he feels he's too busy to
begin such a regime now. He anticipates receiving a
full pension when he retires and that it will continue
to meet his needs. After retirement, he will continue
to volunteer his time to the State as his health permits.

After spending the summer at NEIT, talking with
President Bi was like talking with a neighbor. His informality and warmth contributed to his strength and
reputation as a fine leader.

A Big-Nose* Yankee in Nanhu Park

An American resident of Shenyang observed that a
million dollars could easily be made by airlifting
Nanhu Park with all of its action and setting it down
in New York. The following vignettes will, I hope, illustrate the kaleidoscope of life, movement and health
which, taken together, make the park a fountain of
well-being.

*   *   *   *   *

Beginning about 4:00 in the morning in the summer
months, people are everywhere in the park moving at
different paces and in different ways. A deep, operat-
ic voice cuts across the voices of families and friends
engaged in non-stop conversation. The baritone singing
was so commanding that I assumed it was projected via
an elaborate sound system. This was incorrect. One

---

*Big-nose is a slang term for Caucasian.

morning I tracked the sound to a thick clump of bushes
through which I could see neither microphone nor loud-
speaker--only a pair of man's legs. That was all of
him I was ever able to view. When multi-generational
and extended families share two to three rooms at the
most, a place to stretch, exercise, sing, read (without
waking others with a light), have a good laugh or cry,
or share a secret adds immeasurably to the quality of
life. There is a direct connection to Spirit in Nanhu
Park--even if all you can glimpse are the legs!

* * * * *

Another song was being sung on the other side of
the lake. An old woman in her 70s was bidding goodbye
to her close friends. She was leaving the home of one
child for that of another and to each of her friends
she sang words of caution and advice having to do with
relationships within families and among neighbors.
Tears silently rolled down the cheeks of her old friends
as they listened to her Oriental chant. Her back was to
the rows and rows of chrysanthemums planted and tended
by such groups as employees of a downtown department
store that closes a few days per year for all the workers to do "physical labor" in the park. While others
exercised their bodies, these women shared their souls
--untying the knots of life's complexities. They were
there every morning willing to understand and soothe.

* * * * *

One grandmother in the group often brought me bags
of delicious roasted peanuts--treasure in a land where
protein is scarce. After a few weeks, when they felt
secure about my coming each morning, these old women
gave in to their inquisitiveness and began to feel my
body and hair. The two male students who accompanied
me to translate became embarrassed and disappeared, but
that morning I became an accepted adjunct to the small
circle of old women. I was chastised when they felt I
wasn't dressed warmly enough; I had to report where I'd
been the day before; how much I'd slept; what my life
in America was like . . . .

* * * * *

The bicycle adaptations for the handicapped which
can be seen in Nanhu Park are wonderful. Many are large
tricycles (so one needn't worry about balance) with cart
structures over the rear two wheels. Brakes and pedal
mechanisms are often placed where they can be hand-oper-
ated. As I joined 200 others for an exercise routine
each morning in front of a beautiful rose garden, a
handicapped man would go by with a little prancing puppy

tied to the rear of his tricycle. The pace was just
right for them both.

                    *   *   *   *   *

    Colors these days are a mixture of army green,
uniform blue, white, gray and shocking rose. Black arm-
bands mark those in mourning and red insignia highlight
social and political roles, authority and honor. Some
of the young women cutting through the park on their
way to work have beautifully coiffed hairstyles, high
heels and print dresses--some even above the knee. De-
signer jeans, sent from relatives in Taiwan or Hong
Kong, occasionally mix with the sports clothes of the
young and the tailored pants and blouses of the majority.

                    *   *   *   *   *

    The lake is lined with older men scooping up silt
with nets fastened to the end of bamboo poles. They're
searching for goldfish food. Even as the mornings got
chilly, some would wade out above waist-level in the
water.

                    *   *   *   *   *

    Although Mr. Feng had fainted at his home the day
before, he came to the park to ask me to walk for a
while with him. He had brought a bag full of gifts for
me--ginseng to put in accompanying bottles of bamboo
liquor for my husband and some jasmine tea in an ancient container. He gave it to a teacher who was with
me so it was one Chinese to another. Mr. Feng had been
"criticized" for talking so often with a foreigner, but
he exploded in response and argued that if I was there
it was because I had the official permission of the
government and it was his attacker who had proven himself to be "unsocialistic!" My companion thought that
as an intellectual, Mr. Feng had probably suffered terribly during the Cultural Revolution. I pointed out
that he was 76 when it started, but Mr. Yang replied
that no one had escaped.

                    *   *   *   *   *

    There was a week when no one had seen Feng Xi-chen.
I asked some students to help me find his home to make
sure he was all right. His health at 93 was failing
and I was worried something had happened to him. I had
his address from a poem he'd written and given to me.
The Foreign Affairs Office began to get hassled by all
the students' concerns and finally said to just go. We
were very warmly welcomed. It seemed like an everyday

occurrence--visiting a sick friend--but the neighborhood was abuzz on our departure.

Customs are often such serious concerns. The idea
of taking flowers to Mr. Feng when he was sick brought
peals of laughter from my students, while their custom
of taking food, especially fruit, to a sick or hospi-
talized person worried me because of my notion of prescribed diets.

* * * * *

My students think exercise is for the old. Although *taijiquan* has a three hundred year old history,
it wasn't until after the Cultural Revolution that it
became so popular. A beautiful series of slow movements, this most graceful of martial arts promotes a
peaceful ambiance in the park. Individuals or groups
tuck themselves into niches dotted around the park
where they can achieve full concentration. The two
most important principles which extend across all the
various schools of *t'ai-ji* are relaxation and serenity.
It's widely considered a therapeutic sport which can
prevent and cure illness. A Chinese explanation is appropriate:

> *Taijiquan* is an integrated exercise for
> training the body, the mind and the "vital
> energy," with the main emphasis on the mind.
> The body is to follow the mind wherever the
> mind goes. Since *taijiquan* stresses this men-
> tal aspect rather than strength, it is not
> without reason that some people call it an
> exercise of the mind.
> It is believed that with attention highly
> concentrated on the physical movements, cere-
> bral cells can recover from over-excitement
> and functional disorders, which can in turn
> alter stubborn physiological patterns and help
> treat such physical disorders as neurasthenia,
> high blood pressure and ulcers. *Taijiquan* can
> be practiced by both men and women, old and
> young, the physically strong or weak. It is
> most suitable for the elderly, sufferers of
> chronic ailments and those who engage in in-
> tellectual work.[17]

* * * * *

In front of the beautiful statue of Model Soldier
Lei Feng with other citizens and children, a more
jolting sight is the practice of *qigong*. Part of traditional Chinese medicine, *qigong*, too, is supposed to
relax both body and mind, cultivate internal vitality
and strength, and cure disease. Although it can

involve the use of bioelectricity to treat specific
diseases, what is seen in the park are people in
trance-like states which they achieve through shaking
and jerking arhythmic movements, focused attention and
regulated breathing. No one does *gigong* alone. As in
weightlifting or gymnastics, a "spotter" is required.

*   *   *   *   *

The most visually impressive martial art to me is
the practice of *wushu*, complete with tailed sword. The
most hierarchical, or nonegalitarian, activity I saw in
Nanhu Park was the ranking of *wushu* practitioners.
There was a veteran *wushu* master whose teaching and
support were very important. Homage and respect were
never more evident than towards him. I obviously enjoyed watching these men and one young woman practice--
so much so, in fact, that I was asked to join. A crowd
of over 100 would circle to watch me have my lesson.
Laughing at myself made the spectators feel comfortable
enough to laugh as well. *Wushu* exercises contain many
beautiful body movements and have been incorporated into Chinese opera (for fighting scenes), drama and acrobatics. Occasionally an older man will be seen teaching *wushu* movements to a group of sword-bearing pre-
teens. *Wushu* is not practiced widely in the park. It
is the province of a few longstanding enthusiasts and
their followers.

*   *   *   *   *

In every direction, the Nanhu Park people can be
seen doing pull-ups on tree limbs and push-ups against
the trunks. Other activities are nestled here and
there: wrestling, amateur Beijing Opera performances,
stand-up comedy, cards, mah-jong, Go (the oldest game
in the world) and a grandfather teaching his "double-
jointed" young grandchildren the secrets of balance and
acrobatics in order to pass on the family tradition.
In a more isolated area, old men brought their pet
birds out "to air" and to sing. Only here did I feel
my presence was definitely unwanted for the birds were
immediately covered when I'd stop to look!
More often than not, activities are age and sex
segregated. The young are more bent on studying and
recitation; the old on movement, games and visiting.
Growth becomes visual as you view the generations. Aging in Nanhu Park is a gradual movement along a continuum towards old age where the fullness of adulthood is
seen in the warmth and beauty of the old wrinkled
faces.

*   *   *   *   *

*Getting weighed and measured
for 2 fen in Nanhu Park*

So the day begins. Around six the groups begin to
disperse and return to their old-style bungalows or
apartment blocks to immerse themselves in the day's affairs. As one old woman stated: "We're in charge of
everything related to family peace"--a responsibility
far more complex than just holding babies--the Occidental image of the Chinese elder.

It starts to drizzle. Within minutes a fleet of
middle-aged men arrive on bicycles from all directions
to rescue their parents from the rain. A 50+-year-old
son-in-law lifts my friend, his heavy-set, well groomed
mother-in-law, onto the back of his bike. Together
(she riding side-saddle) they scurry off out of Nanhu
Park and into the grey mist of a Shenyang morning.

Attitudes Toward the Elderly

In addition to interviewing old people in a variety of settings in Shenyang, it was important to understand how younger Chinese viewed the aged and the aging process. Attitudes *toward* the elderly interact with attitudes *of* the elderly and together they help shape the boundaries of a sense of well-being. After all, it takes an unusually strong self-image for an old person to remain unaffected (positively or negatively) by societal and familial messages about his or her value.

It is Kenneth Boulding's proposition that behavior depends on "the image"--that is, the subjective knowledge structure of both facts and values.[18] In other words, how we view something determines in large measure what we do in relation to it. A stock of images defines a society, but the communication processes and the succession of generations continually reshape them.

Changing societal attitudes affect individual attitudes, lifestyles and support structures. For example, during the Cultural Revolution the elderly represented a world contrary to the political ideals of the era. As attitudes changed during this period, the well-being of the elderly--in both subjective and objective terms--took a plunge. Though still wounded in the heart and bitter over the sense of lost time and opportunities, the old people who survived are continuing with their work and coping amidst a society which has now returned to its tradition of respecting and honoring them. Again, changes in post-Cultural Revolution attitudes triggered major changes in the realities of life for the elderly. The lesson is that attitudes are not to be taken lightly for they are both a harbinger and a reflection of the movement of societies--especially in one as volatile as the People's Republic of China.

The people with whom I spoke were unanimous in declaring that the degradation of the elderly during the Cultural Revolution was an aberration that would not happen again. This consensus, in and of itself, can be seen as a powerful defense against a repetition of this breach of Chinese custom.

The dominant attitude towards the elderly encouraged and reinforced by the State now is more than benign. It is actively supportive of the aged and of the notion that younger people--whether family or not--should do what they can to improve the quality of life for their elders. The three articles quoted below express the "correct" attitude toward old people and describe how this attitude should be made manifest in behavior. Although the specific examples cited are not from Shenyang or Liaoning Province, they corroborate attitudes and behavior I regularly witnessed there. The point is not that these particular activities

exist across China (they don't) but rather that they
are indicative of the kind of attitudes and innovations
the State wishes to promulgate on behalf of old people.
Since these attitudes and behaviors also stem from
long-standing cultural patterns in China, they meet
with little resistance. For the State then, the challenge is not to overcome resistance--it is to spur ac-
tivism.

The first of these three examples is taken from a
1983 article emphasizing the rural sector. In this
case, good treatment of the elderly is tied to the success of the one-child family policy, and the author argues that:

> Providing better security for rural people in
> their old age is important if they are to lose
> their fear of being childless. Local govern-
> ments or collectives already provide the basic
> support set by law to ensure aged people with-
> out children a livelihood at least equal to the
> average in that locality. Some better-off
> places now have simple but comfortable retire-
> ment homes to take care of such elderly people.
> More than half the counties in the rural areas
> around Shanghai and in Yantai district in Shan-
> dong province--the two are model areas both in
> production and birth control work--have now
> instituted a pension and retirement system for
> all commune workers.
> In Nangong County, Henan Province, and
> other places, primary and middle school students
> have been systematically mobilized for spare-
> time help to older people. Teams of them regu-
> larly fetch water, clean house and do other
> chores for the elderly. Newspapers carry heart-
> warming stories about young people who have
> "adopted" childless senior citizens.[19]

The second and third articles are taken from 1983
editions of China Daily. They describe exemplary attitudes and actions in different city settings, as follows:

SOCIAL AID FOR AGED

> More than 26,000 young workers in Beijing
> have voluntarily organized themselves into
> groups to provide services for 5,200 families
> of senior citizens in the city and its inner
> suburbs, according to the Municipal Committee
> of the Chinese Communist Youth League.
> They sign contracts with neighbourhood
> committees which have investigated and regis-
> tered the families of revolutionary martyrs,

widows or widowers, the old and disabled and
helpless retired workers. Local Youth League
organizations check up on their work on a
regular basis.

One such family is 79-year-old Sun Xingwu
and his wife in downtown Dashanian Street.
Their son died during the War of Liberation in
the late 1940s.

Young workers from a local grain store
bring them rice and flour at the beginning of
each month, and young salesmen from groceries
bring them pork, fish, fruit and vegetables.

Li Maolin, a 75-year-old retired worker,
whose wife died last March, is also under the
care of youngsters along the Beixinqiao in the
northern part of the city. Young women in the
locality go to wash his clothes and tidy his
house every week.

There are also 166 centres in Beijing's
suburbs, with some 2,000 aged people who have
no children or other relatives to turn to, and
around 60 percent of rural communes on the outskirts have built special homes for senior citizens, manned by 700 peasants.

The municipal civil administration department has allocated more than one million yuan
[about $500,000] in recent years to help rural
communes build such homes for helpless senior
villagers.[20]

SERVICE WITH A SMILE FOR GUANGZHOU ELDERLY

Service with a smile--and a cup of tea as
well--has returned for the elderly customers
of a department store in Guangzhou, capital of
Guangdong Province.

In June, the Zhongshan Fifth Street Department Store opened a special counter to serve
the city's aged residents. It sells 200 different items, including clothing in traditional
southern Chinese styles, shoes, eyeglasses,
hearing aids, pipes, walking sticks and a soap
made according to a Qing Dynasty court recipe.

Some garments and articles in short supply can be ordered or made to measure.

Sales assistants are chosen for their care
and patience in dealing with older people. They
draw up chairs or serve tea as customers carefully choose their purchases.

Some run errands to other departments in
the store, buying items for the less-mobile
elderly.

The store's approach has so far hit a

responsive note here. Its sales have increased from about 300 yuan [about $150] a
day in June to 600 yuan in August.[21]

These types of "instructional" or "inspirational"
stories about the elderly are common features of the
Chinese media. Even during my stay in Shenyang, examples abounded. For instance, the newspaper reported
that a Beijing neighborhood had set up a laundry service for its senior members and visited 74 households
to wash quilts and clothing.[22] In the summer heat
wave, the media announced that some government departments cut their work day back to six hours and elderly
people were allowed to work only half a day.[23] There
are often stories written about people who would have
liked to retire, but because of their skills were persuaded to remain working.[24]
In order to explore the issue of attitudes toward
the elderly in a little more depth, I both solicited
brief essays from my students at the Northeast Institute of Technology and conducted a modest survey.[25]
Some highlights are noted below.
First, attitudes towards retirement were measured
among 109 white collar workers studying English in a
summer session at NEIT. Sixty-five percent were teachers; 28% did research and technical work in engineering,
designing and programming; and 6% were translators.
The proportion of male to female and married to single
were both 3 to 1. Sixty-four percent were city-born,
24% were from the countryside, and 11% were raised in
county towns. At present, 95% are city dwellers. Thus,
the sample was dominated by married males and by educated city dwellers.

When eligible to retire (which, among this
group, is at age 60 for males and 55 for
females):
    46% anticipate working part-time in
        the same position
    32% think they will work or advise
        without pay
    18% believe they will withdraw from
        the workforce and stay at home
     4% will look for other paid employment

When asked why it was they wanted to keep working after retirement:
    57% found work enjoyable and something
        they wanted to continue to do
    22% wanted to pass their skills on to
        others
    18% valued a continuation in developing
        their abilities

2% believed that their families might
need the extra money

When asked how they saw old age compared to
their lives now (35% were in their 20s; 39% in
their 30s; and 26% in their 40s):
    71% answered perhaps more satisfying
    29% answered perhaps somewhat boring

The above-noted attitudes are those of an educated
stratum within the "iron rice bowl." Nevertheless, as
education and white collar jobs become more pervasive,
these attitudes may be representative of an increasing
proportion of China's population. Such attitudinal
profiles are worth monitoring and exploring.
One interesting indicator of shifting societal attitudes affecting the elderly can be found in the desire among young Chinese to live in nuclear, as opposed
to multi-generational, family units. China Reconstructs
reports a survey taken in Beijing that indicated that
of those between the ages of 15 and 25, nearly 90 percent hope to set up their own independent family structure in the future.[26] The actual figures in Beijing,
according to the municipal census office, mirror the
national statistic: 70 percent of the population live
in nuclear families (made up of a couple or a couple
with their children). The figure is over 75 percent in
Liaoning Province.[27]
According to Fei Xiaotong, China's leading sociologist, the extended family is on the decrease for the
following reasons: the limited housing space makes it
very difficult for workers to house their married children and their families; present job opportunities make
it possible for young couples to support themselves;
and elderly people sometimes prefer to live more quiet-
ly.[28] According to polls by Beijing's Statistics Bureau, the size of an average Beijing worker's family
was 3.8 persons in August 1983 while 3.87 in August
1982. In each family 2.3 people are employed and each
employed person supports 1.61 people including himself.[29]
While the above statistics indicate the increasing
nucleation of families, it still would be interesting
to know the percentage of elderly who in fact do not
live with one of their children. There may be reasons
to believe that the growth of the nuclear family is an
important trend in China that correlates with economic
development. Concerning their preference for a living
situation upon retirement, the respondents to my survey
in Shenyang can be categorized as follows:

    63% of the males ⎤
              and   ⎬--want to live near to or
    74% of the females ⎦ close by their children

```
33% of the males ⌐
        and        ⎤--want to live with one of
22% of the females ⌐  their children

 3% of the males ⌐
        and        ⎤--want to live in a retire-
none of the females ⌐  ment home

 1% of the males ⌐
        and        ⎤--want to live by themselves
 4% of the females ⌐  or just with their spouse
```

The family of my colleague Shen Guojun

The sample of student writings appearing on the following pages is an interesting adjunct to the survey results and to the Party line on attitudes toward the elderly. The individual perspectives expressed through these brief essays confirm the extent to which either the current mass line has been internalized or the ancient cultural positivism about growing old has stayed intact--or, of course, the degree to which these two influences are mutually reinforcing.

My Mother

If anyone asks me "Whom do you love deeply?" I would answer that I love my mother best. Why do I say so? Here is a story about my family. After reading my story I think you will know why.

I was born in 1941 in a small village in Hebei Province. It was before Liberation. My father died three months before I was born, so I never saw him. My mother was a hardworking Chinese countryside woman. I have three sisters. All of them are older than I am.

My mother worked in the fields all day long, but she couldn't support the family. Mrs. Sher, you know old China was very poor and backward. In the country-side, all farmwork had to be done using hand tools. So that was hard work for a woman. My sisters worked in the fields to help my mother though they were very young. I was too small to do anything then.

My mother had a strong will. She was determined to send me to school so that we could change our condi-tions in the future. Life was very hard. Sometimes we had no food to eat. We had to live on wild herbs.

In 1954 we moved to Shanhaiguan, a small city in Hebei Province. The Chinese meaning of Shanhaiguan is mountain, sea and gate in the Great Wall. The sea is in the south. The mountains lie north of the city. It is a small beautiful city.

You may ask why my family moved there. It is be-cause I have an aunt who worked there in a bank. She could help us. My mother then worked as a dry nurse for others. She could get 25 yuan a month. At that time there were four people in my family. You can imagine how we managed our life with only 25 yuan.

In 1959 my youngest elder sister graduated from Shanhaiguan Railway Technical School. Then she was sent to Changsindian--a suburb of Beijing. She worked in a locomotive factory. Then our family moved there. Our life was better than before. In 1962 I entered Beijing Institute of Foreign Trade and graduated in 1967.

Now we are living a happy life. My pay is 78 yuan a month. My wife's pay is equal to mine. Now there are five people in my family, my mother, my wife, my son, my daughter and me. Now we get nearly 200 yuan a month, 40 yuan for each person. But in the fifties we only got 5 yuan for each person. What a change this is! Now my mother is 75 years old. It is not easy for her to look after us at this time. So I must do my best to satisfy her, to make her happy.

From this story you may know why I say, "I love my mother deeply."

Wang Xing-hua

What Will My Remaining Years Be Like?

I'm 45 years old now, but I'm sure I can answer what my remaining years will be like. I guess that when I'm 65 years old that may be my retirement age. I will be self-satisfied. Of course, I will be too old to work hard, but I will be able to concentrate my efforts on many interesting things. I believe I will have a happy, wonderful, and glorious life in my remaining years.

In China, there are many graceful traditional ideas and customs; that is, the old people are respected and revered by society and supported by young people who regard supporting their parents as a duty and a virtue. Therefore I will live with my son or daughter to enjoy a delightful family and never feel unaided or lonely. I will dedicate myself to training and bringing up successors, making them into useful powerful people and receive great joy.

If it is possible to select the environment I live in, I prefer living in suburban areas or small towns to the big city. I'd like to be close to nature. I love natural scenery, high mountains, clear rivers, green forests, limitless fields and fresh air. When I take walks with my grandson or granddaughter, how pleased I will be! I will talk to them about how our motherland had been before she changed her face and how I had worked hard to change her for a long time. She will be more beautiful than any when her change is complete.

I am reminded of a poem written by the great poet of the U.S., Robert Frost. A line of that is "and miles to go before I sleep." When I look back throughout my life, I won't regret anything. I will have done all that should have been done, because the present goal of my life is to bring benefit to people.

An Yunpei

Thoughts on Aging

Everyone has three periods: early youth, youth, and old age. And everyone hopes their old age to be better because the lifetime of people is very short in the universe. From birth to death people have different experiences in different countries. Some countries make people feel better. Some others make people feel bad. In my country, it is just between better and bad. On TV, I usually see some of the needy countries of Africa. There are people who have no food, no medicine, no job, and so on. I think their lifetimes are shorter than other countries.

In China, this is no problem. In my country, the

old people are very free and unfettered. But they need
a good economic situation. If they don't have that,
they must look for a proper job for making money. Now
my thoughts go to myself. What about my economic situation
when I am that age? What will my life be like in
the future? I can only think of the possibilities.
These questions are difficult to answer, aren't they?

Wang Tie Fu

Summer Evenings

I live in Anshan. Anshan is a city in northeast
China. Though it is very cold in winter and winter is
very long, summer is still very hot. Lots of people
like to go out for a walk after supper. There is a
small park near my home. It is not very big and it is
not so beautiful.

The most interesting thing is that there are many
retired people. They take their own music instruments
with them and they organize together to play various
kinds of music. Some of them sing opera such as Beijing opera, Ping opera--an opera of Hebei Province, or
Two Persons opera--an opera of Northeast China. Every
evening after supper they go there. They don't ask for
money from the watching people. They do this just because they are fond of it. Since they are retired people, they don't need to do housework at home. I think
doing this refreshes them and it does them a lot of
good. It is good for them and it is good for others.
That is why the retired people do so.

Wang Xing-hua

If I'm 65 Now . . .

Assume you are now 65. What will you be doing?
Will your life be very happy? In this morning's lesson
Teacher Sher gave us this question. How interesting
the question is! But I can't imagine what I'd be doing
if I were 65 now.

If I were 65 now, I think I'd be a very, very old
man, not taller, but thinner. Maybe I'd cough so much
that I couldn't smoke any cigarettes at all. Maybe I'd
cough too much to sleep. No member of my family would
enjoy me at all because I'd be a mad old man with a bad
temper. I'd have to go out of the house and walk about
alone on the street, rain or shine.

Twenty-seven years will have passed when I'm 65
years old. Ten years before my house had double rooms,

and surrounding my house there was a grocery store, a
clinic, a bookshop, etc. But all these have changed
greatly in the last ten years. In this area a large
modern opera theatre has been built. As a result, my
family was moved to the next block. My son got married
five years ago, and my daughter got married over seven
years ago. I've now got a grandson and a granddaughter.
Then, although I'm always satisfied with my life, my
son and his wife aren't. They want a newer and richer
life to come! Thinking it over, I don't want to be an
old man. It's a terrible picture. But it's one of the
natural rules, so no one can be against it.
What would my life be like if I were 65 now? I
think about it over and over, but can't get a good
idea!

Shen Guo-jun

The Life for China's Old Men and Women

I was born and grew up in China. I am often in
touch with old men and women. Sometimes I play chess
and cards with them. Sometimes I have a chat with them.
They like to tell me what they are thinking and what
they want. So I know them as well as I know myself. I
understand their deepest feelings. It must be pointed
out that their life is closely connected with their incomes. Their health is also connected with their life,
because we are living in a society where the people can
change their habits. I must say there are many cities
and towns in the whole of China and the level of life
in each city is a little different. I have been living
in the city of Anshan. So I am very familiar with everything in this city. I can only talk about it.

Sun Bao-yuan

My Fancy

According to my conditions of health, I am afraid
I can't live to age 65. Now suppose I could, what
would I do then? This is indeed an interesting question. As you are a learned woman, you know our Chinese
traditions. From ancient times up til now we Chinese
people have been a hardworking people. We like to live
together with our children and organize a big family,
especially in the countryside. Now in cities, everyone
has his own work. Sometimes the members of a family
don't work in the same city. But they get together for
holidays. Festival Holiday is the year's beginning

according to the Chinese calendar, generally February
5th or 7th. Maybe this holiday is equal to Christmas
in Western countries.

I would like to live with my son and grandsons if
I have any. Generally, the son's wife doesn't like to
live with her father-in-law and mother-in-law, unless
they are in good health (so that they can help her do
some housework) or they have much money. But I think
everything is changing and everything will be better in
the future.

However, if my economic situation is good, I would
like to have a long trip. Maybe I would go to America,
to England or to Europe. I would see with my own eyes
what these countries are like and what people are doing
there. When I travel to America, I will go see you, my
teacher of English. By that time, maybe you won't recognize me because I will be too old.

But I can't throw my bones abroad. As a Chinese
saying says: "No matter how tall a tree is, its leaves
will fall down to its root."

                    Wang Xing-hua

     Another story from the summer of 1983 helps to
clarify the operational attitudes toward the elderly of
the students and administrators at NEIT with whom I
worked. I was accompanied to Shenyang by a 73-year-old
American friend from Paris, who remained at NEIT for
several weeks.

Everyone had a hard time understanding why Ms.
Dwight declined to teach for the role was an entirely
appropriate, familiar and beneficial activity for an
older person. In seeming contrast to the belief that
she could teach very well, if she wanted to, was the
concern that she was "too old." People worried about
her walking distances, handling travel arrangements,
taking crowded buses, etc. Such concern was unsolic-
ited and unwanted; nevertheless the expectation of an
older woman was clear: her physical strength must be
waning, but not her capacity to be productive and contribute.

Only once, in fact, did a "slight" occur and even
then it was unintentional. Frankly, it made us laugh
until we cried. A student wrote how nervous he had
been prior to the first class. His fears, however,
were dissipated when "In walked the old lady and the
miss!"

NOTES

1. Richard Bernstein, From the Center of the Earth:
The Search for the Truth about China (Boston: Little,
Brown, & Co., 1982), p. 11.

2. A Brief Introduction to Shenyang City, published
by the Foreign Affairs Office of Shenyang, Liaoning
Province, PRC.

3. Compiled from the following:

Richard C. Bush and James R. Townsend, The People's Republic of China: A Basic Handbook. Published
in cooperation with the China Council of the Asia Society by the Council on International and Public Affairs,
and distributed by Learning Resources in International
Studies, 777 United Nations Plaza, New York, NY 10017.
A Brief Introduction to Shenyang City, published
by the Foreign Affairs Office of Shenyang, Liaoning
Province, PRC.
"4,000-Year History," China: Facts and Figures.
Edited and published by Foreign Language Press, Beijing.
William Hinton, Shenfan (New York: Random
House, 1983), p. 768.

4. "Party launches rectification," China Daily 3:
640:1, 10/13/83.

5. Another old people's home is described by Lila
Chalpin, "Living is easy in 'respect homes,'" Perspectives on Aging (Washington, DC: The National Council
on the Aging, 600 Maryland Avenue, SW, Nov.-Dec. 1982),
pp. 8-10.

6. "Minister promises a happy life for the old,"
China Daily 3:779:1, 1/25/84.

7. An Zhiguo, "Family Planning," Beijing Review
26:35:4, 8/29/83.

8. There is a slight variation in the listings of
these ideals in the official press. This note is not
meant to lessen the impact of the various campaigns upon the people. They're taken very seriously. The purpose and intent, the honor and rewards, are viewed as
very worthwhile. The Five Traditional Standards officially are: decorum, courtesy, public health, discipline and morals. The Four Beautifications are mind,
language, behavior and environment.

9. The model family is officially judged by the
following Five Points:
    --Love the socialist motherland and the

collectives; observe the rules and laws.
--Work hard and fulfill tasks well.
--Carry out the policy of family planning;
   educate children and practice economy.
--Reform unhealthy customs; stress decorum,
   courtesy and hygiene.
--Respect the old and cherish the young;
   help neighbors.

10. The following excerpts from "Women in Chinese history: A feudal and inhuman concept on chastity," Women of China, 9 Sept. 1983, pp. 40-42, give a clear picture of tradition which so deeply affected the life of this beautiful old woman. Her grace and ability to communicate, her care and concern for others were so extraordinary, yet in her own words she was "a feudal sacrifice" in a family-based and family-structured society:

> A strict ethic affected the girl whose fiancé had died. Her sad lot was to put on mourning clothes and remain single at her parents' home for the rest of her life. Sometimes, she was asked to go to the deceased man's house to kowtow to the departed spirit. And still some girls were forced to perform a wedding ceremony with a wooden puppet or tablet, or even a rooster, as a stand-in for the deceased, after which she would have to stay in the house of her fiance to serve his family. In the most extreme cases, the girl would be forced to give her life for her betrothed, whom she had never seen. Whether she gave her life willingly or not, the sacrifice would bring honor to her and her family, and she was assured that a wooden board with an inscription like: "May Her Act of Chastity be Followed" or "A Reputation That Will Go Down Through Posterity" would be placed on her family gate. By the same token, if a widow had an illicit affair, then she had disgraced her family and was considered rebellious. In such cases she might be sentenced to death by the head of the clan at a family meeting held in the ancestral hall. Sometimes the woman was nailed down into a coffin and buried alive or was thrown into a river with a weight tied to her.
> And so from the middle of the Song Dynasty onward, the ethics guiding women's behavior became stricter. It was considered a great humiliation for a widow to have any body contact with a man, or for any part of her skin to be seen by a stranger. Stories like that about the widow Ma, who suffered from an abscess in

her breast but couldn't bring herself to see a male doctor and died, were not unusual in old China.

The codes of chastity were greatly advocated by rules of the Ming and Qing dynasties (1368-1911). An imperial edict issued in the first year of the reign of the first Ming emperor stated that a widow who lost her husband before thirty and remained single till fifty should be publicly honored and her family members exempted from corvée. This was the first official regulation made which systematized the bestowing of material and spiritual rewards upon women who did not remarry. As is written in the Biography of Women Martyrs in Ming Dynasty, "To ensure adherence to these regulations, local officials on inspection tour should make annual reports about the virtuous women under their jurisdiction, and magnificent memorial temples should be built in honor of outstanding women, while memorial arches should be built for more common women." For this reason, "Even girls from poor families living in remote regions began to discipline themselves according to the rules of chastity, and the names of tens of thousands of them went down in local historical records," while many more were lost to antiquity.

During the Qing Dynasty, the court made further efforts to spread such concepts through commendation on a broader scale. Some of the regulations issued went as follows:

"A girl who starves herself to death to show her faithfulness to her deceased fiancé should be duly honored."

11. Peng Zhen, Concluding Speech at the First Session of the Sixth National People's Congress of the People's Republic of China, June 21, 1983 (Beijing: Foreign Languages Press, 1983), p. 141.

12. "Retirement means new life for millions of workers," China Daily 3:706:3, 11/1/83.

13. Dan Jacobson, "Fatigue-producing factors in industrial work and pre-retirement attitudes," Occupational Psychology, 1972, 46, 193-200.

14. The "5 supports" or "5 guarantees," as they are more commonly called, are food, clothing, housing, medical treatment and burial expenses. If someone is unable to provide for him- or herself or does not have family to do so, the government, through the local work unit, guarantees that these needs will be met.

15. In 1977, the State Council designated certain colleges and universities as "key" institutions. They were to be administered directly by various ministries rather than by provincial or municipality governments. NEIT operates directly under the auspices of the Ministry of Metallurgy in Beijing.
According to Victor and Ruth Sidel in The Health of China (Boston: Beacon Press, 1982), p. 165, "key" universities receive increased budgets for teaching and research, preferences in enrollment of undergraduate and graduate students, preferences in faculty assignments, first right to send faculty and students abroad and in receiving foreign experts. It is hoped that these "key" schools will produce highly trained specialists to lead in the modernization movement.

16. The difficulty in finding professors willing to participate in my study should be mentioned. Had I been working in their (scientific or technological) fields, more of them would have been interested, but as it was, many didn't see aging (a given in the order of things) as a subject worth their time. For many, it was summer vacation; for some, the weeks had been set aside for university research; and others flatly refused. The Personnel Administration Office prepared very carefully for me and took time away from their many responsibilities as the beginning of a new academic year approached. Dr. Zhu Quan, Chairman of the Department of Steel Processing, was asked to participate as he was using the typewriter in the Foreign Affairs Office, a special privilege. I learned a great deal from him and from his excellent interpreter, but he complained that such a discussion was a waste of his time. On the other hand, the three professors from the Mining Department didn't have such a bad time; in fact, it was a delightful and uplifting exchange. Always, I remain appreciative of the time and observations of my first contacts with the university: President Bi, Vice-President Su and Mr. Lao, who, here again, did nothing but try to enhance my study by their candid remarks and warm hospitality.

17. "Traditional Sports," China Facts and Figures (Beijing: Foreign Languages Press, May 1982), p. 2.

18. Kenneth Boulding, The Image: Knowledge in Life and Society (Ann Arbor: University of Michigan Press, 1956).

19. Yan Keqing, "Problems and Prospects in Population Planning," China Reconstructs XXXII:6:31, June 1983.

20. "Social aid for the aged," China Daily 3:679:3, 9/30/83.

21. "Service with a smile for Guangzhou elderly," China Daily 3:670:3, 8/16/83.

22. "Laundry for aged," China Daily 3:642:3, 8/18/83.

23. "Heat wave hits Beijing residents' water supply," China Daily 3:621:1, 7/25/83.

24. For example, "Xiao learned his skill in secret," China Daily 3:604:6, 7/5/83.

25. I would like to acknowledge the kind assistance of Don Woods, a very knowledgeable resource for me on both statistics and Shenyang. Dr. Woods has been a computer specialist in residence at the Northeast Institute of Technology in Shenyang for three years.

26. Zeng Shuzhi, "China's Senior Citizens," China Reconstructs XXXII:1:9, January 1983.

27. "Tradition Changes in Beijing," China Daily 3:802:3, 2/21/84.

28. Ibid. See also Fei Xiaotong, "Changes in Chinese Family Structure," China Reconstructs XXXI:7:23-26, July 1982.

29. "Beijing residents better off," China Daily 3:680:1, 10/1/83.

IV
Analysis and Implications

INTRODUCTION

Nanhu Park is more than a gathering place for old
people. It is a metaphor for the role the elderly play
in Shenyang's daily life and development. Nanhu Park
is to the city's physical environment what the elderly
are to Shenyang's social environment.

By Occidental standards, neither one is materially
well-endowed, yet both are repositories of a spiritual
richness. Neither one is blessed with beautiful or
tranquil surroundings, yet both have within them a level of serenity and joyful activity that transcends the
harshness and turbulence of their environments. Neither one can thrive without careful tending by families,
neighborhood organizations, local units and the State,
yet both give back more than they take from each generation that looks after their needs. And finally, neither one is at the front of local or national drives
for modernization, yet the tangible and intangible support, comfort, perspective and sense of optimism both
provide to the people of Shenyang make them invaluable
and irreplacable in the process of development.

Old age for people of all societies is a time of
increasing loss--loss of family and friends, physical
capabilities and strength. How the individual and how
the society adapt and respond to these losses determines, in large measure, the extent of "well-being."
What has been reported here represents a positive adap-
tation. Certainly the negative side exists. All people do not cope well; all needs are not met by a society. But within each life described is a spark which
infuses life with meaning and patterns the way towards
health and longevity. It is better to understand how
societies can serve to ignite that spark that makes
living a "soaring flight of rich fulfillment," to use
Colin Turnbull's phrase, than to consider how they fail.
That is what I have tried to do in the pages that follow.

It is currently fashionable to be very circumspect about the "lessons" one can draw from the reality of one country and apply to another nation. There is a good reason for this reticence. To assume that because a particular policy, program or innovation "works" in place X, it will automatically "work" in places Y and Z is wrong. The empirical evidence from agriculture to education and from religion to health care has substantiated the fallacy of this assumption.

Third World countries are still paying the price for having agreed (at the insistence of the "developed" nations) to simply *adopt* foreign practices and systems rather than taking the time to sensibly *adapt* them to local realities--if they are appropriate at all. Accordingly, there will be no grand pronouncements here about the need for the United States or other nations of the world to immediately implement such Chinese practices as using the elderly to mediate disputes.

And yet, as crazy as it would be to proclaim that the positive aspects of being old in the PRC could, or should, be transplanted elsewhere in their entirety, it is even crazier to believe that there is nothing of value to learn from the successes the Chinese have achieved in this area. My contention is that what I read, observed, heard and experienced concerning the aged in Shenyang *does* have relevance and significance to other areas of China and to other nations as well.

One final word of caution: I cannot predict what will happen next in the United States--the society in which I've grown up and spent most of my adult life. To pretend to be certain about the course of events likely to unfold in a nation as huge, complex and volatile as the People's Republic of China would indeed be foolish. Accordingly, I share the reservations so many researchers and authors express about the generalizability, replicability and durability of their observations and experiences. My data and my knowledge are, by nature, limited; but, as T. H. Huxley once observed: "If a little knowledge is dangerous, where is the man who has so much as to be out of danger?" The challenge is to try to make sense of the data that are available and to investigate the implications of what we do know--all the while recognizing the need to learn more.

A SPECIAL GENERATION

The elderly in Shenyang are part of a generation unlike any before them in China's long history and probably unlike any that will follow. They are the only generation to spend their prime years of adulthood in both pre- and post-Liberation China. They are the only generation whose lives span the transition from a traditional feudal society to an (almost) modern

Communist one. They are the only generation to have both first-hand knowledge of the deprivations of the old society and first-hand experience with the fruits of post-Mao China. In short, they are China's revolutionary generation.

Understanding their special place in history is the key to understanding the sense of well-being they experience and exhibit today. There are many levels of "knowing" history. For example, I can read about the malnutrition and starvation plaguing China earlier in the 20th century. Today's young Shenyangese can hear about it from their families and teachers. My information may be more objectively correct, but theirs will carry more emotional weight. Still, in both cases, our knowledge of this period's problems is second-hand and, thus, somewhat abstract. The elderly, however, lived this history, suffered its consequences and witnessed its toll. Their knowledge is more profound and more likely to have shaped their worldview and their behavior than is the case for anyone whose knowledge is less concrete.

This may sound like a simple point, but its implications for how the elderly and the State view each other cannot be overstated. Over and over, the old people expressed a gratitude for the changes wrought by the 1949 Revolution that went well beyond what was politically correct, expected, or expedient to say to a foreigner.

The political commitment of the younger adults I encountered seemed largely ideologic--that is, a result of the beliefs developed through formal and informal processes of socialization. If anything, having the Cultural Revolution rather than the 1949 Revolution as their primary personal reference point meant that the young people viewed the State with greater detachment (if not suspicion) and with less affection than their elders. It also meant that they tended to compare the present situation not with the realities of the old society, but rather with their images of the Occidental nations (or Occidentally-influenced places like Hong Kong or Tokyo).

By contrast, the political commitment of the old people was almost palpable. Their fervor was not based on theory. The foundation of their loyalty to the State and what it represented was entirely concrete and reality-based. They saw the Liberation of 1949 as having rescued them in a direct and personal way. Having come of age in a society in which the average life expectancy was 35 years, they often attributed their survival into old age--their very existence--to the good works of the Party and the State. People with the kinds of personal histories of those I interviewed tend not to take for granted even the simplest pleasures of regular meals, adequate clothing, basic medical care and a place to live. Moreover, people who feel it is a stroke of good fortune that they are alive at all are inclined toward feeling a real sense of well-being.

Of course, the State has recognized the allegiance of the elderly. As detailed in earlier chapters, it has reinforced this bond by instituting a variety of special measures to support and enhance the status of the aged in Shenyang and elsewhere. Why has the PRC bothered to invest so much in its senior citizens? Neither humanitarianism nor tradition is an adequate explanation, for the State repeatedly has shown a willingness to put aside both of these principles when it has been deemed advantageous to do so.

The post-Mao regime emphasizes its pragmatism. Consequently, it makes sense to look for the pragmatic reasons behind the State's active beneficence toward the elderly. My work suggests the following:

First, the State wants, and needs, the political support of its senior citizens. Although the government is not enamored with traditions *per se*, it recognizes that respect for the elderly is a traditional social value that continues to be widely held and deeply felt among the Chinese people. Violating this tradition, as happened during the Cultural Revolution, would serve mainly to alienate the masses and undermine the State's credibility. Obviously, this is highly counterproductive. On the other hand, it is very useful to do everything possible for the aged so that they, in turn, will continue to sing the State's praises and remind impressionable younger family members and fellow workers of the comparative advantages of the current government.

Second, the State realized that ensuring a good life for old people was vital to the accomplishment of one of its most eagerly sought goals: the one-child family. China cannot achieve the Four Modernizations or win the Race to the Year 2000 if its already enormous population continues to increase at a rapid pace. Thus, birth control and the one-child family have been top priorities of the post-Mao government. The elderly play critical roles in this campaign, ranging from advocating and enforcing the official policies within their own families to helping with the family planning efforts of their residents' and Street committees.

Yet, the connection between the one-child family policy and the positive treatment of the elderly runs deeper than the operational roles old people play. Remember that for thousands of years the family has been the most important social, political, educational and economic unit in Chinese society. Children have been seen as the only hope for economic security and quality care in one's old age. The clear incentive has always been to have lots of children (especially male) in order to increase the odds that at least one would take

responsibility for the parents as they became more dependent.

One powerful way of countering the perceived need
for many children is for the State to demonstrate its
willingness--and capacity--to ensure the well-being of
all elderly people, regardless of the number of children they may have. Therefore, by strongly supporting
the elderly, the State is reinforcing the message that
the quality of life in one's later years is *not* a function of the number of children one has. Only by prov-
ing that adults will not be placing themselves in jeop-
ardy because of too few children can the State expect
widespread compliance with the one-child family policy.
And here we have the beginnings of the transference to
the State of what have traditionally been family responsibilities.

The third rationale for the PRC's support for the
elderly is that their skills, knowledge and experience
have made them very valuable in the push for the Four
Modernizations. Many of the old people I interviewed
in Shenyang had been asked to delay retirement or to
continue working on the second or third line, not for
sentimental reasons, but because they were genuinely
needed.

The Cultural Revolution brought scientific and
technical training and research to a standstill for
more than a decade. This fact, combined with the post-
Mao push to expand productivity quickly and to promote
rapid development, meant that large numbers of older
workers had become, quite literally, irreplaceable.
The nation's economic goals could only be achieved with
the active cooperation and assistance of her senior
citizens. Even those older people not having special
skills or experience were needed to labor in the home
and in the community to make it possible for young people to participate in work and training programs that
further the country's economic development.

The need for the knowledge and labor of the elderly is not limited to the economic sector. Old people
are called upon to perform a host of service and civic
functions, e.g., organizing and conducting neighborhood
beautification drives, political education sessions and
recreational activities. Having old people carry out
these functions frees up the second generation to engage in economically productive labor while simultaneously enhancing the quality of community life. The
fact that this activity and participation benefit the
elderly as well as the society is a happy coincidence--
but a coincidence nonetheless.

The fourth, and final, explanation is that the
cost/benefit ratio of supporting the elderly has been
very advantageous for the State. Given the reasons
noted above, it should be obvious that no other investment in the nation's human resources could have yielded

such high dividends so quickly. The social and economic benefits of investments in the elderly--especially
since they currently constitute only eight percent of
China's population--were, and are, very favorable compared to either the cost of foregoing their contributions or the cost of training another segment of society to take their place and assume their role.

The "bottom line" here is that for a series of
very pragmatic reasons, the State and the elderly in
Shenyang have evolved a mutually supportive and mutually beneficial relationship. Each one has wanted, needed, and been grateful for the other.

Today's elderly represent a special--and perhaps
unique--generation in China's history. The good news
is that this specialness has been recognized and amply
rewarded by the larger society. The bad news is that
there is no guarantee that the special regard accorded
the elderly at present will be extended to successive
generations. In order to examine the possibilities for
the future, two divergent scenarios for future generations in Shenyang follow.

THE SCENARIO OF DECLINING STATUS

The current generation of elderly Shenyangese enjoys a special status and special support both from the
State and from the younger generations. Yet, their
specialness raises questions about exactly what they
represent. Are the respect they receive and the roles
they play an historical fluke or are these standards of
treatment successive generations can expect when they
reach retirement age? Will the sense of well-being
felt by old people in Shenyang today also be characteristic of the city's next generation of senior citizens?
Do the social and economic changes sure to come to China in the years ahead bode well or ill for the aged in
places like Shenyang?

Obviously such questions are not answerable. The
best one can do is to examine the available evidence,
take likely developments into account, and then try to
imagine both positive and negative scenarios. Let us
begin by constructing the less favorable alternative,
for indeed there are societal factors and trends that
make a scenario of declining status a plausible one.

Ironically, if this negative vision comes to pass,
the chief culprit will be the very thing young and old
alike are striving so hard to achieve--that is, modernization. Modernization may be "good" for China as a
whole, but there is a fair chance the cost will include
the well-being of an even larger elderly population.
Such an unintended negative consequence is reminiscent
of the warning of Saint Theresa (by way of Truman
Capote) that "more tears have been shed over answered

prayers than unanswered ones!"

Intergenerational dependency is high in Shenyang for reasons of: (1) pooled income and the consolidation of expenses; (2) the supportive roles retired people play in child care, housework, home administration, marketing and food preparation (thereby allowing the middle generation family members to work outside the home); (3) the present shortage of housing space (this factor works both ways, as noted previously); and (4) the spiritual and psychological satisfactions of close familial relationships.

However, the situation is likely to change as the urban economies of China move further into their industrial phases. The economic value of the older generation is presently very high--and a real boon to families--in a society where, in general, incomes are barely adequate, and very often the sum of many small parts. The issue is whether modernization (i.e., the social changes that precede, accompany, and follow economic development) will necessarily lead to a Westernization of family relationships and structures.

It is John Caldwell's thesis that a fair degree of emotional nucleation precedes economic nucleation.[1] His research on intergenerational wealth flows has shown that in all traditional societies the flow has been from younger to older generations. This wealth flow from children to parents historically has been the economic rationale for high levels of fertility. However, in the process of development, there comes a point at which a "great divide" occurs. Caldwell posits social, psychological and physiological reasons for this rift as it affects the traditional structure of families--and eventually of societies.

Families begin to nucleate emotionally and then economically as wealth flows reverse direction and take a downward turn from adults to children. Fertility also declines as more investment is made in each offspring. Thus, social and familial change, according to the theory, precedes economic development. The point is that Caldwell attributes this emotional nucleation to Westernization, which he defines as "the transmittal of European cultural traditions" (and to which I would add American lifestyles). Because of the overwhelming economic strength the West derived from the Industrial Revolution, it has been able to export not only its material goods, but also its social structures and values.

"From the demographic viewpoint," Caldwell states, "the most important social exports have been the concept of the predominance of the nuclear family with its strong conjugal tie and the concept of concentrating concern and expenditures on one's children."[2] Networks of relatives remain important in transitional societies, as we currently see in China, but as full development occurs, what can be projected? Caldwell cites two relevant studies:

> In one of the major texts on social change in
> the Third World, Alex Inkeles and David Smith
> fleetingly recognized that the difference in
> their division of the world into that which
> was modernized and that which was not was al-
> most entirely a contrast between the West and
> the rest: "With the exception of Japan . . .
> all the major nations which we can consider
> modernized are part of the European tradition."
> Rather than pursue this theme, they decided
> not to be "arrogant" and instead broke up the
> Western tradition into components that could
> be used for measuring not "Westernization" but
> "modernization." Throughout William Goode's
> important study, World Revolution and Family
> Patterns, with its investigation of recent
> family changes in the Arab, Sub-Saharan Afri-
> can, Indian and Chinese world, "revolution,"
> except in the discussion of slower growth over
> a longer period in the West, is a synonym for
> "Westernization."[3]

While the old compare their lives to those of their
parents in the old society and feel gratitude, the young
compare their lives to those they envision in the West
and feel dissatisfied. The old work to contribute; the
young work to compete. The old work to reinforce ground
that has been gained; the young work to gain new ground
(as well as computers, washing machines, curling irons,
etc.). The old have a strong sense of socialist consciousness; the young have a stronger materialistic and
individualistic orientation.

As commodities become more readily available, desires begin to revolve more and more around a cash economy. Ninety percent of Beijing's residents, for example, own television sets.[4] Whether television brings
families together or serves to partition them (or whether it serves an educational, political or recreational
purpose) is not as relevant as the fact that the univer-
sality of home televisions represents an emerging consumerism. Buying a television is followed closely by
the purchase of washing machines and other laborsaving
devices.

There is no doubt that a subsistence economy pre-
dominantly based on familial interdependence is one in
which the productive capacities of the older generation
count very heavily. By contrast, a more developed and
modern economy with goods and services readily available
to anyone with cash is one in which individualism and
nucleation are fostered. The desire to "live near"
rather than *with* the older generation--as was repeatedly expressed in my survey and student interviews--is a

gradual step toward the independence of generations
seen as normal in Occidental nations. Certainly attitudes toward extended families and intergenerational
housing will be subject to alteration once necessity is
no longer their *raison d'etre*.

Two correlaries of modernization--better health
and better education--are worth special attention in
this discussion. Both are undeniably beneficial to
China as a whole, and yet, both may prove to be very
mixed blessings for the status and well-being of the
elderly.

Living Longer but Enjoying it Less?

The "problem" with better personal health, better
public health, and better health care for all people is
that it will result in more people living longer than
ever before. Needless to say, this will not strike the
individual beneficiaries as bad news or as a result to
be shunned. While the old people I talked to expressed
no particular fear of dying (regarding it as a "natural
law" and an inevitability),neither did they welcome it.
Their attitude toward dying is perhaps akin to Tevye's
attitude toward poverty--"It's no shame, but it's no
great honor either."

Nevertheless, there is a real risk that better
health will serve to devalue the elderly and to transform them from a collective asset to a collective burden. Up until now, the elderly have been a powerful
resource for, rather than a drag upon, economic development. Will this continue to be true when the number
of senior citizens is so much greater in both absolute
and relative terms?

Remember that life expectancy in the PRC has doubled in the last 30 years, as has the number of people
over 60 years of age. Whereas there were only four
million people over 75 years old in 1950, the projections are for a ten-fold increase in this age cohort
(to 40+ million) by 2010. Being 75 in a society in
which the average life expectancy is 35 rates as quite
an accomplishment--and as a phenomenon automatically
inspiring a certain degree of respect and admiration.

It is hard to believe that being 75 in a society
in which the average life expectancy is quickly ap-
proaching 70 will so readily evoke respect and deference from the young. After all, rarity is one of the
standards by which societies establish anything's, or
anyone's, worth. When being elderly becomes common-
place in Shenyang, will the younger generations assign
old people the same value and importance as they currently enjoy?

Even more to the point, will a still relatively
poor nation be able to bear the cost of supporting tens

of millions of new retirees--no matter how positive the
societal attitudes and inclinations might be? The current financial problems with the PRC's limited pension
scheme encourage a negative response. China Daily
openly discussed this phenomenon as shown in the following excerpt from an article entitled "Pensions: New
Problem for Enterprises":

> Since liberation, retired people in commerce
> and the service trades have received their pen-
> sions from units where they originally worked.
> In the past, pensioners were few and units
> found little difficulty in making payment.
> But in recent years, especially since 1979,
> the number of pensioners has increased sharp-
> ly.
>   For example, in Beijing's West District
> in 1978, units belonging to financial and com-
> mercial departments had 3,909 pensioners--11.9
> per cent of the total workforce. By the end
> of 1982, pensioners increased to 8,624, and the
> percentage to 23.
>   Money paid to pensioners in 1978 was
> 1,698,000 yuan. In 1982, it rose to 5,496,000
> yuan, a 2.2 fold increase. This sharp increase
> was a heavy burden, especially to small enter-
> prises engaged in tailoring, haircutting, re-
> pairs and other service trades . . .
>   Such heavy burdens deprived many collec-
> tively-owned enterprises of funds to enlarge
> production. Equipment could not be renewed,
> nor dilapidated buildings rebuilt, and labour
> and living conditions of workers remained un-
> improved.
>   For instance, the domestic coal depart-
> ment of the district has not built a single
> apartment house for its staff in the past 20
> years. All the buildings, machinery and vehi-
> cles date to the 1950s. Because of a poor en-
> vironment, and hard working conditions, this
> trade finds it hard to recruit new workers.[5]

Davis-Friedman's conclusions on this subject are
also instructive:

> Because China first implemented a national re-
> tirement program several decades after most
> European nations (but only a decade after the
> United States), she modeled many of her poli-
> cies after those of economically more developed
> and prosperous nations. As a result, proposed
> benefit levels exceed the nation's ability to
> pay. Another consequence of economic weakness
> is that retirement programs have been restricted

to the small minority of workers in the modern
State sector. Barring radically reduced benefit levels or drastically improved productivity,
it seems likely that retirement will remain a
privilege of a labor elite for the next two
generations of workers. Thus poverty and overly ambitious expectations for long term economic
growth have forged a distinctive Chinese experience.[6]

So, as health and health care improve, more Shenyangese will survive to old age and tomorrow's elderly
will live for more years beyond retirement than today's
retirees. However, the ability of either families or
the State to cope with this "graying" of China is suspect. In addition, there is a possibility that the
sheer number of old people will force a downgrading of
their position within Chinese society. Respect, like
money, may prove to be a finite entity that will become
thinner as it is spread more widely.

Valuing Expertise over Experience

The role of education and technical training in
the scenario of declining status for the elderly is also critical. Like better health, better education will
speed the modernization process and raise the overall
standard of living. However, as with better health,
the rewards of better education and training will not
be distributed uniformly across all segments of society.
There is a reasonable chance the elderly in Shenyang
and other urban areas will be the net losers.
As explained earlier, Shenyang (and indeed all of
China) has genuinely needed the skills, knowledge and
experience of its senior citizens in order to keep its
economy alive and move toward achievement of the Four
Modernizations. The Cultural Revolution greatly aggra-
vated an already critical shortage of highly trained
and highly productive individuals. Thus, some old people have been encouraged to stay on their jobs, to
train new workers or to serve as advisors well beyond
the official retirement ages.
Greater access to higher levels, and more sophisticated types, of education might serve to alter the
intergenerational balance in fundamental ways--strength-
ening the relative position of the young graduates while
simultaneously undercutting the position of their elders. Shenyang has already experienced the beginning
stages of this process. Increasingly, older workers
are being encouraged to "step aside" in order to make
room for the better educated, more technically advanced
young workers.
If this trend continues, one can envision a day in

the not too distant future when the great majority of
older workers will not be needed at all in their own
industries, when their advice and assistance will be
neither required nor solicited, and when they (in Brit-
ish terminology) will become "redundant." Will the PRC
continue to rush to help, or lavish praise upon, its
older workers if their productive contributions are
seen as being marginal and their relative economic
utility has significantly diminished?

One way in which education undermines families,
and thereby the elderly, is through the job assignment
system. The common practice is for the State to control where the highly educated and/or highly skilled
Chinese work upon graduation. The physical separation
of families made possible by the education and training
the young receive sometimes results in a weakening of
the bonds among generations. Still, for the elderly,
the primary negative dimension of the push for better
education is also the most subtle and insidious. In
China today, the relentless pursuit of modernization
has put a premium on the acquisition of technical
skills and information. The Occidental nations are
looked to for the technical assistance and technical
know-how they can contribute to the Four Modernizations.
Mao's dictum to "seek truth from facts" seems less in
keeping with the technocratic mentality of the current
regime than "see facts as truth."

The danger here is simple. If technical knowledge
and professional skills supplant the wisdom born of experience, then the elderly will be swiftly and defini-
tively devalued. After all, why respect people you see
not as wise, but simply old-fashioned; not venerable,
but merely out of date? One key reason that old people
are "put out to pasture" so often in the Occidental nations is not because they have nothing to contribute,
but rather because we rarely take seriously the contributions they *can* make. The West is so enamored with
expertise that there is precious little value placed
upon wisdom. And, when a society stops genuinely be-
lieving in wisdom it has cut itself off from the power
and energy the elderly can provide.

By ascribing wisdom to the elderly, I do not mean
to suggest that they necessarily have surer knowledge
or firmer facts to offer. Rather, by wisdom, I am referring to the perspective gained through a lifetime of
experience. If the trend toward valuing and rewarding
technical expertise continues unchecked, then the respect accorded to the life experiences of old people
may well decline.

Implications

Modernization is a double-edged sword. If the PRC

follows a course of economic and technological development that carries within it the seeds of Westernization,
it will jeopardize one of its great successes--i.e.,
making the transition from a traditional to a relatively modern society without having abandoned or marginal-
ized her senior citizens.

It is no accident that the status and well-being
of the elderly in Occidental nations are so often pre-
carious. We even have fancy labels for the process we
promote, expect and encourage: deculturation and disengagement. As cultural gerontologist Lowell Holmes
argues:

> Not only does retirement in America rob the
> individual of a most important source of sta-
> tus and identity--the work role--but according
> to Anderson, retirement is a period of life
> when people are systematically forced to under-
> go *deculturation*. That is to say, they are
> required to relinquish cherished values and
> goals and accept a secondary social and eco-
> nomic role. Gerontologists Cumming and Henry
> suggest that there is a universal and natural
> tendency, which they label *disengagement*, for
> aged individuals to withdraw socially, eco-
> nomically and politically. They see such
> behavior as "mutually advantageous" for both
> the elderly and the society. Although they
> claim that this phenomenon is found in all
> societies, anthropological data prove that if
> the concept is valid at all, it is characteris-
> tically Western.[7]

Deculturation and disengagement certainly have not
been characteristic of China's elderly. Heading in
this direction is counterproductive in a country that
must maximize the contribution of every segment of the
population in order to realize its ambitious goals.
Should this scenario of declining status become a reality, it is clear that the physical and mental health
(as well as the overall sense of well-being) currently
experienced by Shenyang's aged would plunge dramatically.

The Shenyang experience reveals a high level of
expressed well-being among the elderly despite margin-
ally adequate material standards of living. It is an
Occidental assumption that one's material possessions
and one's sense of well-being are intimately inter-
twined. In the case of the PRC, it is plausible that
raising the general standard of living through economic
modernization, better health, and better education actually will *lower* the sense of well-being felt by old
people. The critical factor will be the choices made
about which development path the Chinese should follow

--or blaze for themselves. Inevitably, the status of
the elderly is a by-product of larger political decisions about the nature and direction of development.

THE SCENARIO OF CONTINUED WELL-BEING

While the preceding negative scenario is plausible,
it is by no means inevitable. The influences discussed
above might diminish, be neutralized by positive factors, or prove to be less powerful and pervasive than
they appear at present. Moreover, China already has
the ingredients necessary to ensure that the aged
emerge from this phase of national development with
both their objective and subjective well-being pre-
served, and perhaps even enhanced.

There are three grounds for maintaining optimism.
The first can be found in the enduring traditions and
values of Chinese society. Throughout the twentieth
century, the people of Shenyang have been inundated by
wave after wave of social and economic change. The
corresponding political reforms have washed away the
debris of the old society, but retained several key aspects of China's ancient civilization.

This valuable inheritance includes respect for the
elderly, close-knit extended families and a deep undercurrent of social consciousness. All of these may have
been born of economic necessity or equally harsh realities, but over the course of centuries each has taken
on a life of its own that exists apart from the circumstances of its origin.

For example, historians and psychologists may have
divergent views of why the Chinese are characteristically far more "other-directed" and far less "individu-
ally-oriented" than Americans, but they would not dis-
pute the existence of the characteristic itself. The
social consciousness of the Chinese--i.e., the ethic of
putting familial or group needs and desires ahead of
one's own--is so deeply imbedded in the collective culture and individual psyches of the Chinese that no government could easily counter it (even if so inclined).
The strains and pressures of modernization may bend
this social consciousness into particular channels at
particular times, but it is by no means certain that
rising consumerism will replace these deeper traditions
and values.

Respect for, and assistance to, the aged may be
too deep-seated a Chinese social value to be whisked
(or wished) away. The State has already thrown its
considerable weight behind the ethic of promoting well-
being among old people. Even if the numbers expand and
the circumstances change, there is no reason to believe
that either the State or the masses would be able to
construct a rationale persuasive enough to overcome

both the cultural inclination and the existing commitment to support the elderly.

The State is discovering that it may not be able
to afford large, European-style pensions for its retirees. But it also knows that for a host of political,
economic and cultural reasons, it absolutely cannot afford to abandon support of the elderly, waste their labor and experience, or bear the burden of the ill-health
and ill-will caused by breaking the social contract to
maintain their well-being.

The solution may be for the State to continue to
reinforce the ideals of self-reliance and familial allegiance. The creation of the new production responsibility system is a step in this direction, as is the
experiment underway to allow a sample of university
graduates to select their own jobs and elect to remain
in their home cities with their families. As G. M.
Ssenkoloto advises:

> While it is easy to say that support must be
> provided by the family members, this is not
> specific enough. We need to stress the idea
> of the corporate family which is organized
> around a number of important activities, such
> as performing important rituals, rearing its
> children and "supporting" its aging. In this
> context, therefore, each member of the family
> has to play a particular role in supporting
> the elderly materially and nonmaterially,
> though in varying degrees and employing vari-
> ous means. Jointly, members of a family can
> and should provide psychological security,
> physical security and cultural satisfaction.
> These are tremendously treasured among the
> aging population in the Third World. Those
> who are better able to offer economic support
> to the aging should be willing to transfer
> some of their wealth, income or resources to
> the elderly or, better still, to invest it
> for the benefit of the aging.
>   Age-old values are changing. Adverse
> economic forces, the misallocation of resources,
> the yearning for material things, the struggle
> for self-esteem and status--all these factors
> are overtaking the traditional positive values
> as regards support for the elderly.
>   How can this trend be checked? Particu-
> larly in the Third World, the extended family
> with all its ramifications should be upheld,
> valued, respected, preserved in terms of its
> positive aspects; and it should be provided
> with the means and backing it needs to take
> care of its old people. Through a process of
> learning, both informally and formally, the

younger population need to acquire knowledge,
skills, acceptable beliefs, values, customs
or practices that emphasize how valuable and
admirable it is to support the aging . . .
If only we can lend realistic, valued and
timely support for all various aspects of the
life of the aging, "more life will be added
to years."[8]

Ssenkoloto's advice would not strike people in
Shenyang as news or as anything more than an affirma-
tion of what happens there already. Witness, for example, the following excerpt from an interview with
Mr. Sui Zhitong, a professor at NEIT:

There is only one municipal home for the elderly in all of Shenyang. With a population
of almost five million, not very many people
are cared for in this fashion. The rest are
cared for by their families. Families are
expected to fulfill this function, not the
State. People who do not care for their
families are criticized severely . . . I
don't think the status of the elderly will
decline with modernization because of the
strong effect of criticism and because of the
helpful role expected by the society of the
elderly in the home situation and in the
neighborhood situation, too.

The kinds of attitudes and expectations reflected
in Mr. Sui's statement seem unlikely to disappear.
There is a positive self-fulfilling prophecy at work.
The mass line on the roles and status of the elderly
has created a common vision among the State, the young
adults of Shenyang and the elderly themselves. This
vision then shapes the objective reality—which ends up
reinforcing and validating the vision. It creates a
social fabric that will be very difficult to unravel,
even if the growing ranks of the aged make them less
special and more "inconvenient."
The second reason for optimism about a scenario of
continued well-being is that the State and the society
will continue to need the active participation of senior citizens well into the future. The roles the aged
play in Shenyang may increasingly move out of the factories and into the communities (i.e., from the economic to the service sector), but the overwhelming likelihood is that there will be important and valued roles
for them somewhere. There is so much that needs to be
done—and that the elderly can do successfully—that it
would be imprudent and counterproductive to discourage
them from making any and all contributions they are
able to make in the push for Shenyang's development.

Given the pragmatism of the current regime, it is highly unlikely that the government will choose to forego
this vital resource that the older population represent.

As described earlier, Shenyang's elderly, through
their roles in their families, in their former workplaces, and in their residents' committees, have been
able to stay active and productive. They are involved
in family and community planning, settling disputes,
counseling the young, beautifying and sanitizing the
environment, policing, caring, building their own activity centers, etc. They have legitimate roles.
Their work is central, not marginal, to the quality of
life of their families and communities. This activity
is vital not only to the pursuit of modernization, but
also to the well-being of the elderly themselves.
Though I cannot say what percentage the system works
for, who's left out and why, I can verify through my
research and experience that the potential to be involved not only exists, but beckons.

It is clear that being active and remaining productive keep older people healthier. They say so; they
live so. Many of the retirees I interviewed remarked
on how their health had improved since retirement,
largely (they say) because of their exercise programs.
Activity is recognized as having both prophylactic and
therapeutic benefits for degenerative and chronic diseases in the physical realm and for "a right attitude"
in the psychological realm. Inactivity is correctly
viewed as dangerous to one's health. In addition, the
social network built up by the elderly takes care of
manageable emotional and mental health needs. The re-
ciprocal of the support structure for problem-solving
is the group's authority to set limits on behavior, to
"criticize" and to seek conformity.

The people with whom I spoke have adequate incomes
and have been freed from the burden of fighting for
survival. This, in turn, has allowed them to choose to
take active roles in community life. Their "pursuit of
happiness" has lead them to contribute to the welfare
of others.

The heart of Chinese socialism is the commitment
to the collective welfare of the people. The strong
desire of many old Shenyangese to continue working as
volunteers shows money is not the key to motivation or
to work satisfaction. Now that their physical needs
are being met, the elderly are assessing and designing
active roles for themselves. Based upon the ethic of
self-reliance, *they* are defining the arena of their
contribution to society.

In other words, the elderly of Shenyang have
forged a sense of purpose and a sense of place that allow them to progress up the steps of Maslow's hierarchy
of needs:

Self-Actualization (the
achievement of the inner
self)

Esteem (worth, competency,
respect)

Belongingness and Love (the basic
social needs)

Safety (actual safety from injury and
feeling safe from injury)

Physiological (food, shelter, body needs)[9]

Having acquired a sense of well-being--and being
cognizant of what is necessary to sustain it--the elderly are most likely not going to passively relinquish
their gains. Their keen determination to keep on "doing well by doing good" should inhibit any attempts to
diminish their connection to the life around them.

The third factor supporting the scenario of continued well-being is more speculative. It hinges on
the State's willingness to use education (in its formal,
non-formal and informal manifestations) to intentional-
ly bolster the elderly.

As education becomes more widespread the government has the opportunity to determine more consistently
who learns what and who does what. If the education
system is used to train young people to replace the elderly not only in industry but in the community as well
--for instance, by training young "professional" social
workers--the sphere of influence of the aged will be
narrowed. Not only will there be an adverse impact on
the elderly, but the talent of these young professionals will be wasted by assigning them to duties already
performed well by their elders.

However, this need not occur. Instead, the State
could decide to train the young to run the productive
sector of the economy while making an equally explicit
decision to empower the elderly to run the full gamut
of social and community services. New training programs could be developed with the elderly as both teachers and clientele. In the Occidental nations, "senior
citizen" is a euphemism for "burned-out old person."
In Shenyang, where there is a firmly-entrenched culture

in which aging is seen as part of a continuum rather
than a downhill curve, there is an opportunity for *Senior Citizen* to connote something far more useful and
positive than has been achieved in the West. Whether
this potential will be realized is a function of what
direction the State decides to take as it builds the
nation's educational systems.

In a sense, this example illustrates my overall
conclusion about being old in the People's Republic of
China. The PRC is a nation in which the State is as
omnipresent as one could ever imagine. After all this
is a government that prominently displays charts of
women's menstrual cycles as part of the one-child family policy. This is a government that regulates the
daily lives of more than one billion human beings and
directly controls who eats what, who works where and
who may visit whom when! And yet, it is also a government that has made it possible for millions of elderly
people to achieve a standard of living, a degree of social integration, and a sense of well-being that would
have been beyond the imagination of their parents and
that legitimately can be admired by far wealthier Occidental nations.

As perhaps befits a revolutionary society, China
seems to be perpetually at critical crossroads. The
challenge and the excitement of China today are that it
appears to be charting a unique course toward national
development and modernization--a course that might help
the Chinese reap the rewards of economic progress without falling prey to the trap of discarding their own
culture in favor of wholesale Westernization. If the
Chinese can succeed in reconciling the seeming contradictions between economic modernization and "socialist
spiritual civilization" they will add a new chapter to
the history of Third World development.

Already, the experience of the People's Republic
of China dramatically demonstrates that the quality of
life for the elderly is neither a function, nor even a
corollary, of Western-style wealth and living standards.
Beyond a modest level of the "basics"--that is, food,
shelter, clothing and health care--the well-being of
the old people of Shenyang was far more dependent upon
their degree of active participation and level of social status than upon their material possessions or
economic power. Accordingly, the elderly of Shenyang
serve as a powerful reminder that a sense of well-being
does not hinge upon massive new outlays of scarce financial resources, but rather upon personal and societal commitments to accord the elderly a place of importance and respect in the lives of their families,
their communities and their nation.

NOTES

1. John C. Caldwell, "Toward a restatement of demographic transition theory," Population and Development Review 2:3-4:321-366, Sept.-Dec. 1976. See also: Caldwell, "A theory of fertility" 4:4:553-577, Dec. 1978; and Caldwell, "The mechanisms of demographic change in historical perspective," Population Studies 35:1:5-27, 1981.

2. Caldwell, "Toward a restatement," p. 356.

3. Ibid., p. 353. Caldwell is referring to the following studies: Alex Inkeles and David H. Smith, Becoming Modern: Individual Change in Six Developing Countries (London: Heinemann, 1974), 17-18; and William J. Goode, World Revolution and Family Patterns (Glencoe: Free Press, 1963).

4. "Color TV in demand," China Daily 3:698, 10/22/83.

5. "Pensions: New problems for enterprises," China Daily, 10/25/83.

6. Deborah Davis-Friedmann, "Retirement Practices in China: Recent Developments," speech given at the conference, "Aging and Retirement in Cross-Cultural Perspectives," Rockefeller Study and Conference Center, Bellagio, Italy, June 22-26, 1981.

7. Lowell D. Holmes, Other Cultures, Elder Years: An Introduction to Cultural Gerontology (Minneapolis: Burgess Publishing Company, 1983), p. 52. Cited studies are B. G. Anderson, "Deculturation among the Aged," Anthropological Quarterly 45:209-216, 1972; and E. Cumming and W. E. Henry, Growing Old: The Process of Disengagement (New York: Basic Books, 1961).

8. G. M. Ssenkoloto, "Family support for the elderly," World Health, May 1982, pp. 22-26.

9. Abraham H. Maslow, Motivation and Personality (New York: Harper, 1954).

Appendix A:
Methodology

THE ETIC PERSPECTIVE

Data on the interface of public policy and ordinary life in the PRC have been very difficult to obtain.
When the Shanghai Communiqué opened China's doors to
the West in 1972, the country itself was still in the
midst of the Cultural Revolution, a period disavowing
the merits of "intellectualism." Universities were
closed from 1966 to 1976 and scientists, scholars, and
students were ordered to the countryside to be reeducated and to "serve the people."
Huan Xiang describes the impact of the Cultural
Revolution in "Social Science and the Modernization of
China" as follows:

> Social science research was disrupted to the
> point of stagnation and even retrogression,
> while China's national economy was pushed to
> the brink of collapse. It was only after the
> fall of the Gang of Four and their cultural
> autocracy in 1976 that social sciences in
> China were able to flourish again.[1]

Thus, Chinese behavioral and social scientists have
just recently begun the research needed to understand
and document the social and demographic characteristics
of contemporary Chinese life.
Western reports on China in the 70s were full of
hope. When Mao came to power, China was characterized
by overwhelming illiteracy, disease, misery, hunger,
high unemployment, and corruption. By 1980, through
policies in support of local determination and self-
reliance, infant mortality had fallen to less than one-
tenth the 1949 rate and infectious diseases, childbirth,
and TB were no longer common causes of death.[2] The
three top killers had become more developed country
phenomena: 1980 figures from Shanghai County showed
that malignant tumors accounted for 23.5 percent of all

deaths, heart disease for 20.1 percent, and cerebrovascular disease for 19 percent.[3] The statistics gave
credence to the claimed benefits of Mao's liberation of
China and the Marco Polos of the late 70s came back
marvelling at the wonders of the Orient.

In regard to the elderly, who, as every American
schoolchild knows, get treated with "respect" in Eastern societies, deeply ingrained respectful attitudes
were reported to have survived a period of profound revolutionary change. The roles, identities, and behaviors
of the Confucian ethical system (with its supportive
normative and legal structures) were altered. A traditional authoritarianism on the part of old people was
replaced with equality, but the integrity of the elderly as an important part of Chinese life seemed to be
intact.

Although Western technical assistance in matters of
science and technology has been increasingly sought in
recent years, opportunities for research in China by
Western social scientists have remained very limited and
controlled. The way in which much of the recent research has been done is by refugee interviews in Hong
Kong--a technique posing serious problems of representa-
tiveness, political bias, authenticity, and otherwise
skewed samples. Competitive Comrades: Career Incentives and Student Strategies in China by Susan Shirk[4]
was based upon 34 paid refugee interviews. Deborah
Davis-Friedmann relied upon the Chinese press and public
broadcast system, drama and fiction, and 29 interviews
in Hong Kong with visitors and emigrants who had left
China since 1970 for Old People and Their Families in
the People's Republic of China.[5] Parish and Whyte,
whose well known book Village and Family in Contemporary
China was based on transcripts of paid interviews with
65 refugees, note that:

> Without the possibility of conducting empirical
> social science research in China--which we do
> not see arising in the foreseeable future--we
> feel that careful refugee interviewing provides
> the richest source of information about contem-
> porary Chinese life.[6]

Even a cursory review of the recent research on
China reveals a widespread agreement among researchers
that refugee interviews and the variety of secondary
sources routinely used are not ideal. They have been
employed because they have been the best data sources
to which Western social scientists have had access.
However, a consensus remains as to the desirability and
scholarly merit of conducting ethnographic studies within China's borders and especially within her cities.

China was closed to the West for nearly 30 years.
Exchanges did not begin to any significant degree until

late 1978. By the late 70s, the Chinese, in need of both foreign technology and currency (for their modernization efforts) thought these needs could be met by opening their doors to journalists, scholars and tourists. What emerged from the new foreign correspondents in Beijing, however, were not only news stories, but such books as China, Alive in the Bitter Sea, 1983 Pulitzer Prize Winner by Fox Butterfield, New York Times; From the Center of the Earth: The Search for the Truth about China, by Richard Bernstein, Time; and The Chinese, by David Bonavia, London Times. Each attempted to describe the underside of the earlier stories of China's revolutionary successes.

These journalistic accounts have been supplemented by the reports of Western visitors and special interest delegations assessing the work of the Chinese in their own particular fields. Yet, so elusive is the image of a land that serves approximately one-quarter of the world's population that Westerners are still rather at a loss to comprehend either the totality or the "nitty-gritty" of everyday life in China. "China Stinks,"[7] "Dissent and Compromise in the New China: Conversations with Li Gongsu,"[8] and "Critical Care in Tianjin's First Central Hospital and the Fourth Modernization"[9] all make very negative assessments. The question becomes whether they provide the balance of the truth.

Beyond the baseline research and data analysis which the Chinese (and such external agencies as the World Bank) gather, there is a need for qualitative assessments of Chinese life in the post-Mao era. A need also arises for micro-level studies that both extend and refine macro-level data gathering (such as the 1982 population census). This need has been advanced in several recent books. For example, Wai-ken Che concludes The Modern Chinese Family with the following recommendation:

> Changes in the age and sex hierarchies have
> been generated by the Communist Government;
> and it is essential to observe the impacts
> and influences of such changes in the age and
> sex hierarchies in the family. It would be
> rewarding to examine the closeness of the
> ideal and the actual structures . . . .
> Since survey research is not allowed to be
> conducted in Communist China by outsiders
> . . . . Studies on the social changes in the
> urban areas would be rewarding because many
> of the important political and social activi-
> ties are concentrated in urban areas.[10]

Cross-cultural comparisons of "objective" data and quantitative indicators, e.g., per capita income, are insufficient in examining the actual quality of life

experienced by the elderly in different societies. After all, the meanings and manifestations of "well-being"
are culture specific rather than universal. Therefore,
it is to an internal (i.e., an emic) perspective we
must turn.

THE EMIC PERSPECTIVE

As a branch of anthropology, the methodology of
qualitative field research is well suited to the study
of cultural gerontology. The work herein--a consideration of the quality of life experienced by the elderly
in Shenyang--is a study of cultural phenomena. Arthur
Kleinman, Harvard medical anthropologist and psychiatrist, calls anthropology "the queen of the social sciences because, though her methods are weak, she asks
the right questions."11 A qualitative study like mine
describes a culture from the view and concepts of the
informants themselves. A particular context is defined
and the unique patterns which give shape to the culture
are identified. Based upon the realities of the unit
of analysis, the research is both holistic and relativ-
istic. As many components of the group situation as
possible are considered and the value systems, world
views and norms of behavior outlined. The degree of
congruence between the ideal and real culture is ex-
plored and diversity noted. The results are based upon
a "triangulation"12 of observation, interviews and surveys carried out in the field and both supported by and
grounded in an analysis of available literature. I
fully believe the "emic" perspective generated by such
a methodology has a distinct advantage over the "etic"
view when attempting to understand what is important
and distinct about a group of people, a community or
social phenomena in a culture different from one's own.
The task of this study was to establish the national context; observe and interact with people at an
illustrative local site; and then return to the macro-
level in order to generate additional research questions from the data discovered in the natural setting.
By examining the ethical and cultural foundations of
policies on the one hand and by investigating the extent to which the objectives of policies were actually
made manifest in the lives of their intended beneficiaries on the other, it was my intention to untangle
the web of issues which impact upon the degree of well-
being among the elderly in China today.
The research question was whether--because of the
extent to which respect for, and participation of, the
elderly is operationalized--old people in a typical industrial city in China have a higher level of perceived
well-being than one might expect given their material
standard of living. I felt that by examining how

another culture establishes the relationship between material and psychological well-being, our own handling of this delicate interaction might become more clear. As Ruth Benedict stated in <u>Patterns of Culture</u>, "Comparative studies release us from boundaries of our habits of thought, and show us the wide gamut of patterns possible in human interaction."[13] Change is rapid in China and it is important to document the steps of transition. I hope for this document to first communicate the particular corner on life and humanity held by the elderly Shenyangese in 1983 and then to help focus the planning efforts of those researchers who follow.

> Know then thyself, presume not God to scan;
> The proper study of mankind is man.
>
> Alexander Pope
> <u>An Essay on Man</u>[14]

THE RESEARCH DESIGN

No methodology is ever problem-free, but this one had some interesting developments and complications.

According to protocol, my research design was submitted for review to the Chinese government through the International Center for the Exchange of Learning and Research at the Northeast Institute of Technology (NEIT), my base in China. I had asked for permission to individually interview 20 retired Chinese from a factory unit and 20 from a university unit, each four times, concerning a different aspect of well-being. Consequently accepted, I presumed the design had received approval.

What actually happened, I was told at the conclusion of my stay, was that no factory had wanted to be bothered by an intensive interview schedule. Even in the university setting, where it proved difficult to get interviews with faculty members, I was told that, being technologically-minded, the professors hadn't wanted to be bothered with so "common" a subject as "aging." It seems that if I had been in their field and interested in doing collaborative research, it would have been a different story. Thus, in an attempt to support my work, the decision was made by the Chinese prior to my arrival that I could better achieve my goal by interviewing a cross-section of retired workers in seven different settings, as follows:

- a machine tool factory
- a woolen factory
- an electric cable plant
- an old people's home
- a residents' committee

- a university unit
- a commune

Initial arrangements were made prior to my arrival, and a provincial level psychologist, Wang Shu-mao, was asked to help facilitate my work.[15] Translators and drivers were to be provided and every effort was to be made to assist me in my efforts.

In order to help the psychologist and translators with the nuances of my work, I drew up a list of 80 questions (see Appendix B) under the general headings of aging and well-being; social concerns; health; labor; economics and retirement; political role and ideology; and philosophy. My intention was to discuss the list at length with them to test the culture specificity and relevance of each topic of concern. Without my knowledge, but in an attempt to help me, these questions were sent to the machine tool factory and the old age home in which I was to interview. When I found this out, I was quite afraid the length alone would scare people off. The questions had specifically been written (and translated) to communicate the kinds of issues in which I was interested--not as a refined interview schedule.

The response from the two sites was that their old people were largely uneducated and could not answer such questions. In truth, life was the teacher and the best qualification was age. (These sites, however, turned out to be the most successful--possibly because of this prior contact. I was far less threatening in person than my questions!) Rather than conducting a formal, structured interview, however, we felt the best and most comfortable situation in which to elicit honest and spontaneous information would be an open forum, talking informally and allowing the conversation to pursue interesting points. We all agreed that during the actual interviews the questions would be used just for reference.

An open format has the additional benefit of allowing informants to fill in and compensate for limitations in the researcher's perception of issues. As the literature reflects, an interviewer must attempt to see things through the eyes of the interviewees and understand a culture as it is lived.[16] The symbols of a society must not be misinterpreted by an Occidental interpretation nor should the "public" side of life be confused with the "private." The goal of cross-cultural interviewing is to elicit the unique perceptions, perspectives, time and place of the subjects--to understand their relation to the processes of life as they experience them. The subsequent documentation must then become an authentic representation of unique phenomena.

I have a very strong commitment to the ideal that cross-cultural interviewing should aim at leaving everyone with the sense of having deeply communicated in a way that each person feels upgraded, understood and enhanced. Of secondary consideration should be the gathering of academic information. I feel it is wrong to imperialistically exploit native peoples through domination techniques and position power and/or to impose your own ethnocentric standards and mindset and set out to confirm them through concepts, constructs, models and theories.

Joan Cassell notes that:

> Anthropology has been called "a child of Western imperialism"; there is the image of the ethnographer at the outposts of the empire, sitting on the veranda, sipping gin and bitters, asking the District Officer to send over a few "natives" to question. Whether this scene reflects myth or history, such a relationship is entirely untenable in today's "revolutionary and proto-revolutionary world."[17]

She points out, and rightfully in the case of China, that the observed and the observer are exposed to injury, both during the interaction and when the data become public. Even though the subject of well-being among the elderly is far less controversial, or potentially explosive, than that of infanticide or third-semester abortions, there is no denying the fear I occasionally felt that I would make some inadvertent error and get someone into trouble.

The interview situation turned out to be a group affair--an entourage, in fact. Usually included were at least two representatives of the plant administration, a worker's union representative,[18] six retired workers, Mr. Wang, at least one translator, a driver, Ms. Dwight[19] and myself. After six interviews in this fashion, I insisted on being able to talk privately at the next interview site. I was asked if I didn't consider my request rather impolite. Interestingly enough, I didn't feel I was able to elicit any new information or communicate any better in the limited setting (as had been predicted by my Chinese hosts). The private situation was just not that different from the public given the parameters of my interests. The group situation made me wary that the results might be biased by subjects' fear they would do "poorly"; that the internal validity might be affected by the group pressure for the "right" response; or that there would be apprehension in being evaluated by everyone present (especially in a society where "saving face" and the welfare of the group are more valued than revelation of the "self").

The goal of research is to build an increasingly sophisticated and consonant body of knowledge. Without

internal validity, there can be no external validity.
In my interviews I truly encountered a cross-section of
people and situations; still, they all had in common
the fact that they were "survivors," that is, people
who had the inner resources to make it through hard
times and to a mentally healthy old age.

Gail Sheehy defines well-being as "an accumulated
attitude, a sustained background tone of equanimity behind the more intense contrasts of daily events, behind
even periods of unhappiness."[20] Sheehy compared the
experiences of people who felt exceptionally good about
themselves and the qualities of mind and heart they
called upon at important crossroads of their lives. My
sample was similar. The people to whom I was given access were representative of those who embodied what the
culture defined as well-being.

The interviewees were picked by the "contact" at
the location based on who was available, willing to
participate, and (I presume) a good risk in their eyes.
The various reasons people agreed to participate were
that they wanted to contribute to the prestige of their
unit; being interviewed by a foreigner was the most interesting thing going that day; or simply that they
were asked and felt obliged to agree.

No money was involved, contrary to the practice in
the refugee social science research which has been done.
In the university, people usually participated as part
of an exchange of favors. For example, I gave a special English examination to eight faculty members of a
certain department to help determine who would go
abroad. One of their older faculty members reciproca-
ted by agreeing to be interviewed. The case study itself delineates the wide gamut of people with whom I
spoke--from a well-traveled university president to a
30-year resident of an old people's home.

To supplement the formal interviewing, I followed
the same route in a park near the university most every
morning at daybreak. Old people routinely start gathering about 4 a.m. and the park is astonishingly full
during the early morning hours. I would exercise with
the same groups of old people daily and, with at least
one student to translate, visit the same old men and
women. This was my favorite time of day. If I didn't
appear, total strangers would approach me around town
to inquire after my well-being and report back to my
morning friends. (Communication without telephone is
amazing--relying so much more on perception, patience,
and chain communication.) Much of my informal interviewing was thus done in the park where I was privy to
more emotion, inquisitiveness and acceptance.

A contract had been signed between the Northeast
Institute of Technology and Anshan Iron and Steel Company, the largest producer of steel in the country, for
a class to be given in intermediate conversational

English. As part of the Faculty-Exchange Agreement I
took responsibility for the class and attempted to provide an English-speaking environment for the students
to meet the needs for an intensive course. I lived in
the same dormitory as my 24 Chinese students, aged 28
to 51, which gave me a wonderful opportunity to learn
through informal discussion some practical sides to Chinese family and social structure, living situations,
and views toward the elderly. My students and other
Chinese with whom I had regular, informal interactions
ended up playing the role of "barefoot" sociologists
and assisted me in the development of culturally-rele-
vant interview and survey questions and procedures. In
addition, I gained insight and information about life
in Shenyang where knowledge has always been most readily available--on the street!

To complement the field study, I administered a
survey to 109 people in their 20s, 30s and 40s regarding their attitudes toward aging and their own retirement. A field study should serve to identify the
unique patterns and features of a unit of analysis. A
survey can substantiate the reality of those patterns,
inclinations and configurations. The two methodologies
complement each other quite well--the field study iden-
tifying the characteristics and the survey measuring
the independent variable.

EVALUATION

Mao remarked that "a revolution is not a dinner
party,"[21] but, believe me, conducting field research in
post-Mao China is no picnic either!

Although I reviewed the pertinent literature on
qualitative and survey research methodology prior to my
fieldwork in Shenyang, the truth is that while it was
useful in helping develop a strategy and thinking
through parameters of various designs, its utility did
not go past the theoretical level. In fact, my attempt
at one site to adhere as strictly as humanly possible
to the "dos" and "don'ts" offered in one handbook on
case study methodology all but ruined my ability to
leave with useful data or insights. While the handbook
might have had practical utility in Occidental societies, in the context of Shenyang in 1983, the sugges-
tions, strategies and warnings were misleading.

On the other hand, actual anthropological and/or
data-gathering works of such people as Margaret Mead,
Colin Turnbull, William Hinton, Victor and Ruth Sidel,
and Laurence Wylie equipped me with a more personalized
sense of style and spirit, and I must credit their
roles in shaping my work in the field.

Looked at from a "worst case" viewpoint, the ob-
stacles and constraints I faced were formidable ones.

I didn't speak Chinese, and thus, was at the mercy of my interpreters' level of competence and honesty.[22] I didn't get to implement my original research design, even though I was under the impression that I had received "approval" of it from the Chinese authorities before leaving the United States. I didn't have the opportunity to select my own sites or subjects, at least for the formal phase of my interviewing.

Instead, I was given numerous chances to memorize two key phrases whenever I sought to proceed as the research literature suggested I should. The first response to many of my research plans was the oft-heard "*anzhao womendi guilii*" (i.e., "according to our regulations . . ."包). The alternative response received was the ever-popular "*bu da fangbian*" (i.e., "It's not very convenient")--an innocuous sounding barrier but one that proved impenetrable on several occasions.

Being a foreigner inevitably placed a veil between the Chinese with whom I interacted and me--a veil that would not have been present conducting interviews in North Carolina. Sometimes this veil was transparent, occasionally it was opaque, but most often it was gently translucent--major features were easily discernible but subtler details were doubtless obscured.

This inherent distancing was compounded by the cultural and political realities of modern Chinese society. Especially during the Cultural Revolution, China's xenophobia was so profound that foreign influences and foreign contacts were viewed with automatic suspicion if not rejected out of hand. Although a new, more favorable perspective on foreigners has been promulgated in recent years--and has gained widespread acceptance, especially in Beijing, Shanghai, Shenyang and other major cities in the eastern part of the PRC--the legacy of historic antipathy toward foreign ways and justifiable fears of foreign domination (now in the socio-cultural domain) remain. While my own experiences persuade me to view it as an overstatement of the situation today, there is still an element of truth in David Bonavia's observation that:

> Much more important than violence, in the
> defenses of the modern Chinese State, is secre-
> cy. This is one of the outstanding features
> of all socialist states, and in China it has
> been compounded by the traditional mistrust of
> foreigners (which at one point in Chinese history
> was taken to the extreme of forbidding the
> teaching of the Chinese language to them). From
> the arrogance of the old imperial attitude,
> which held that Chinese culture was a sacred
> mystery beyond the reach of all but a few of
> the most gifted and privileged foreigners, the
> Communist Party has shifted to the role of

custodian of all secrets which foreigners
might use to harm its own authority or sub-
jugate the Chinese people.

The general public has mostly collabo-
rated in the Party's attempt to keep foreigners
from learning more about China than they are
supposed to. Through a complex, nationwide
system of background briefings and hearsay,
the Party has established a remarkable degree
of discreet communication between the leaders,
the officials, and the masses, nearly all of
whom assume without question that it is bad to
let outsiders know too much about the way Chinese society works.23

These, then, were the barriers I encountered in
the course of my research--barriers that the existing
methodological literature ill-prepared and ill-equipped
me to handle. Taken together, I had every reason to
fail and an abundant rationale for having done so. And
yet . . . .

I came away from this experience feeling as though
I had learned a tremendous amount. Several factors
contributed to my belief that the research undertaken
represented a net gain for current Occidental understanding of the reality of being old in China today.

The first was that I selected a topic about which
little is known, and even less is written, inside or
outside of China. The available information about the
elderly in the PRC consists of minimal aggregate national data, refugee interviews and inferences drawn
from media and literary sources. What have been con-
spicuous in their absence are firsthand observations of,
and discussions with, aged Chinese still living in
China. Even if I didn't see everything that (in theory)
could have been seen had I not experienced the constraints noted above, this does not change the fact
that I have probably seen more than any other Occidental
researcher working in this particular field.

The second factor is related to the first. Access
is generally limited for foreigners in China, yet I was
given extraordinarily open access to people and places
in Shenyang. I had, and took advantage of, complete
freedom of movement in the city. Several hours most
days were spent exploring Shenyang--riding buses, walking around neighborhoods, going into shops, restaurants
and public buildings, exercising in the park--and im-
mersing myself in the local environment. In addition
to meeting with various administrators and listening to
them explain what was happening, I saw for myself how
old people interacted with each other, with their families, and with those who were part of their daily lives.
While I was often noticed (American women are a rarity
in Shenyang), it is hard to believe that my presence

altered people's behavior in any fundamental way as
they went about their normal business. In fact, Americans are such a rarity that ordinary people would not
have known how to alter their behavior to "please" me,
even if they had desired to do so.

At the formal level, as well, President Bi and my
other NEIT hosts made every effort to be accommodating
to my research interests--within the bounds of what was
considered politically appropriate and acceptable.
They went to a good deal of trouble on my behalf to arrange a series of site visits and interview opportunities they believed to be representative of the situation of Shenyang's elderly residents. My sense is that
they not only bent some of the normal rules applied to
foreigners, but also went above and beyond the call of
duty (and the terms of the NEIT-Appalachian State exchange agreement) to assist me in my work. The fact
that my research was on a topic close to the people and
about which they feel justifiable pride doubtless made
everyone extra accommodating, but this in no way belit-
tles the degree of friendly assistance I was given.
Again, my access may have been more circumscribed than
one would normally expect in the West, but it was more
open than foreigners are usually accorded in China.

The third factor enhancing my research was my relationship with my 25 students at NEIT. All but one
were employees of the Anshan Iron and Steel Company and
were living away from home themselves during these
months. My interaction with them was not limited to
our time together in the classroom. We lived in the
same dormitory and shared many hours of informal conversation in our rooms, at meals, going swimming or
exploring Shenyang. They told me a great deal about
their families and their thoughts about aging and the
aged. In addition, they assisted me in shaping my interview questions and served as a test group for my
survey. They became friends and in many respects were
as much teachers of mine as I was a teacher of theirs.

The fourth, and final, positive factor I can cite
had to do with the extensive and varied kinds of preparation I had been fortunate enough to acquire before
arriving in Shenyang. My courses at the University of
North Carolina on aging, China, cross-cultural and
qualitative research and policy analysis were invaluable reference points. My research on a series of related topics helped create a context for what I would
later witness in the PRC. I also had the benefit of a
health study tour of China with the Sidels the previous
summer and three weeks at a Salzburg Seminar with the
representatives from eighteen nations comparing perspectives on health, productivity and aging prior to
leaving for China. Because I didn't walk into the situation in Shenyang "cold," I didn't waste a lot of time
and energy trying to acclimate myself to the environment

or to the tasks I faced.

In summary, my methodology was an eclectic one based on careful preparation, interviews, observations, surveys, and a wide range of both formal and informal interactions with a spectrum of Chinese elders, officials, experts and students. It may not have precisely followed an established procedure for qualitative fieldwork, it may not have been elegant, and it may not have been ideal. Nevertheless, my methodology had one major quality to commend it--it worked! I learned a great deal about life among the elderly in a corner of the People's Republic of China.

NOTES

1. Huan Xiang, "Social Science and the Modernization of China," Social Sciences and Public Policy in the Developing World. Edited by Laurence Stifel, Ralph Davidson, and James Coleman (Lexington, MA: Lexington Books, 1982), p. 16.

2. Ruth Sidel and Victor W. Sidel, Serve the People: Observations on Medicine in the People's Republic of China (Boston: Beacon Press, 1973). Ruth Sidel and Victor W. Sidel, The Health of China: Current Conflicts in Medical and Human Services for One Billion People (Boston: Beacon Press, 1982). M. Gregg Bloche, "China Discovers Health Perils Accompanying Modernization," Washington Post, August 19, 1979. M. Gregg Bloche, "Hypertension on the Rise in Modern China," Washington Post, August 20, 1979.

3. Gu Xing-yuan and Chen Mai-ling, "Vital Statistics," American Journal of Public Health, September 1982, Vol. 72, Supplement on "Health Services in Shanghai County," p. 21.

4. Susan Shirk, Competitive Comrades: Career Incentives and Student Strategies in China (Berkeley: University of California Press, 1981).

5. Deborah Davis-Friedmann, "Old People and Their Families in the People's Republic of China." Unpublished Ph.D. dissertation, Boston University, 1979.

6. W.L. Parish and M.K. Whyte, "Health, Education, and Welfare Policies," Chapter 6, Village and Family in Contemporary China (Chicago: University of Chicago Press, 1978).

7. J. Kenneson, "China Stinks," Harper's Magazine, 164:13-18, April 1982.

8. R. Terrill, "Dissent and Compromise in the New China: Conversations with Li Gongsu," Boston Globe Magazine, August 15, 1982, pp. 10-14.

9. R.C. Fox and J.P. Swazey, "Critical Care in Tianjin's First Central Hospital and the Fourth Modernization," Science, 1982, 217 and 700-705.

10. Wai-ken Che, The Modern Chinese Family (Palo Alto: R & E Research Association, Inc., 1979), pp. 141-142.

11. Arthur M. Kleinman, M.D., "Illness Meanings: The Role of Culture in the Experience of Illness and Medical Practice in the United States and China." A lecture given at Duke University, October 12, 1983, for the Society for Culture, Illness and Healing.

12. See Henry Wolcott, "Study Guide for Ethnographic Research Methods in Education," Alternative Methodologies in Educational Research. Richard M. Jaeger (ed.), American Educational Research Association, p. F-3, for further discussion of the value of "triangulation" of data and the value in combining various techniques.

13. Ruth Benedict, Patterns of Culture (Boston: Houghton Mifflin, 1934).

14. Alexander Pope, "Epistle II: Of the nature and state of man with respect to himself as an individual," An Essay on Man. See The Complete Poetical Works of Pope, Henry W. Boynton (ed.) (Boston: Houghton Mifflin, 1903), p. 142.

15. The following biographical sketch was condensed from an interview I conducted with Mr. Wang in July of 1983. I have included it here because of the high interest in the state of psychology and the field of mental health in China.

Wang Shu-mao is an Associate Professor at the Academy of Social Sciences of Liaoning Province located in Shenyang, a city in the northeast of the People's Republic of China. He attended Beijing University from 1958 to 1963 majoring in Psychology which, at that time, was included in the Philosophy Department. His graduate work, also at Beijing University, was in Experimental Psychology. He studied under the guidance of Zhou Xiangene who is considered one of the forefathers of psychology in China. Mr. Zhou, now 85, received his Ph.D. from Columbia in 1936 and

specialized in research on emotion and skin
electricity. Mr. Wang completed his work in
1966 at the beginning of the Cultural Revolution. No degrees were given at that time.
    Considered a "small intellectual,"
Mr. Wang was ordered to a factory from 1968 to
1970 to receive reeducation from the workers.
Standing all day to do his work at a grinding
machine in a machine tool factory, his legs
were very swollen and painful. The other
workers, who treated him well, made him a
stool, but being "reeducated," he didn't dare
use it, choosing rather to endure the pain.
He was eventually sent back to Liaoning Province to be a propagandist of Marxism, Leninism,
and Mao Zedong Thought for the duration of the
Cultural Revolution.
    Politically speaking, the "left line" from
the 50s to the smashing of the Gang of Four in
1976 indicated that only political teaching and
not the study of psychology be conducted at
the University, hence Mr. Wang's study of psychology with the Department of Philosophy.
There are presently 1,100 psychologists, most
of them in educational psychology, in China
with a population of 1,031,800,000. Participation in psychology was controlled after
Liberation with only ten persons per year
admitted to study at Beijing University, the
sole institution in China to offer psychology.
During the Cultural Revolution, the speciality
was cut out altogether.
    Times have changed and since 1976 four
universities have added a Department of Psychology. The State is now emphasizing its
value, in fact, to cadres, medical doctors,
teachers, militarists, lawyers and engineers.
    Mr. Wang has been with the Academy of
Social Sciences since 1979, and, in addition
to his writing and research, teaches a course
in psychology to graduate students at the
Northeast Institute of Technology. He is a
member of the Council of the Liaoning Province
Psychology Association and the only delegate
from the Province to the Chinese Psychological
Society's Basic Theory Speciality Committee.
    His publications include a paper on memory
published in both China and the United States
(American Psychology Digest) in 1964; his Ph.D.
dissertation, The Effect of Lack of Oxygen upon
Brain Function, was published in 1966 under the
label of physiology; Interesting Psychology was
published in 1982 and a recently completed book
Experimental Sciences will be printed in 1984.

194

Mr. Wang is now at work on two volumes: Management Psychology and The Methodology of Psychology.

16. Cassell, Joan, "Risk and Benefit to Subjects of Fieldwork," The American Sociologist, 1978, Vol. 13 (Aug):134-143.
   Dunn, William N., "Qualitative Methodology," Research in Progress, 1983, pp. 591-597.
   Herriott, Robert E., and Firestone, William A., "Multisite Qualitative Policy Research: Optimizing Description and Generalizability," Educational Researcher, Feb. 1983, pp. 14-19.
   LeCompte, Margaret D., and Goetz, Judith P., "Problems of Reliability and Validity in Ethnographic Research," Review of Educational Research (Spring 1982, Vol. 52, No. 1), pp. 31-60.
   Lofland, John, "Styles of Reporting Qualitative Research," The American Sociologist, 1974, Vol. 9 (Aug): 101-111.
   Nisbet, John, and Watt, Joyce, "Case Study," Nov. 1978, Contact Authors at University of Aberdeen.
   Spradley, James P. Participant Observation (New York: Holt, Rinehart and Winston, 1980).
   Spradley, James P. The Ethnographic Interview (New York: Holt, Rinehart and Winston, 1980).
   Spradley, James P., and McCurdy, David W., The Cultural Experience: Culture in Complex Society (Palo Alto: Science Research Association, 1972).
   Stake, Robert E., "The Case Study Method in Social Inquiry," Educational Research, Vol. 7 (No. 2) 1978:5-8.
   Third World Surveys: Survey Research in Developing Nations (Ed.: Gerald Hursh-Cesar and Prodipto Roy.) Published by S.G. Wasani for the Macmillan Company of India, Ltd., 1976.
   Wolcott, Harry, "Study Guide for Ethnographic Research Methods in Education," Alternative Methodologies in Educational Research, Ed. Richard M. Jaeger, available from the American Educational Research Association.
   Zimmerman, Don H., "Ethnomethodology," The American Sociologist, 1978, Vol. 13 (Feb):6-15.

17. Joan Cassell, "Risk and Benefit to Subjects of Fieldwork," The American Sociologist, 1978, Vol. 13 (August), p. 135.

18. Trade unions are characteristically supposed to support the welfare of their members. The following excerpts from "History, goals of China's trade unions," The China Daily, 3:694:4, October 18, 1983, give a governmental perspective.

   Trade unions are mass organizations embracing all workers--the advanced, the middle

and those lagging behind. There are 73.3
million members in 30,000 grassroots union
branches. . . .
Unions are organized both by trade and
by geographical location. Membership is voluntary and open to anyone who applies and
gets permission from the branch where he or
she works. Monthly dues amount to only 0.5
per cent of wages, and they help to cover
basic costs. In addition, unions get financial support from enterprises and funds raised
from recreational activities . . . .
In October 1978 the unions' Ninth National Congress was held to criticize the past
"Left" errors and to explore the correct orientation of a labour movement in a socialist
country. Deng Xiaoping, in his speech at the
congress, outlined the new mission of the
Chinese working class as "to build China into
a modern, strong socialist power by the end
of this century." This mission, Deng said,
requires union members to take an active part
in reforming government and enterprises,
raising political, managerial, technological
and cultural levels of the workers, maintaining
centralized administration and promoting democratic management of enterprises.
In particular, he stressed that trade
unions should work to protect the welfare of
workers, urge and assist the authorities in
enterprises and localities to do everything
possible to improve workers' living and working
conditions, fight for workers' democratic
rights and oppose bureaucracy.

19. Because I tend to be theoretical and to see
things in a positive light, and because (depending upon
who's looking) at 35, I'm young or middle-aged, I invited a 73-year-old American woman who's lived in Paris
for the last nineteen years to accompany me to China.
My theory was that she could help me understand conditions or interpretations of both aging and China that I
was too inexperienced to grasp. She was strong,
healthy, independent, and a frequent visitor to China.
With her, I experienced responsibility, age deference,
the rage of short-term memory loss, and the anger
evoked by ageistic prejudices and practices. Her col-
laboration and corroboration of data were invaluable
(as well as her assistance in teaching).

20. Gail Sheehy, _Pathfinders_ (New York: Bantam,
1982), p. 13.

21. The full quotation is:

A revolution is not a dinner party, or writing an essay, or painting a picture, or doing embroidery; it cannot be so refined, so leisurely and gentle, so temperate, kind, courteous, restrained and magnanimous. A revolution is an insurrection, an act of violence by which one class overthrows another.

Mao Zedong, 1927

22. The high quality translation efforts of Sun Lianying, Li Juen, and Sui Zhitong of the Northeast Institute of Technology made my research possible, and I am greatly indebted to them for their integrity and ability.

23. David Bonavia, The Chinese (New York: Lippincott & Crowell, 1980), pp. 48-49.

Appendix B:
Questions Defining Research Interests for the Case Study of the Meanings and Manifestations of Well-Being Among the Elderly in Shenyang

AGING AND WELL-BEING

1. What does "aging" mean to you?

2. How do you feel about your own aging?

3. What do you expect to happen as you age?

4. In the West, we divide the life cycle into three distinct phases: education, work, and then retirement. Are there such distinct divisions here?

5. Talk about what factors make a good quality of life for older people.

6. What about for you?

7. What can you think of that could harm your quality of life?

8. What could happen to improve your quality of life?

9. What is most important in maintaining your quality of life? For example, is it a function of being surrounded by family? having enough money? access to care? emotional support of your family, friends or unit?

10. Who is responsible for your quality of life and in what ways?

11. How is well-being a function of your own actions?

12. How do things change as people get older?

13. How about for you? How have your perceptions of quality of life changed from ten years ago? How do you expect things to be different ten years from now?

14. Is the quality of life for older people better or worse in the countryside? Why?

15. Some people always seem to do better than others. How does this society protect its vulnerable?

16. Life expectancy in Shenyang is 70. What contributes to a worthwhile, meaningful existence past the age of retirement?

17. What kinds of needs do the elderly have? Are these needs different from the needs of other groups in the society? Are special policies needed to insure the satisfaction of these needs?

18. As the number of children decreases in China, the proportion of elderly increases. How will this new balance affect the way of life?

SOCIAL CONCERNS

19. People need to be part of society in a very human way: we seem to need to be both independent and dependent. What special role do you have in your family and in your unit?

20. When are old people considered a burden?

21. How are the members of your family interdependent? How are they independent?

22. Who is most important to you?

23. Are you valued for your wisdom? Do people seek your advice about life situations?

24. What do you think the society owes old people, and conversely, what do old people owe the society?

25. Some people choose a very active pattern of existence and others choose a quiet, contemplative lifestyle. Are men or women more active? What do they do that's different?

26. Are older people considered to have a productive potential or are they expected to take a reserved place in the society?

27. Do you feel a sense of control over what happens to you?

28. What is expected of you in your family, in your unit, and in your society?

29. What are the barriers to carrying out these roles?

30. What are the rewards for an active social role?

31. What groups, committees, or organizations do you belong to?

32. How are you treated?

33. Do you feel you have a role in the modernization effort?

34. Are elderly men treated differently from elderly women? How? Are the lives of elderly members of your unit different from the lives of elderly in other units you know of? Are the elderly in rural areas treated differently from the elderly in urban areas? Do you think old people are treated differently in other parts of China?

35. Do you think older people in general have any unique qualities or any unique problems?

36. What is your concept of well-being?

HEALTH

37. After retirement, is aging a period of growth or decline?

38. What do you think affects how long you live?

39. What was the impact of retirement upon your health?

40. What type of medical care do you seek? Preventive or curative? Traditional or Western? For acute problems or managing chronic disease?

41. Who takes care of you when you need help?

42. It is believed that activity postpones or even prevents disability and the manifestations of disease. How is activity for old people promoted here in Shenyang?

43. Sometimes a decrease in activity or productivity is due to physical decline, sometimes a personal choice, and at other times, encouraged by society. What changes in your own life have you noticed as you have aged? To what are they due?

44. What work is done to promote good health either by education or propaganda?

LABOR, ECONOMICS AND RETIREMENT

45. What does it mean to retire in Shenyang?

46. What kind of work did you do?

47. Do people over retirement age have the right to work? Who makes the decision about when to retire?

48. Do you think that people who do light work would like to continue to work past retirement age? Would people who do moderate work like to continue working beyond retirement age? What about those who do heavy work?

49. Were you willing or reluctant to retire at the pensionable age? Did you do light, moderate, or heavy work? For you, would the ideal time to retire have been earlier or later?

50. Do you think retirement should be based upon age, health, ability to perform, or the nature of the work itself?

51. What opportunities do you now have for work?

52. How has the modernization effort affected the role and retirement of the elderly?

53. It has been said that the best thing for the elderly and for everyone else in the world is improvement in economic conditions. Do you agree?

54. Do you have financial commitments to anyone other than yourself? Whom do you support? What would happen to them if you died?

55. Did you have the option of passing your job on to your son or daughter when you retired?

56. How much money do you receive each month? What is the total income of your household each month?

57. What has been the effect of the responsibility system on the structure of your family? How has it affected your situation?

58. What are the rewards of productive activity for older men and women?

59. After retirement, is there any possibility of learning new vocational skills leading to other work?

60. What have you done since you retired?

61. Are any special arrangements made in your workplace to accommodate needs of elderly workers (such as shortening work hours)?

POLITICAL ROLE AND IDEOLOGY

62. What activities do you undertake that are of a political nature?

63. In general, do you participate in political life more than, less than, or the same as someone twenty years younger?

64. Do you expect your participation to increase or decrease as you get older?

65. What policies (such as housing or employment) promote or strengthen family relationships and which hinder them?

66. What are the guiding principles, values and policies which affect your life? For example, independence is highly valued in the United States and underlies what happens in the culture. What are the strongest forces outside yourself affecting your life?

PHILOSOPHY

67. You have survived many years, many transitions and many changes. Do you find that as you age your thoughts become more philosophical about what life is all about?

68. Do you fear death?

69. Has your life had meaning and direction?

ADDITIONAL INFORMATION NEEDED FOR RESEARCH

1. What are the main health problems in Shenyang and what are their solutions?

2. What is the life expectancy in Shenyang and what is the source of this information?

3. Can you tell me something about the nutrition of the people of Shenyang?

4. One of the leading gerontologists of Sweden,
   Dr. Alvar Svanborg, has estimated that at age 70,
   18 percent of the elderly are in need of some form
   of mental health support in his country. Manifestations are affective disorders (due to functional
   difficulties and life crisis reactions) and organic
   disorders. In the United States, 5 percent of the
   elderly suffer from Senile Dementia of the
   Alzheimer's Type and 25 percent of all suicides are
   committed by those over 65. What is the incidence
   of mental disorders here and what is done for these
   people? Is there an increasing pathology of mental
   problems in the aging population?

5. What are the morbidity and mortality figures in
   Shenyang? What is the birth rate and rate of
   growth? What are the main public health problems?

6. What is done to promote health in the population,
   especially the elderly population?

7. What is the literacy rate?

8. What is the labor force participation rate of those
   past retirement age?

9. What happens when someone dies?

10. May I please have information on Shenyang and on
    each of the sites I am to use for my research?
    Also on NEIT?

11. May I please have a copy of the information sent to
    each of the sites in which I will interview? It is
    necessary for me to document the process giving
    each step taken.

Appendix C:
Organizations Working in
the Field of Aging in China

1. The National Committee for the Aging (NCA), set up
   in April 1982, aims to investigate and coordinate
   problems associated with aging and seeks to promote
   physical exercise and better medical care to help
   the elderly keep fit. Its director, Yu Guang-han,
   represented China at the 1982 U.N. World Assembly on
   Aging held in Vienna. It was to this organization
   and its intent that he referred in the speech he delivered there:

> China has set up a national committee con-
> sisting of twenty organizations to coordinate
> the related activities throughout the country,
> its members being departmental directors or
> higher officials in the concerned state or-
> gans, scientific research institutions, peo-
> ple's organizations and news media. Now the
> outline of a plan of action concerning the
> question of the aged has been worked out and
> the member departments and institutions of
> the committee will formulate specific plans
> for the gradual unfolding of activities in
> their respective fields concerning adminis-
> trative measures, scientific research, mass
> media and education and mass work.

2. The Chinese Society of Geriatrics of the Chinese
   Medical Association was founded at China's second
   conference on gerontology held in October 1981 in
   Guilin. (The first was held in 1964 in Beijing.)
   With twenty branches in various parts of the country,
   there are 23 gerontological research units under its
   auspices, most of which are attached to provincial
   or municipal hospitals, sanatoriums, medical colleges or other research institutions. Publishes The
   Chinese Journal of Geriatrics.

3. The Chinese Academy of Social Sciences is concerned

with problems of the aging. Some creative ideas
have been contributed by Du Renzhi, a sociologist at
the Academy.

4. Association of Doctors for the Elderly, Xuanwu Hospital of Traditional Medicine, Beijing. Under the
leadership of Dr. Xu Huanyun. See Health Context,
pp. 61-62.

Bibliography

"Add Life to Years." World Health. Geneva: The World
    Organization, Feb.-March 1982.

Ardell, D. High Level Wellness. Emmaus, PA: Rodale
    Press, 1977.

Baines, J. Aging and World Order. East Orange, NJ:
    Global Education Associates, 1980.

Baker, H. D. R. Chinese Family and Kinship. London:
    The Macmillan Press, Ltd., 1979.

A Barefoot Doctor's Manual: A Guide to Traditional
    Chinese and Modern Medicine. Toronto: Coles Pub-
    lishing Co., Ltd., 1980.

Belden, J. China Shakes the World. Harper, 1949; re-
    printed New York: Monthly Review Press, 1970.

Benedict, R. Patterns of Culture. Boston: Houghton
    Mifflin, 1934.

Bernstein, R. From the Center of the Earth: The
    Search for the Truth about China. Boston: Little,
    Brown and Co., 1982.

Birren, J. E. and Renner, V. J. "Concepts and Criteria
    of Mental Health and Aging." Amer. J. Orthopsy-
    chiatry 51:2:242-254, Apr. 1981.

Bonavia, D. The Chinese. New York: Lippincott &
    Crowell, 1980.

Boulding, K. The Image: Knowledge in Life and Society.
    Ann Arbor: Univ. of Michigan Press, 1956.

Butler, R. N. Why Survive? Being Old in America. New
    York: Harper and Row, 1975.

Butler, R. N., Gertman, J. S., Oberlander, D. L.,
    Schlinder, L.   "Self-Care, Self-Help, and the El-
    derly."   Int'l J. Aging and Human Development 10:
    1:95-117, 1979.

Butterfield, F.   China, Alive in the Bitter Sea.   New
    York: Times Books, 1982.

Caldwell, J.   "The Mechanisms of Demographic Change in
    Historical Perspective."   Population Studies 35:1:
    5-27, March 1981.

Chen, P. and Kols, A.   "Population and Birth Planning
    in the People's Republic of China."   Population
    Reports.   Series J:25:603.   Baltimore: Population
    Information Program, The Johns Hopkins Univ.,
    Hampton House, 624 No. Broadway, 21205, Jan.-Feb.
    1982.

Cherry, R. L. and Magnuson-Martinson, S.   "Moderniza-
    tion and Status of the Aged in China: Decline or
    Equalization?"   The Sociological Quarterly 22:253-
    261, Spring 1981.

Coale, A. J.   "Population Trends, Population Policy and
    Population Studies in China."   Pop. & Dev. Review
    7:1:85-97, March 1981.

Cowgill, D. O.   "Aging in Comparative Cultural Perspec-
    tive."   Mid-Amer. Rev. of Sociol. 6:2:1-28, Winter
    1981.

Davis-Friedmann, D.   Long Lives: Chinese Elderly and
    the Communist Revolution.   Cambridge: Harvard
    Univ. Press, 1983.

Demographic Indicators of Countries: Estimates and
    Projections as Assessed in 1980.   New York: Unit-
    ed Nations, 1982.

Dernberger, R., ed.   China's Development Experience in
    Comparative Perspective.   Cambridge: Harvard
    Univ. Press, 1980.

Estes, C. L.   "Austerity and Aging in the U. S.: 1980
    and Beyond."   Int'l. J. Health Services 12:4, 1982.

Etzioni, A.   "Old People and Public Policy."   In
    Reissman, F., ed.   Older Persons: Unused Re-
    sources for Unmet Needs.   Beverly Hills, CA: Sage
    Publications, 1977.

Fairbank, J. K.   The United States and China.   4th ed.
    Cambridge: Harvard Univ. Press, 1980.

Filner, B. and Williams, T. F. "Health Promotion for
    the Elderly: Reducing Functional Dependency." In
    Hamburg, D. A. Healthy People: The Surgeon Gen-
    eral's Report on Health Promotion and Disease Pre-
    vention Background Papers--1979. Washington, D.C.:
    U.S. Department of HEW (PHS) Pub. No. 79-55071A,
    pp. 365-386.

Fischer, D. H. Growing Old in America. New York:
    Oxford Univ. Press, 1978.

Fry, C. L. Aging in Culture and Society: Comparative
    Viewpoints and Strategies. So. Hadley, MA: J. F.
    Bergin Publishers, 1980.

Fry, C. L. Dimensions: Aging, Culture and Health.
    So. Hadley, MA: J. F. Bergin Publishers, 1981.

Fry, C. L. New Methods for Old-Age Research: Anthro-
    pological Alternatives. So. Hadley, MA: J. F.
    Bergin Publishers, 1983.

Gelfand, D. Aging: The Ethnic Factor. Boston:
    Little, Brown and Co., 1982.

Grosse, R. N. and Harkavy, O. "The Role of Health in
    Development." Soc. Sci. and Med. 14C:165-169.
    Great Britain: Pergamon Press, Ltd., 1980.

Guttmacher, S. "Whole in Body, Mind and Spirit: Holis-
    tic Health and the Limits of Medicine." The
    Hastings Center Report. Apr. 1979, pp. 15-21.

Han Suyin. Till Morning Comes. New York: Bantam,
    1982.

Harrison, J. P. The Long March to Power: A History of
    the Chinese Communist Party, 1921-72. New York:
    Praeger, 1972.

Hendricks, J., ed. In the Country of the Old. Farming-
    dale, NY: Baywood Publishing Co., 1980.

Hinton, W. Fanshen: A Documentary of Revolution in a
    Chinese Village. New York: Random House, 1966.

Hinton, W. Shenfan: The Continuing Revolution in a
    Chinese Village. New York: Random House, 1983.

Holmes, L. D. Other Cultures, Elder Years: An Intro-
    duction to Cultural Gerontology. Minneapolis:
    Burgess Publishing Co., 1983.

Horn, J. S. Away with All Pests . . . An English Sur-
    geon in People's China, 1954-1969. New York:
    Monthly Review Press, 1969.

Huan Xiang. "Social Science and the Modernization of
    China." In Stifel, L., Davidson, R., and Coleman,
    J. Social Sciences and Public Policy in the De-
    veloping World. Lexington, MA: Lexington Books,
    1982.

Hudson, R. B. and Binstock, R. H. "Political Systems
    and Aging." In Binstock, R. H. and Shanas, E.,
    eds. Handbook of Aging and the Social Sciences.
    New York: Van Nostrand Reinhold Co., 1976.

Hursh-Cesar, G. and Roy, P., eds. Third World Surveys:
    Survey Research in Developing Nations. Delhi:
    The Macmillan Company of India, Ltd., 1976.

Kayser-Jones, J. S. Old, Alone and Neglected: A Com-
    parison of Being Old in Scotland and the U.S.
    Berkeley: Univ. of California Press, 1981.

Keith, J. Old People as People: Social and Cultural
    Influences on Aging and Old Age. Boston: Little,
    Brown and Co., 1982.

Kelman, H. R. "Health Care of Old People in Scotland:
    Lessons for the United States." J. of Pub. Hlth.
    Policy 1:2:177-186, 1980.

Kleinman, A. Patients and Healers in the Context of
    Culture. Berkeley: Univ. of California Press,
    1980.

Lampton, D. The Politics of Medicine in China: The
    Policy Process, 1949-1977. Boulder, CO: Westview
    Press, 1977.

Liu Zheng, Song Jian, et. al. China's Population:
    Problems and Prospects. Beijing: New World Press,
    1981.

Livingston, M. and Lowinger, P. The Minds of the Chi-
    nese People: Mental Health in New China. Engle-
    wood Cliffs, NJ: Prentice Hall, Inc., 1983.

Lowy, L. Social Policies and Programs on Aging. Lex-
    ington, MA: Lexington Books, 1980.

Maddox, G. L. "Challenge for Health Policy and Plan-
    ning." In Binstock, R., Sun Chow, W. and Schultz,
    J., eds. Int'l. Perspectives on Aging: Population

and Policy Challenges. New York: United Nations
Fund for Population Activities, 1982.

Maddox, G. L. "Measuring the Well-Being of Older
Adults: Conceptualization and Applications." In
Somers, A. and Fabian, D., eds. The Geriatric Im-
perative: An Intro. to Gerontology & Clinical
Geriatrics. New York: Appleton-Century-Crofts,
1981.

Morse, R., ed. The Limits of Reform in China. Boulder,
CO: Westview Press, 1983.

Myrdal, J. Report from a Chinese Village. New York:
Pantheon, 1965.

Neugarten, B. L. and Havinghurst, R. J., eds. Social
Policy, Social Ethics and the Aging Society.
Chicago, IL: Univ. of Chicago, Committee on Human
Dev., 1976.

Omran, A. R., ed. Community Medicine in Developing
Countries. New York: Springer, 1974.

Parish, W. L. and Whyte, M. K. Village and Family in
Contemporary China. Chicago: Univ. of Chicago
Press, 1978.

Peng Zhen. Concluding Speech. The First Session of the
Sixth National People's Congress. Beijing: Foreign Languages Press, 1983.

Peng Zhen. "Report on the Draft of the Revised Consti-
tution of the People's Republic of China." Fifth
Session of the Fifth National People's Congress.
Beijing: Foreign Languages Press, 1983.

Populi: Journal of the United Nations Fund for Popula-
tion Activities 9:4, 1982. (Especially see Salas,
R., "Aging: A Universal Phenomenon," and Acheson,
E. D., "The Crisis of Old Age.")

Pruitt, I. A Daughter of Han: The Autobiography of a
Chinese Working Woman. New Haven: Yale University
Press, 1945.

"Report of the World Assembly on Aging." New York:
United Nations Publication No. E.82.1.16.

Ru Zhijuan et. al. Seven Contemporary Chinese Women
Writers. Beijing: Chinese Literature, 1982.

Salber, E. Don't Bring Me Flowers When I'm Dead--Voices

of the Rural Elderly. Durham, NC: Duke Univ. Press, 1983.

Schell, O. "A Reporter at Large: The Wind of Wanting to Go it Alone." The New Yorker, Jan. 23, 1984.

Sheehy, G. Pathfinders. New York: Bantam, 1982.

Shirk, S. Competitive Comrades: Career Incentives and Student Strategies in China. Berkeley: Univ. of Calif. Press, 1981.

Sidel, Ruth. Families of Fengsheng: Urban Life in China. Baltimore: Penguin Books, 1974.

Sidel, Ruth. Women and Child Care in China. Baltimore: Penguin Books, 1973.

Sidel, Ruth and Sidel, V. W. The Health of China: Current Conflicts in Medical and Human Services for One Billion People. Boston: Beacon Press, 1982.

Sidel, V. W. and Sidel, Ruth. Serve the People: Observations on Medicine in the People's Republic of China. Boston: Beacon Press, 1973.

Siu, H. F. and Stern, Z., eds. Mao's Harvest: Voices from China's New Generation. New York: Oxford University Press, 1983.

Snow, E. Red China Today. New York: Vintage Books, 1971.

Snow, E. Red Star over China. New York: Random House, 1938.

Spence, J. D. The Gate of Heavenly Peace: The Chinese and Their Revolution: 1895-1980. New York: Viking Press, 1981.

Ssenkoloto, G. M. "Family Support of the Elderly." World Health. Geneva: The World Health Organization, May 1981.

Taeuber, C. M. America in Transition: An Aging Society. Washington, D.C.: Current Population Reports, U.S. Department of Commerce, Bureau of the Census, Series P-23, No. 128, Sept. 1983.

Terrill, R., ed. The China Difference: A Portrait of Life Today Inside the Country of One Billion. New York: Harper & Row, 1979.

Thomae, H. and Maddox, G., eds. New Perspectives on Old Age: A Message to Decision-Makers. New York: Springer, 1982.

Tien, H. Y. "How China Treats Its Old People." Asian Profile 5:1:1-8, Feb. 1977.

Townsend, J. R. Politics in China (2nd ed.). Boston: Little, Brown and Co., 1980.

Treas, J. "Socialist Organization and Economic Development in China: Latent Consequences for the Aged." Gerontologist 19:35, 1979.

Turnbull, Colin. The Human Cycle. New York: Simon and Schuster, 1983.

U.S. House of Representatives. 96th Congress. Select Committee on Aging. Future Directions for Aging Policy: A Human Service Model. Washington, D.C.: U.S. Government Printing Office, Comm. Pub. No. 96-226, 1980.

Vepa, R. Mao's China: A Nation in Transition. New Delhi: Abhinov Publications, 1979.

Weisskopf, T. "The Relevance of the Chinese Experience for Third World Economic Development." Theory and Society 9:2, March 1980.

World Bank. World Development Report, 1983. New York: Oxford Univ. Press, 1983.

Yang, C. K. Chinese Communist Society: The Family and the Village. Boston: MIT Press, 1959.

Yang Jiang. A Cadre School Life: Six Chapters (Trans. by Geremie Barme). Hong Kong: Joint Publishing Co., 1982.